A Return to Glory.

Restoring a Classic Dragster

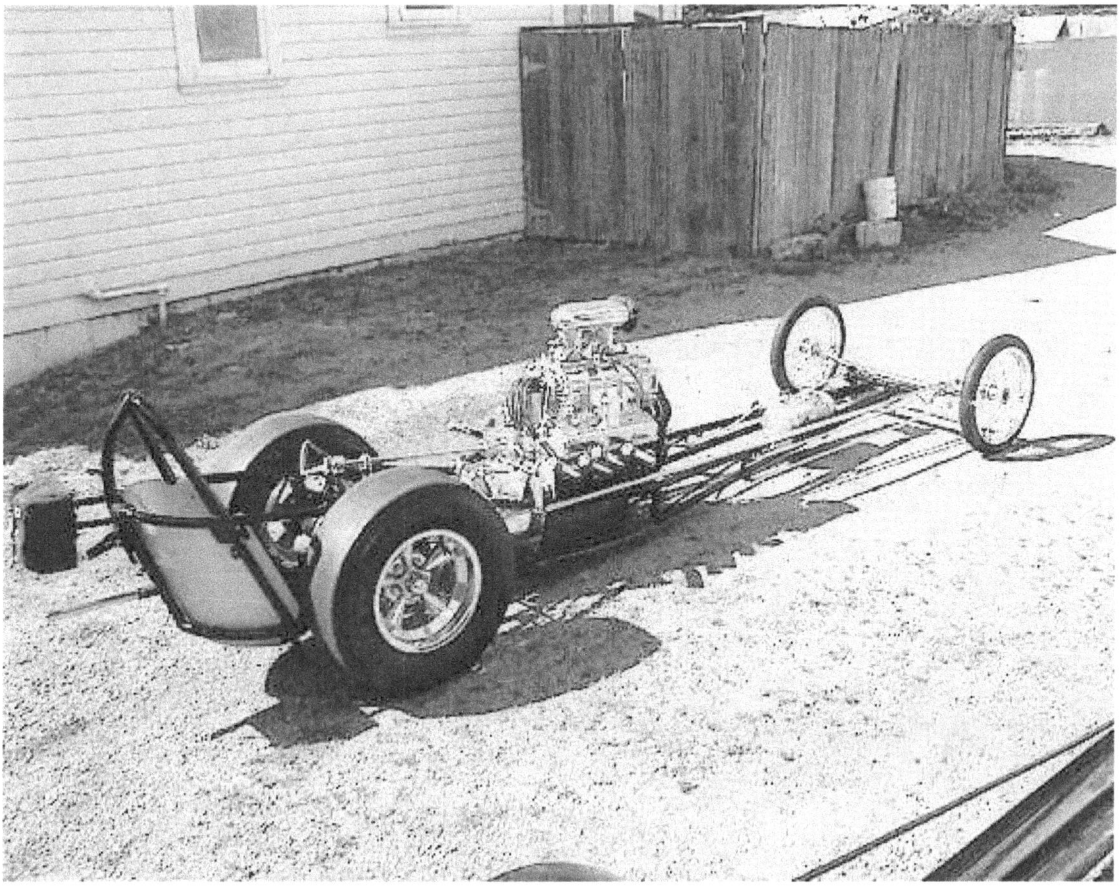

By Fred Vosk

A Return to Glory:
Restoring a Classic Dragster
Copyright 2011
Created by: Fred Vosk
Written by: Fred Vosk
Pictures by: Fred Vosk
Publishing and Editing Assistance by: Jack Troy

Acknowledgements

Thank you to Pete "Pit Crew" Starrett whom without the restoration of the Fuller would not have been possible, and Thank you as well to Kent Fuller, who originally created the Western Manufacture Special. Without either of you this would not have been possible.

The "Western Manufacturing Special" Restoration

AKA "The Little Fuller"

Ya know ... I've restored all sortsa things, Horse Buggy's, Classic Cars, Exotic Sports Cars, ect. - built a bunch of cars 'n' stuff from scratch, too, but this project was especially sweet - cuz it's the favorite car of my favorite digger builder... Kent Fuller built over 250 dragsters, almost all of them during the 60's they were the best of their time, and are now the most coveted by collectors... This car was originally built by Fuller in late 61 or early 62 for Vic Hubbard Speed Shop/Jerry Forsberg as a very light blown Chevy fueler ... The car is restored in the colors of Jon Halstead, who bought the car from Forsberg/Hubbard and ran it first as an injected gas dragster and then for a year or two as a flyweight AA/GD, once again powered by a blown Chevy small block ... the car weighed around 900 pounds in this form... Pete Starrett worked on the car when Halstead had it - - hence his nickname, "Pit Crew Pete" ... At the end of it's noteworthy racing career it was in the hands of Jim Laing - who stored it in the rafters of his garage - - where the little digger hung for the next 30 plus years, untouched - and for the most part - original. Until three years ago when Pete liberated it to be restored for the 2000 California Hot Rod Reunion - - which was honoring Kent Fuller.

Fred Vosk

Pieces of Art like this car are not really owned - - we are just their caretakers...and the caretakers for this jewel are
Kent and Evelyn Fuller
Jim and Diane Laing
Pete and Pam Starrett

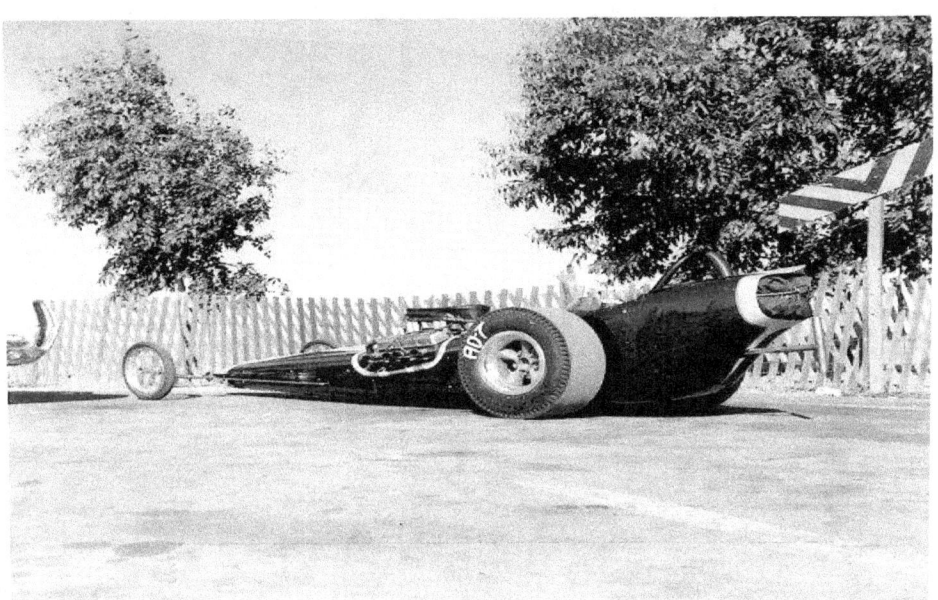

The above photo is the car when Jon Halstead first ran it back in 1964, before he put the supercharger on it.

The Photo below is the car as it was in 1965 ... and what follows is some of the process of bringing it back to that point in time again ... I hope it gives you a little peek into the creative art of Kent Fuller

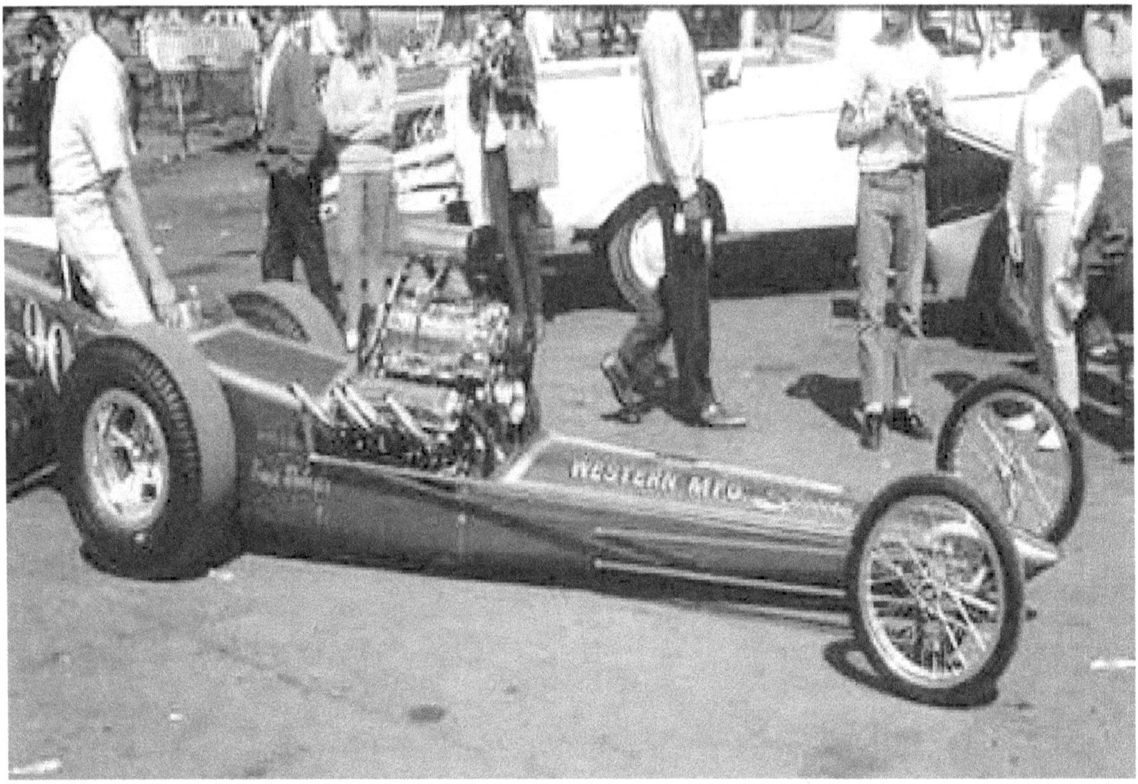

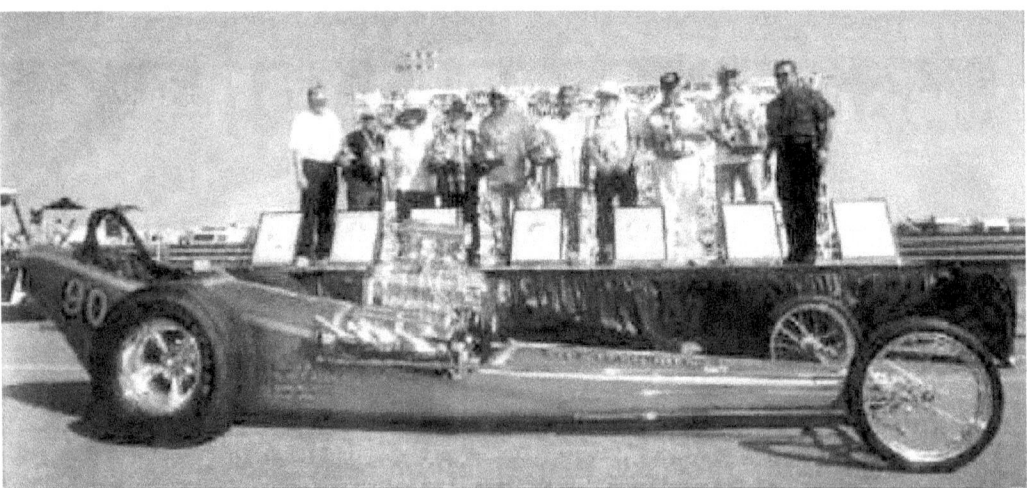

Questions about the restoration of this car? Or any help we can give you with a
project you are doing, (i.e. learn from our disasters), we're always willing to
answer any question we can...
Fred
fredvosk@bikesters.com

Western Mfg. Special

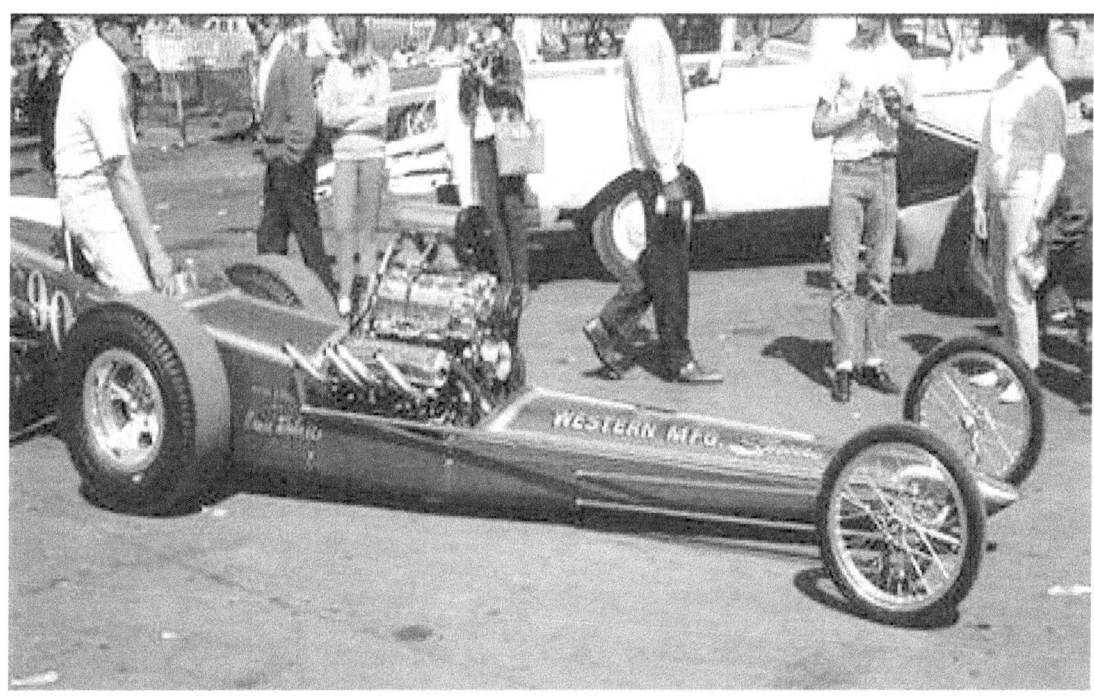

Here we are in 1965 or '66.... Now lets move forward to the year 2000....
Hmmmmmmm.... or is it back to the year 2000---Oh well, back from
now, forward from now...Back To The Future"?? (Disclaimer) The
following photos and text are by me-and I can't resist going for the cheap
laugh when the opportunity presents itself...So live with it... Fred Vosk

The Naked Fuller

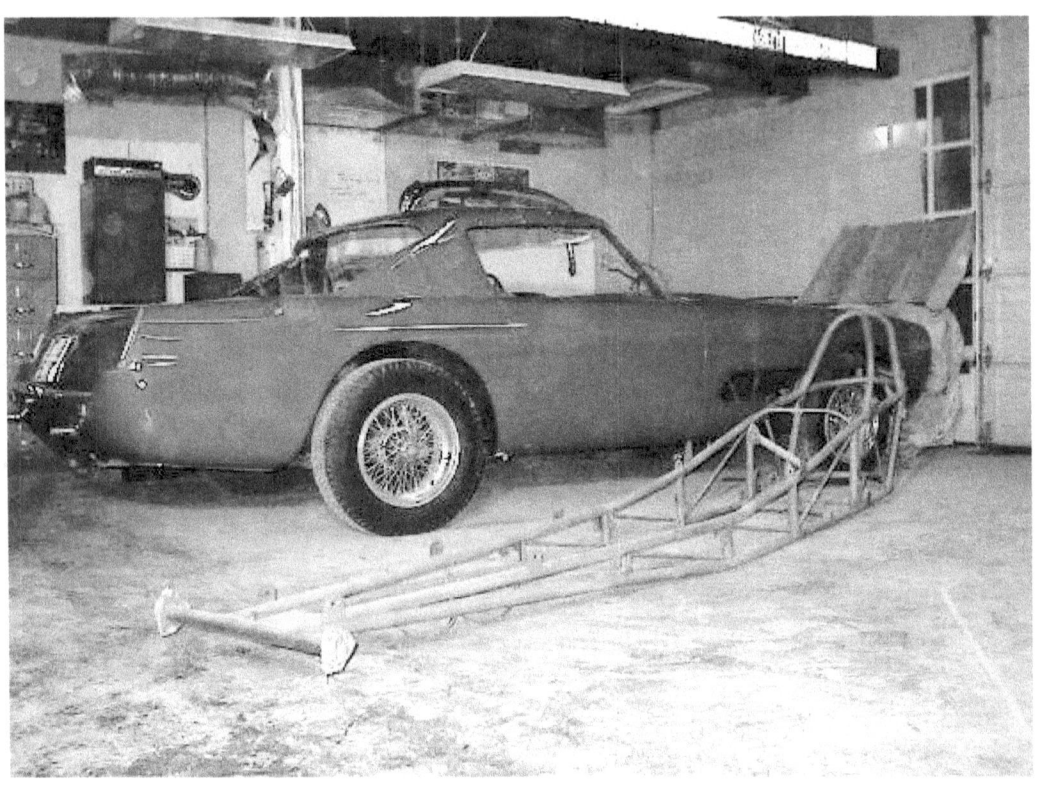

Here's 'The Fuller' - fresh from the media blaster - - hangin out with his Italian 'roomie' - - the very exotic, Gina Ferrari ... ... Next, The Naked Fuller and Barbara Bugatti ... a shocking expose! PS: Gina is a 59 Super America 4.9 liter ... a very rare chick indeed...

The Naked Fuller Returns

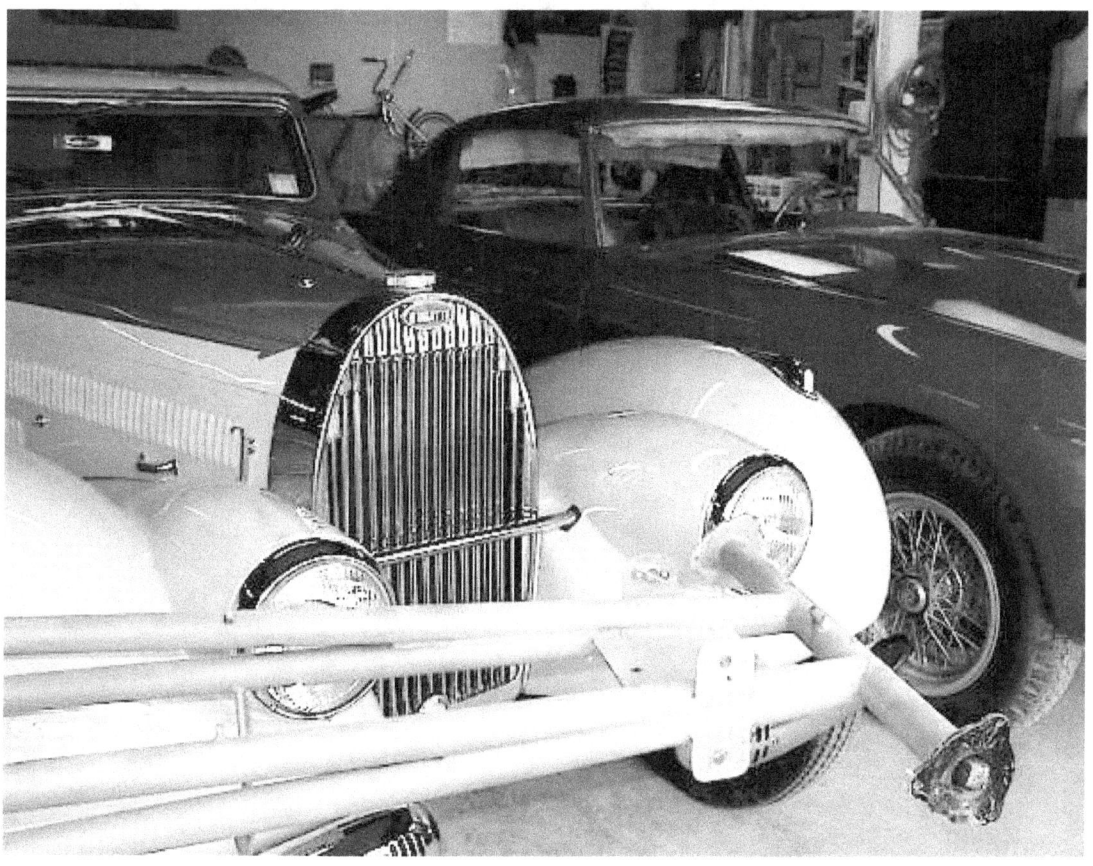

As you can see, the Naked Fuller has acquired a new escort over the week end ... former 'close friend' Gina sulks in the background

More Fuller & Frenchie

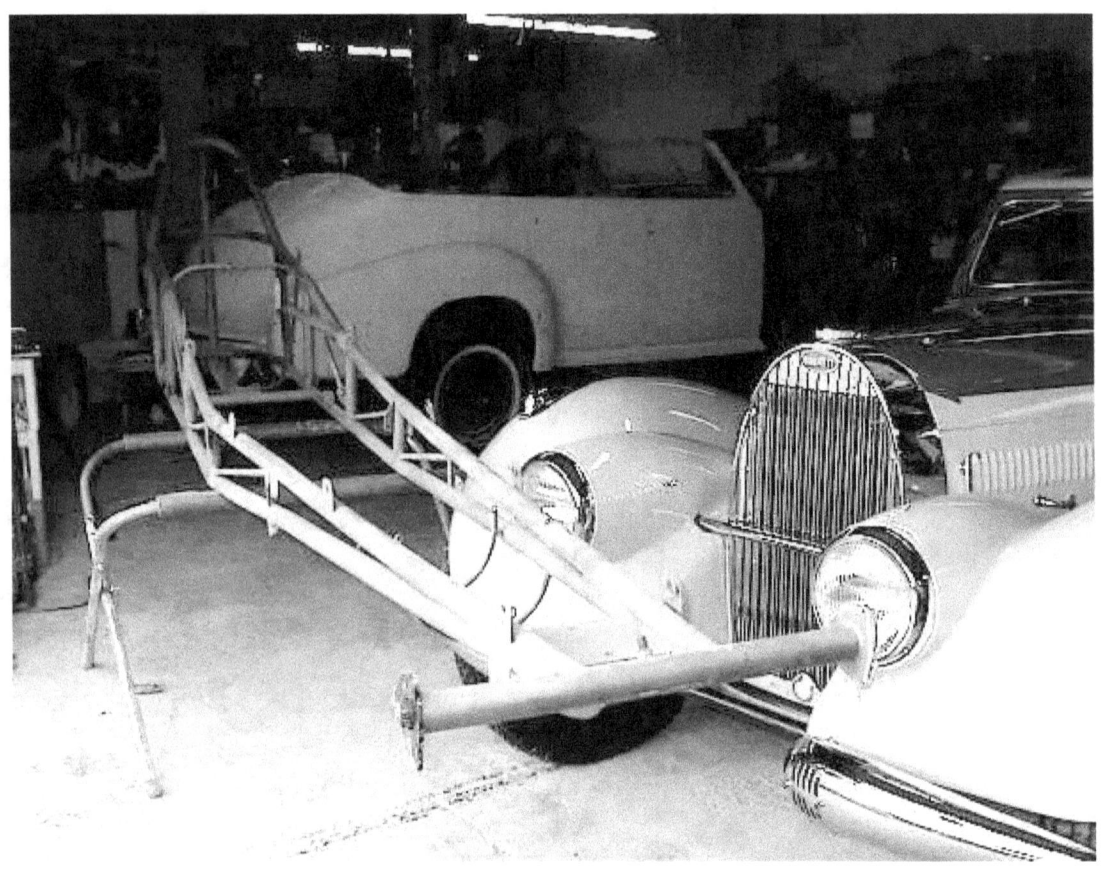

A little more of The Fuller and the French chick

Bottom's Up

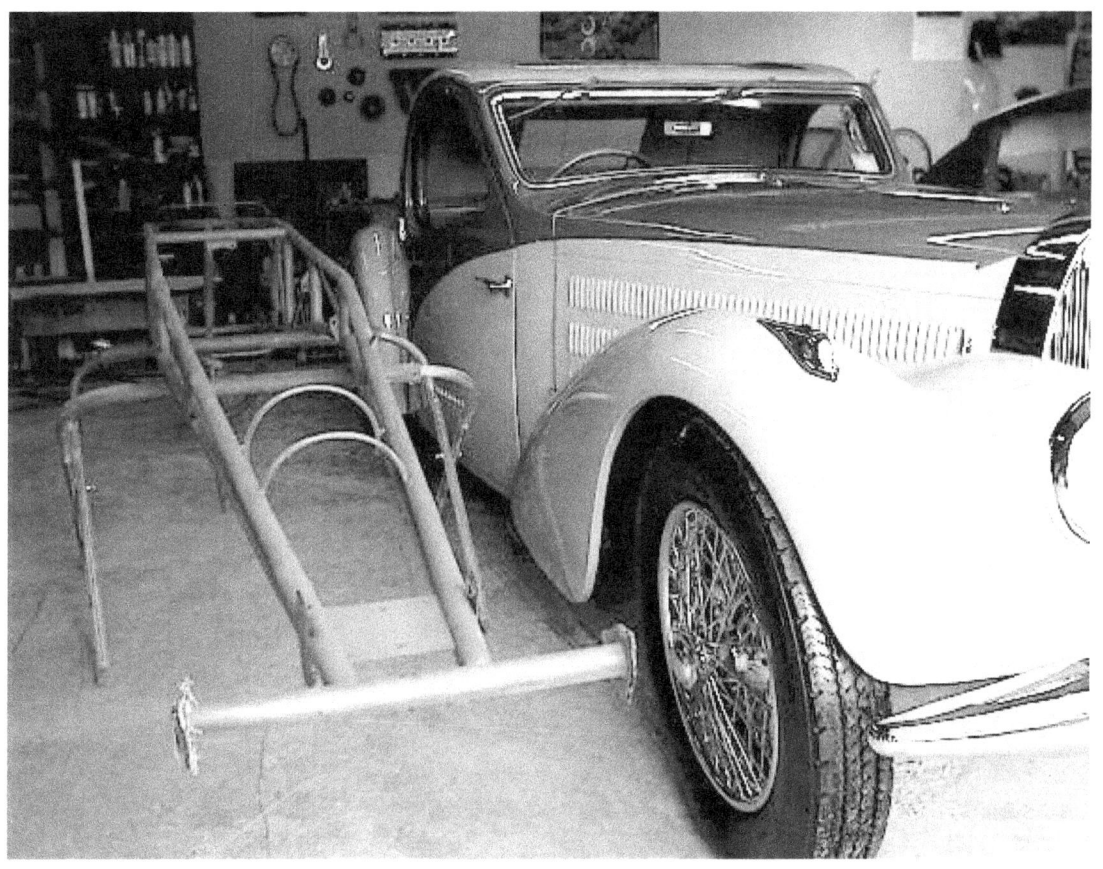

The Fuller snuggles up with the French Chick

Fuller & "Bab's"

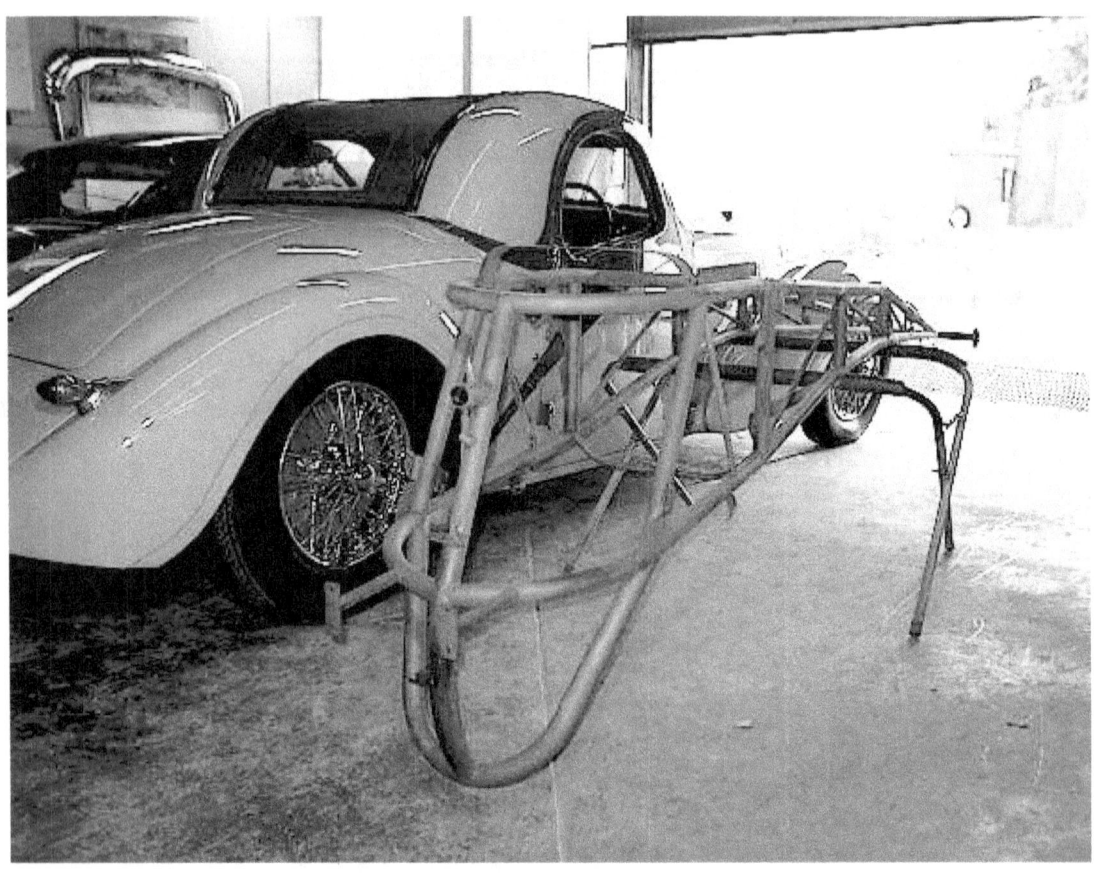

Upsidedown and Backwards ... ... The Naked Fuller showes off for the French Chick..............

Right Side Up

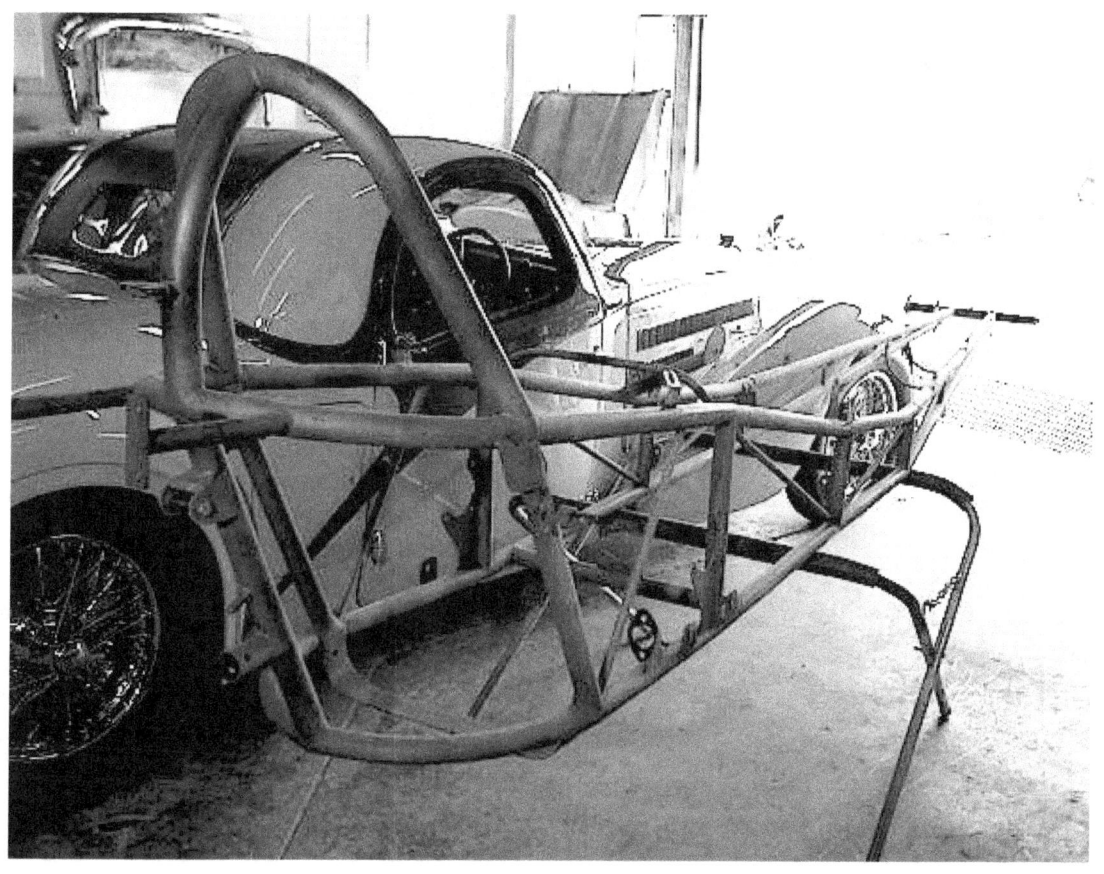

The blood was rushing to his rollbar ... is a 62 FULLER a piece of art - - Or What!!!

Got Ya' Beat

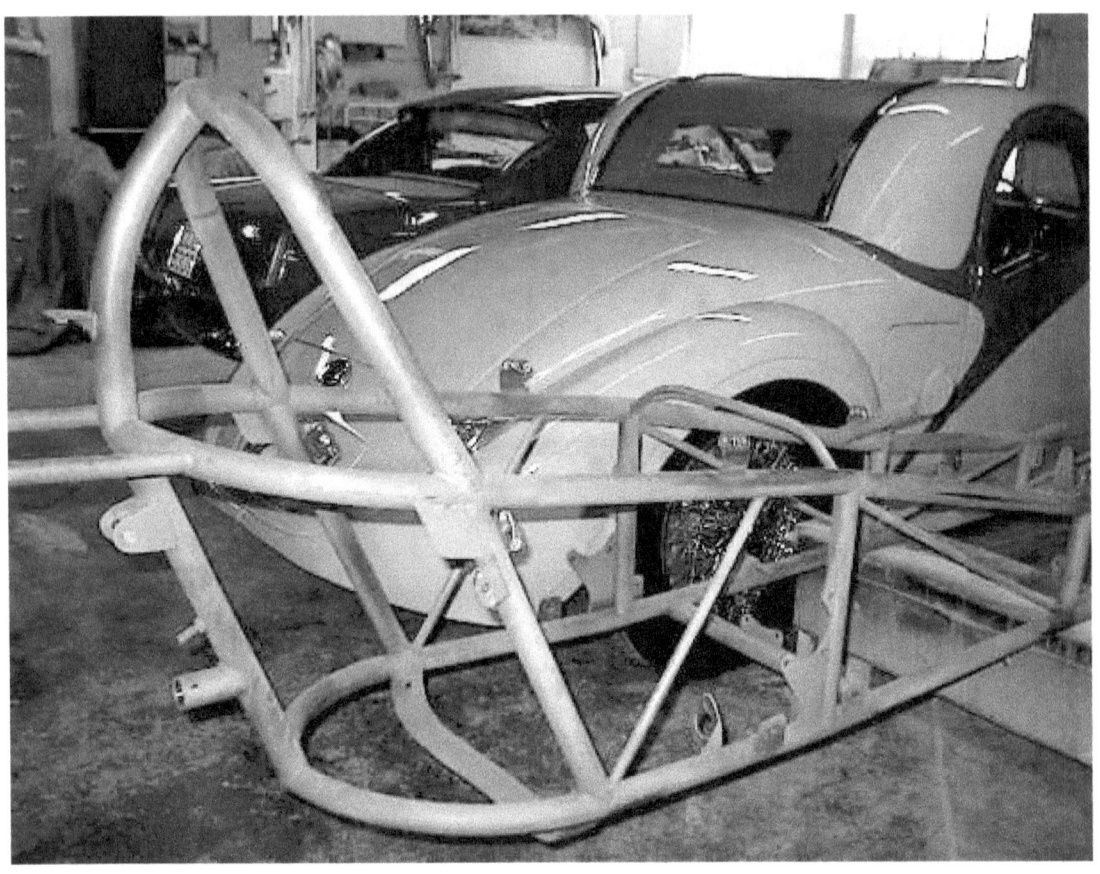

The Fuller and the girls compare booties...

I'll Bring it Back "Honest"

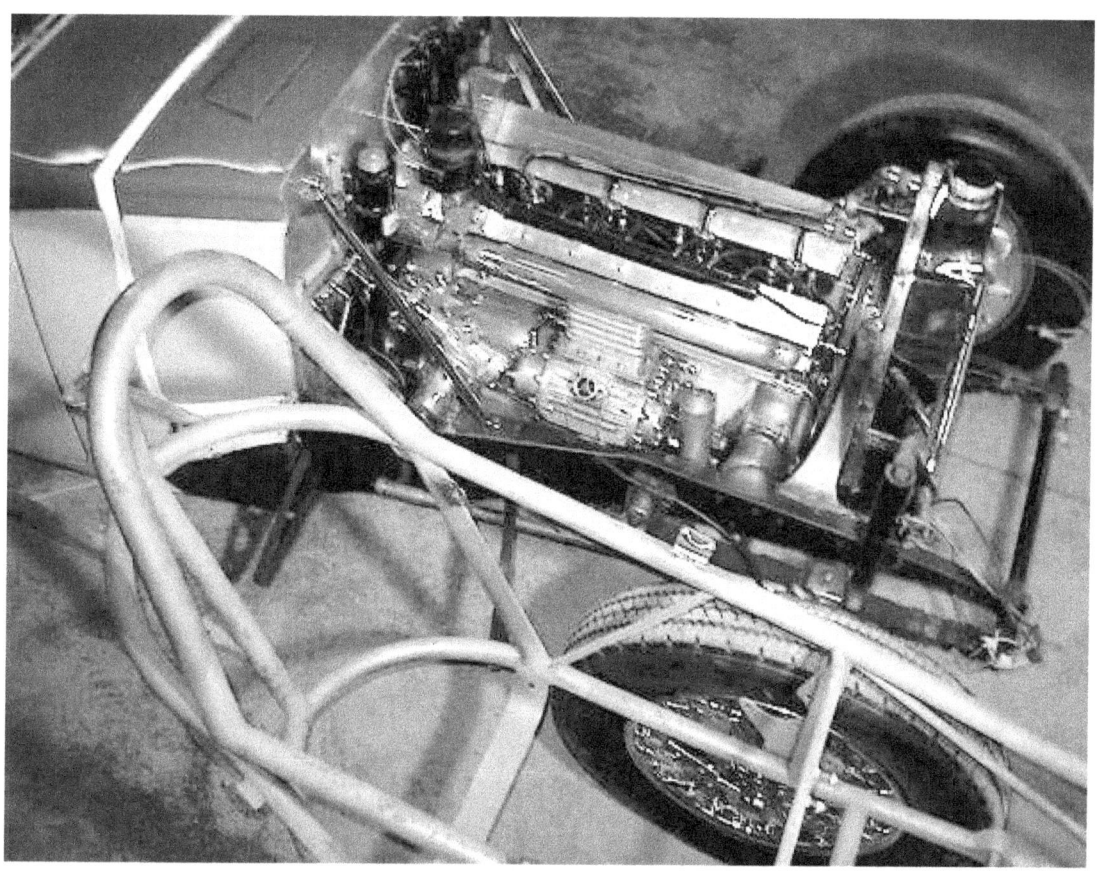

The Naked Fuller hustles 'The Naked Bugatti' for her engine - - She's French ... She's goin' for it ... ... To quote Johnny Cochran, "Your never late - with a straight 8" PS: Barbara is a 1938 type 57C (supercharged)

Chassis Paint Prep

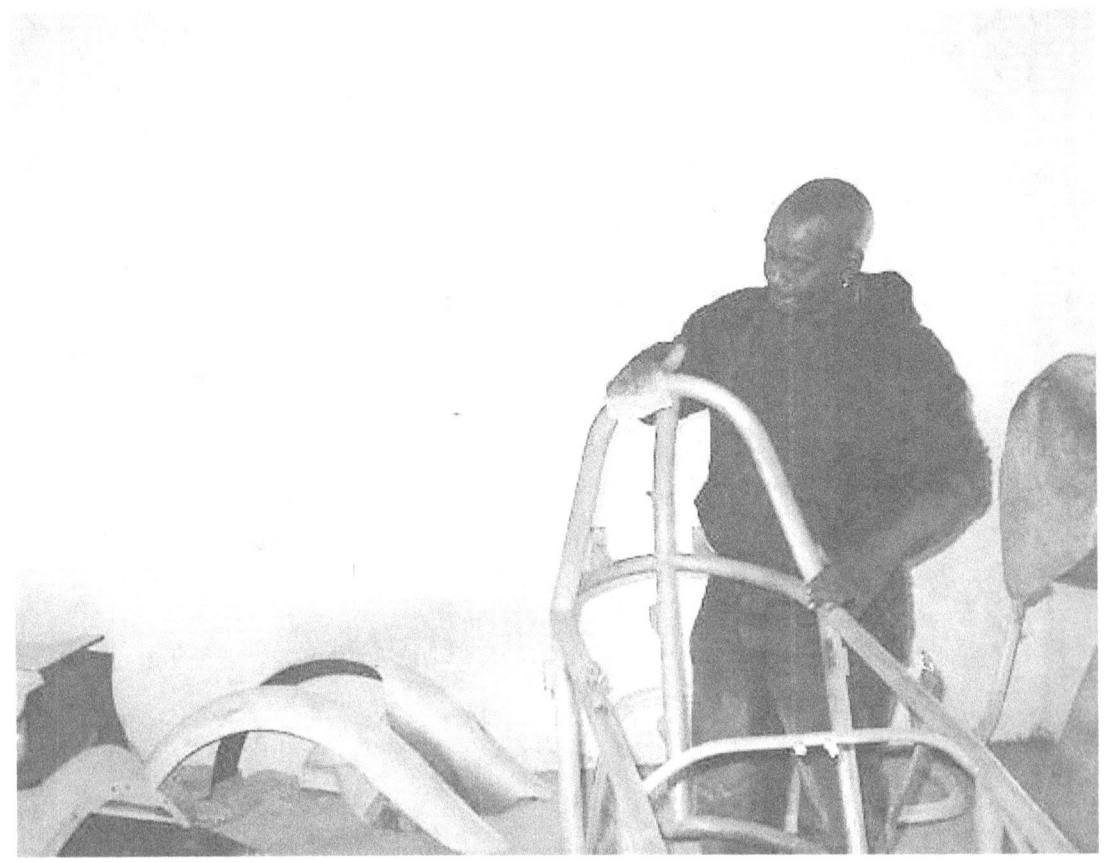

Passed down since the days of Ben-Hur ... ... Chassis painting continues to be one of the sacred arts ... Handling the gun today will be the well-known spraygunoligest - - Eric J. Hayes. As you can see in this first photo, Mr. Hayes is sanding the still naked Fuller with 100 grit ... well you can't really tell that it's 100 grit - but trust me ... it is ... ... this takes off any surface rust that was left after being media blasted, (media blasting doesn't take off rust very well)). Hmmm.... Must have the settings a little off on this Digi Thing ... Eric's photographing kinda dark

More Prep

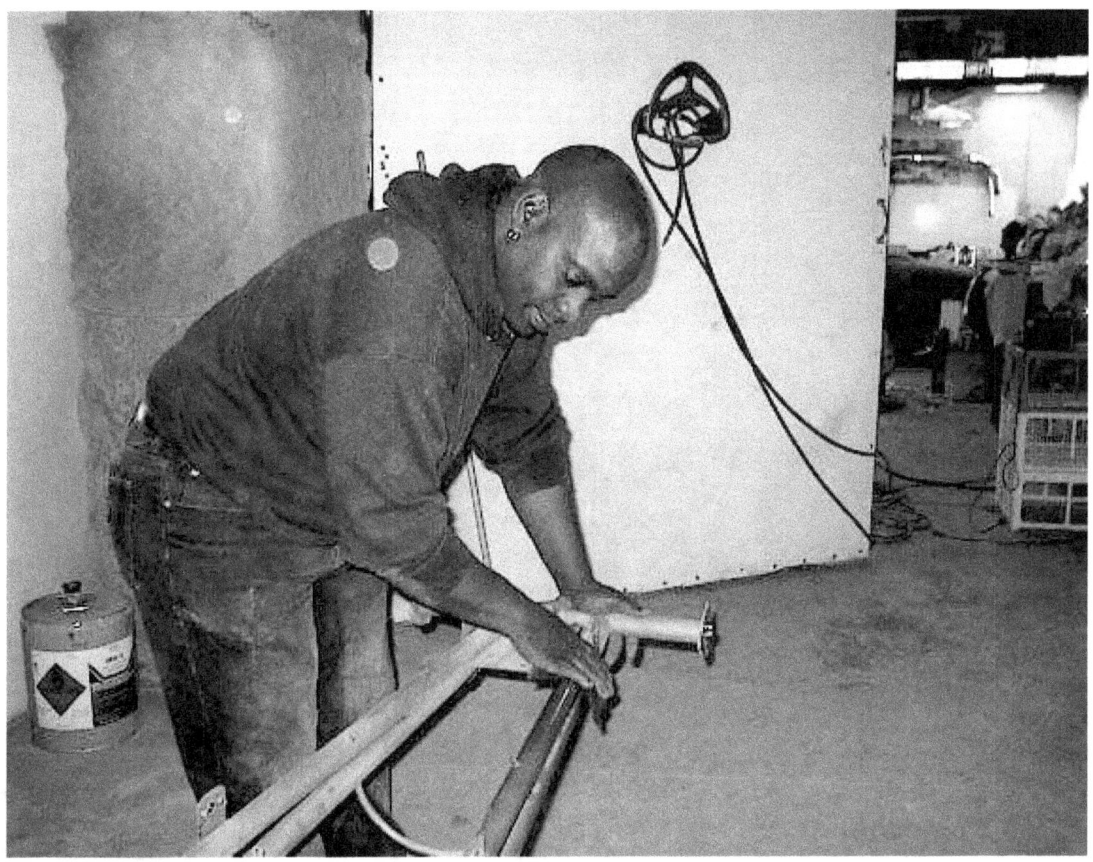

Here we see Eric scrubbing the Fuller with one of those red scotch-brite scrubber things ... and Lacquer thinner ... This not only gets the little spots that were missed by the sand paper - and removes any grease, etc ... but also in the process can get you quite stoned, (note the smile on Mr. Hayes's face). I recommend a fast thinner for this job....

FullerPoxy

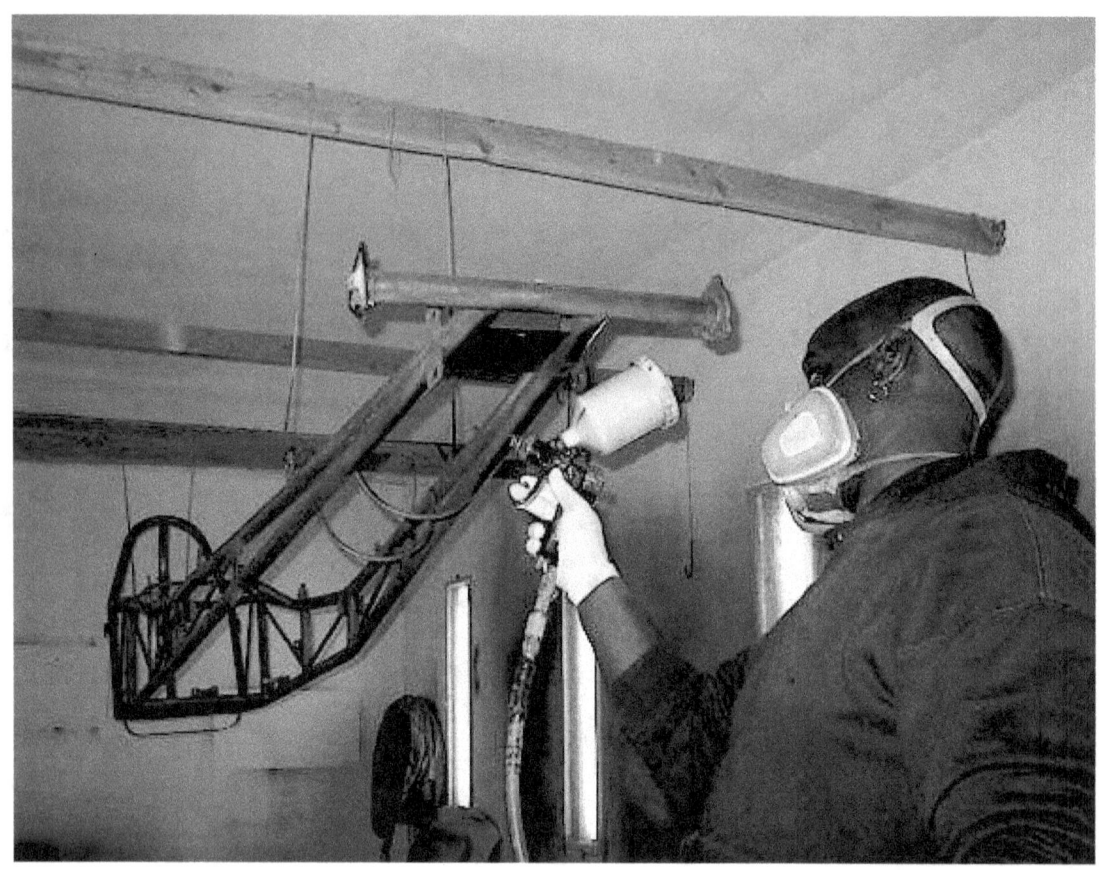

OK ... now we get down to the real stuff ... Here you see Mr. Hayes deftly handling the spray gun - as he sprays (the rapidly becoming former) naked Fuller with (PPG) DP 90 epoxy primer, (I recommend the fast 402 catalyst), note the very special Mickey Mouse type white gloves Eric's wearing... a very 'in' style. These kids today Man! ... gloves - masks - - you'd think they were robbing a 7-11 - not just paintin' somethin' ... in my day we didn't use any of that sissy stuff ... ... Yaaaaah - now if I could just get my lungs to work again...

The Un-naked Fuller

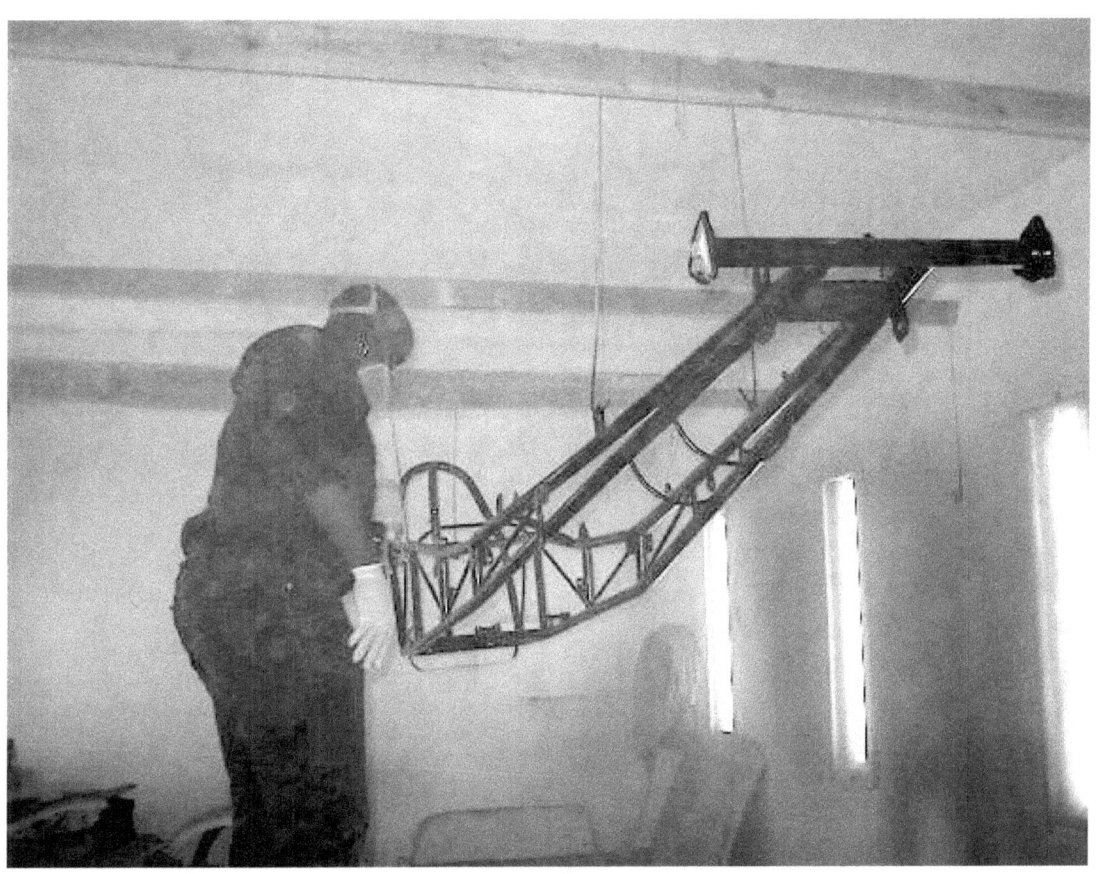

Onward ... Here we see our faithful Indian companion spraying the color - basic black - we use PPG - DBU 9700 base coat ... I could put a pic on here of Eric spraying the clear Urethane top coat over the black ... but it would look much the same, (and yeah - it's true, clear is my favorite color) ... OK - - Powder Coating is tougher - - but this one gets paint ... hey - - didn't have no powder coating in 62...

The Hanging Fuller

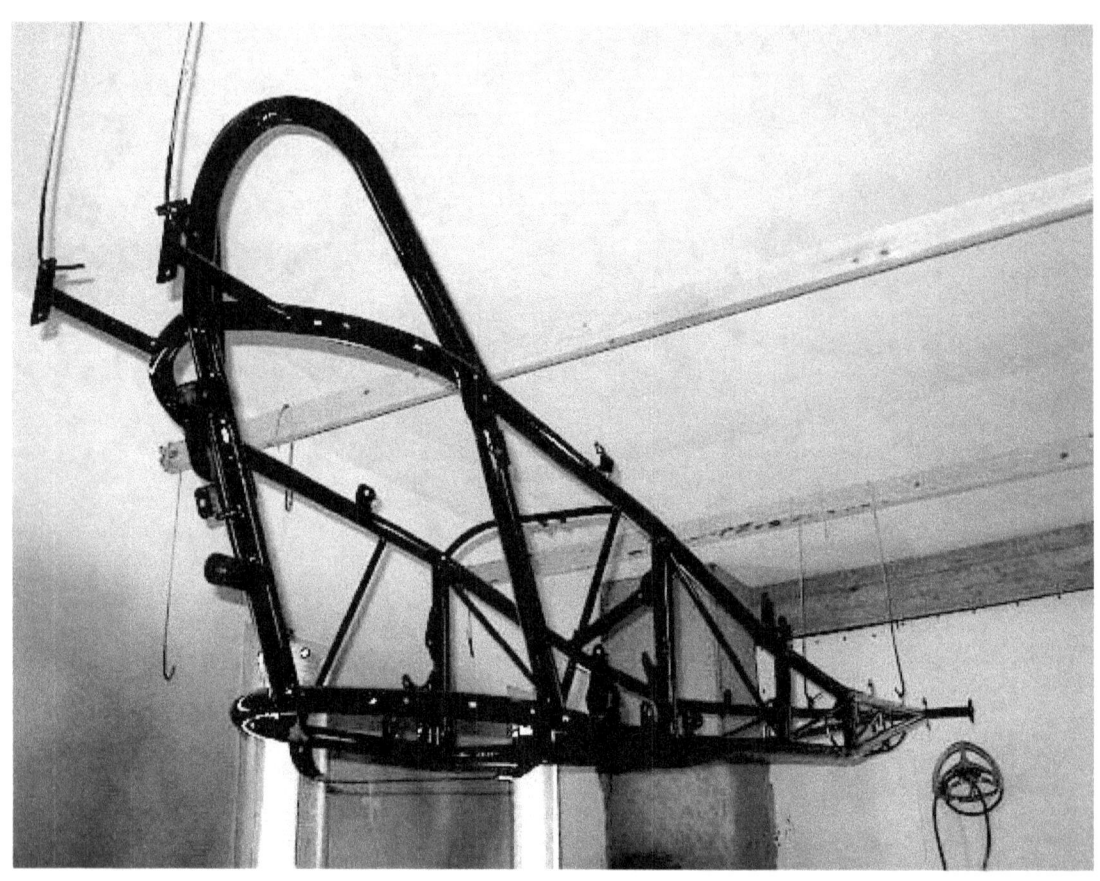

Here we see the re-newed Fuller just hangin' around ... or as Eric say's ...
"He's showin' off his shine"

The Future

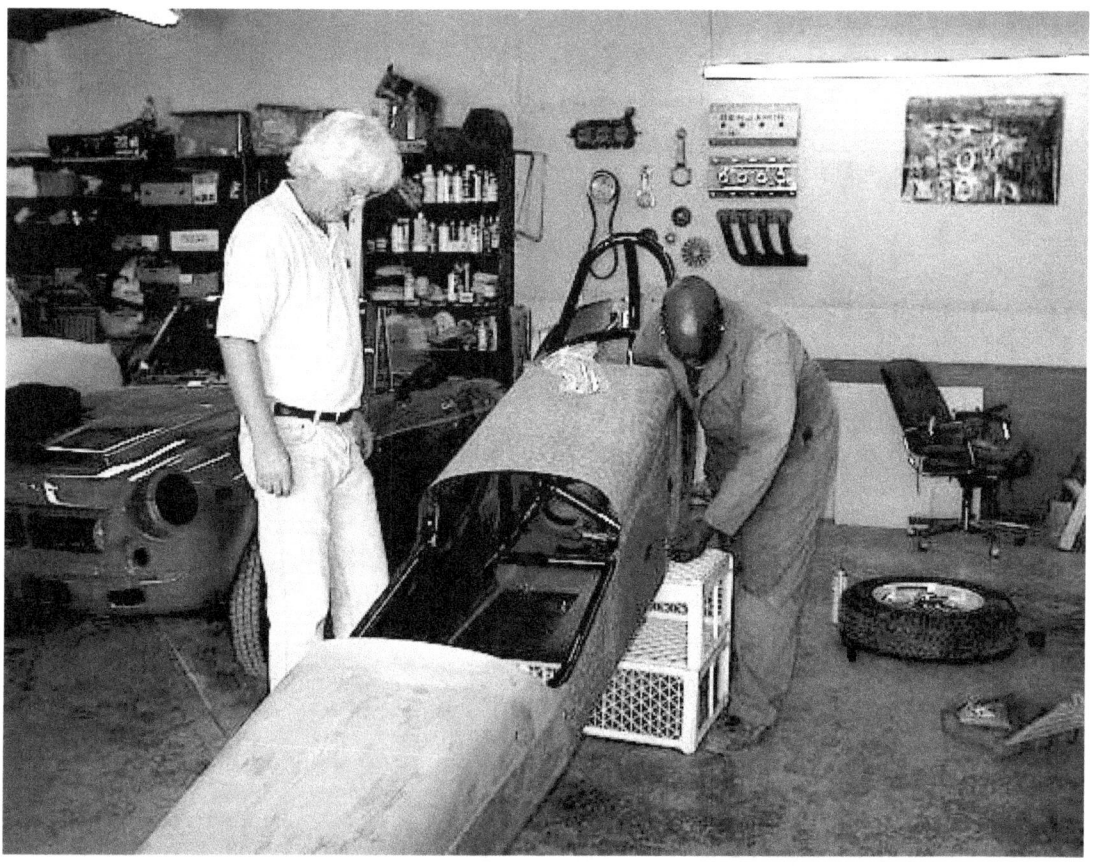

Pit Crew Pete and Eric contemplate the future as they fit the body panels
to the car

How's it fit

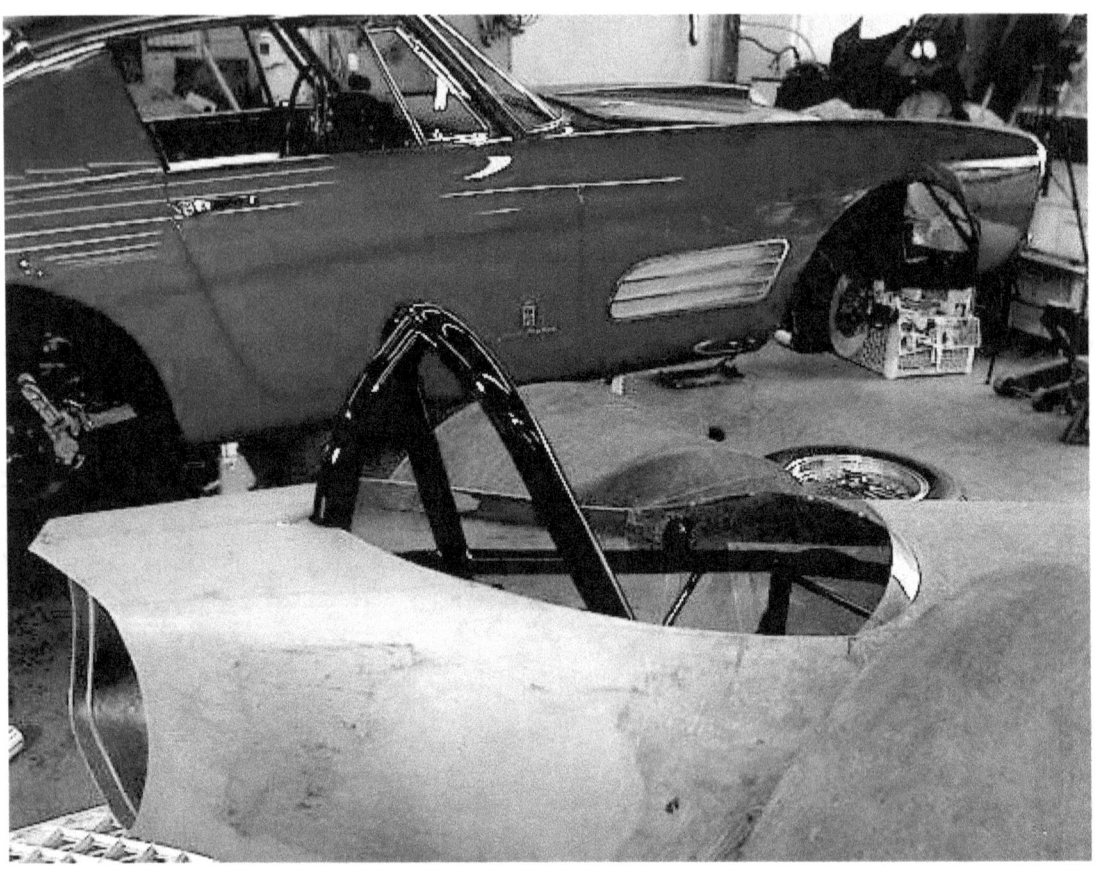

The Fuller slips the ol' tailpiece on for the first time in a few years... note - He's also trying on a couple of SuperBike's spare tires to see how they fit too... Gina is flashed...

The Fuller Makes a Move

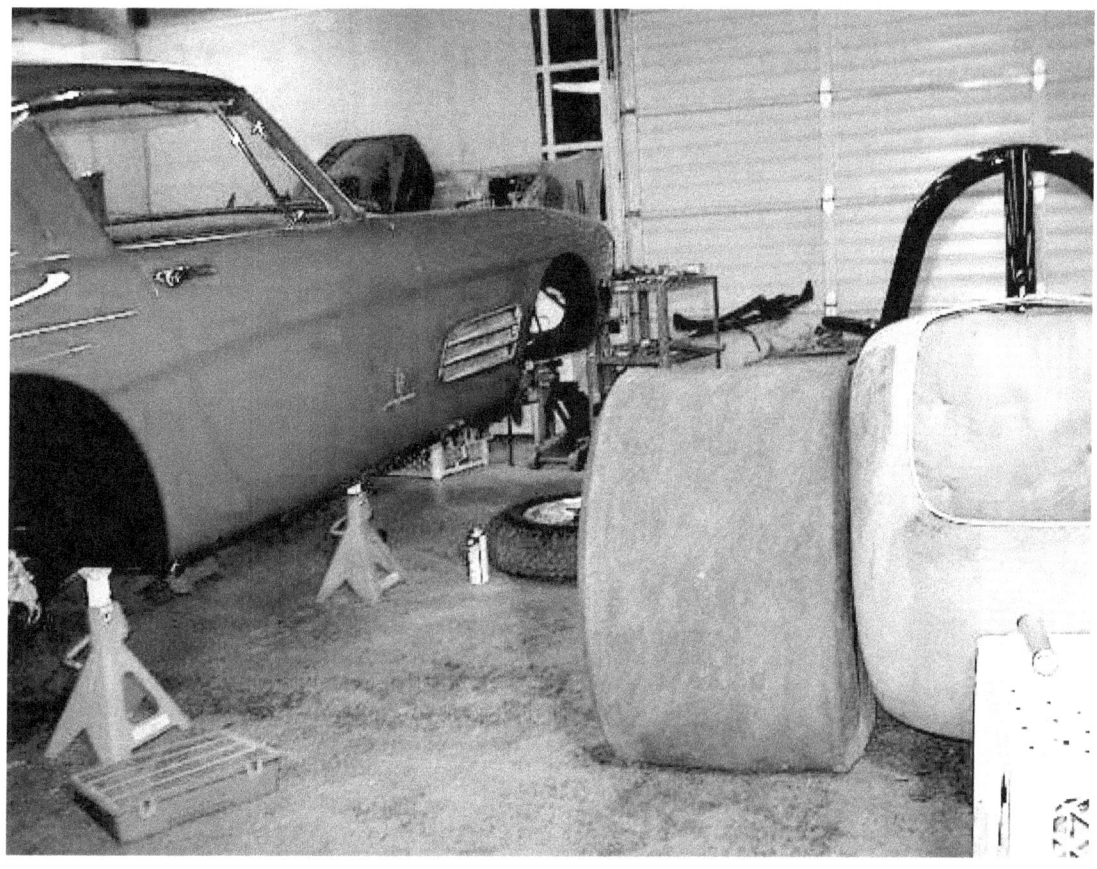

The Fuller shows 'Gina Ferrari' His new 'Big Tires' and designer chute pack. "10 inch tires? ... I use them on my trailer", say's the Fuller ... Gina is impressed!

"BAD"

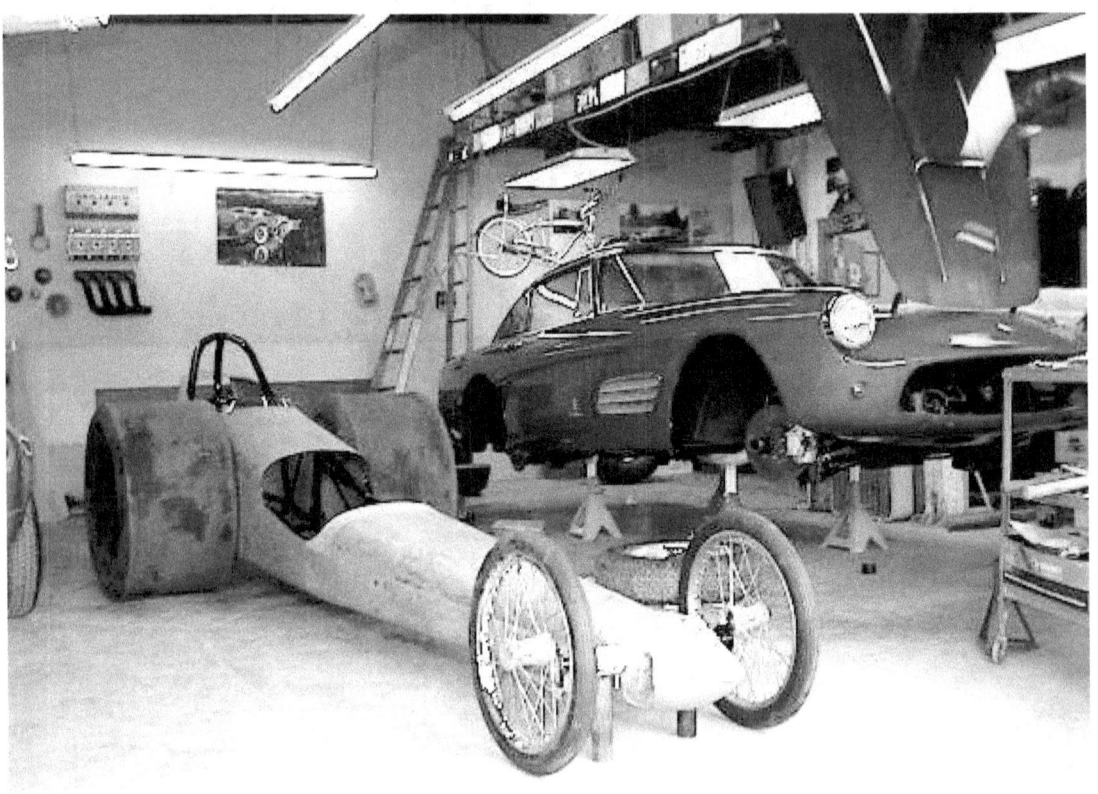

"Am I BAD - or what?" ... thinks The Fuller as he shows off his perfect fit body panels - "35 years and they still fit just right - I haven't gained a pound, and these slicks are too cool - - I mean. is this a look!, or what" Gina is starting to get just a little tired of listening to 'The Fuller' talk about himself............

The Sordid Tale Continues...

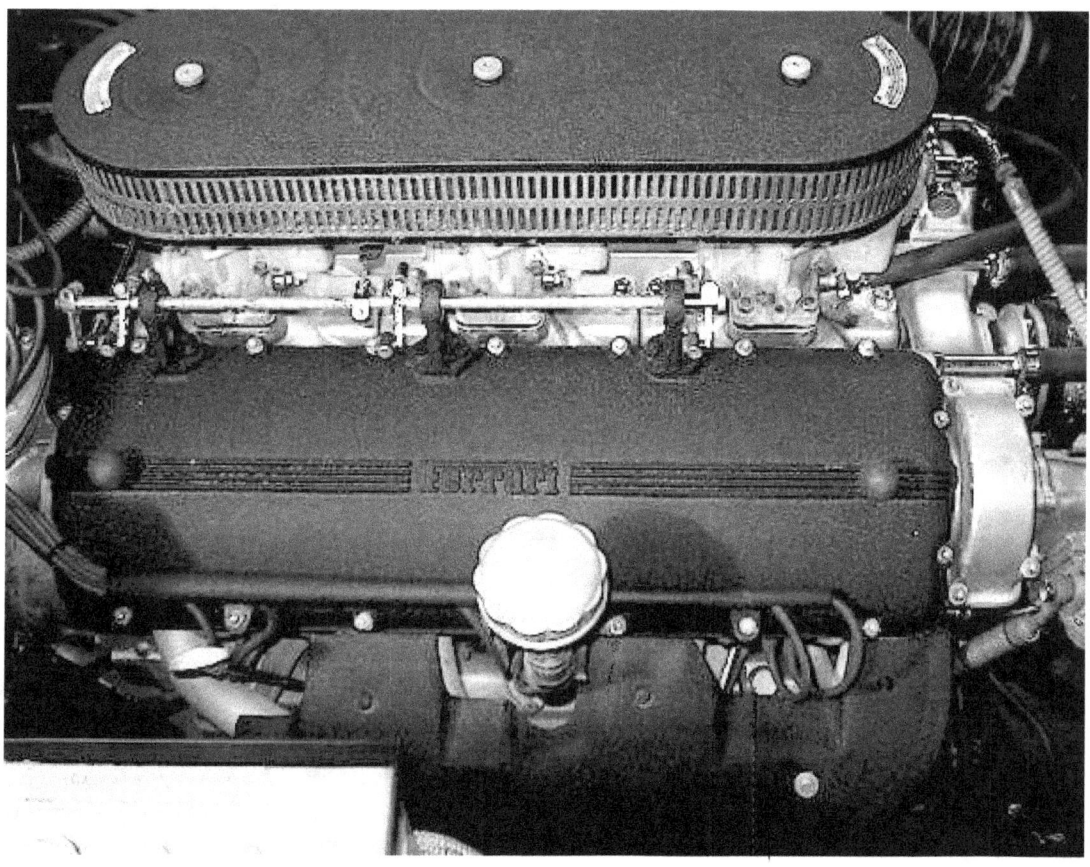

Gina shows him her engine, "Hmmmm....." thinks The Fuller, "I need an engine - looks like a 671 will bolt right on there..."

Hummmmmmmmm...

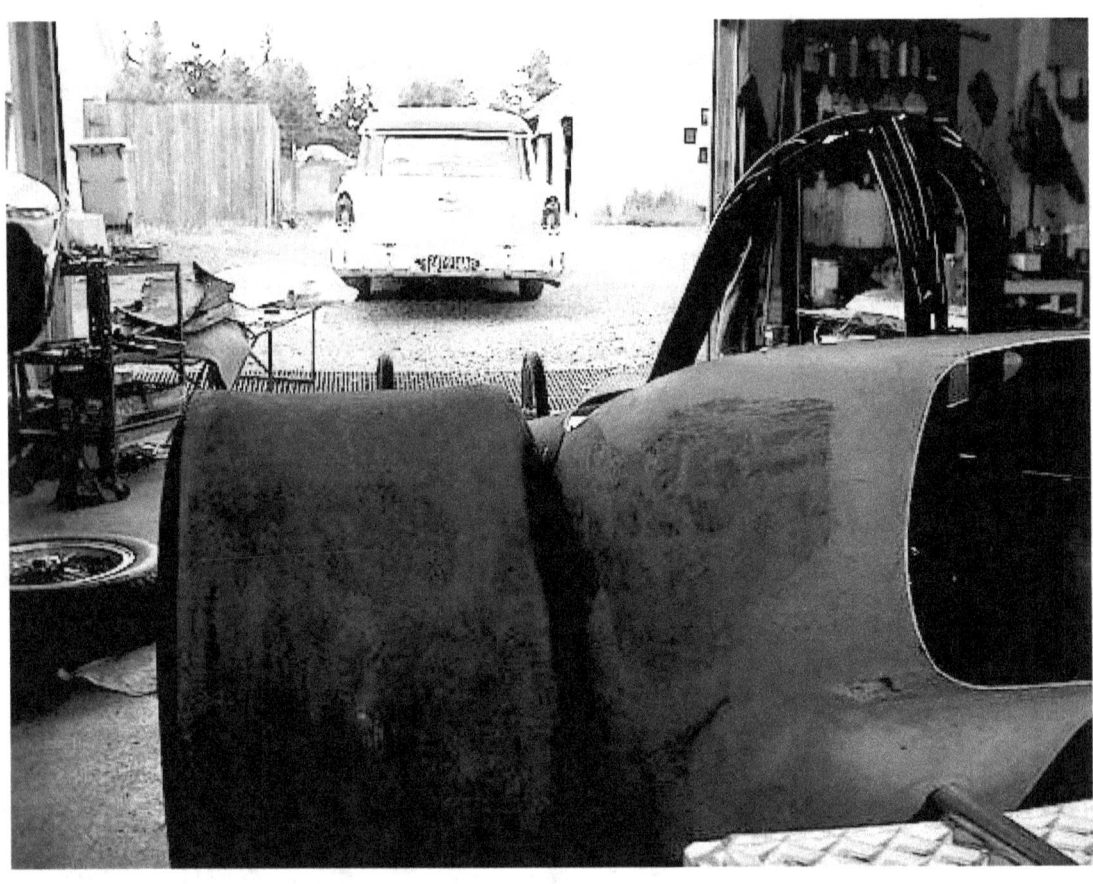

The Fuller looks towards the future... and has his eye on a likely push car candidate... Time to turn on the charm again...

Wanna Race?????

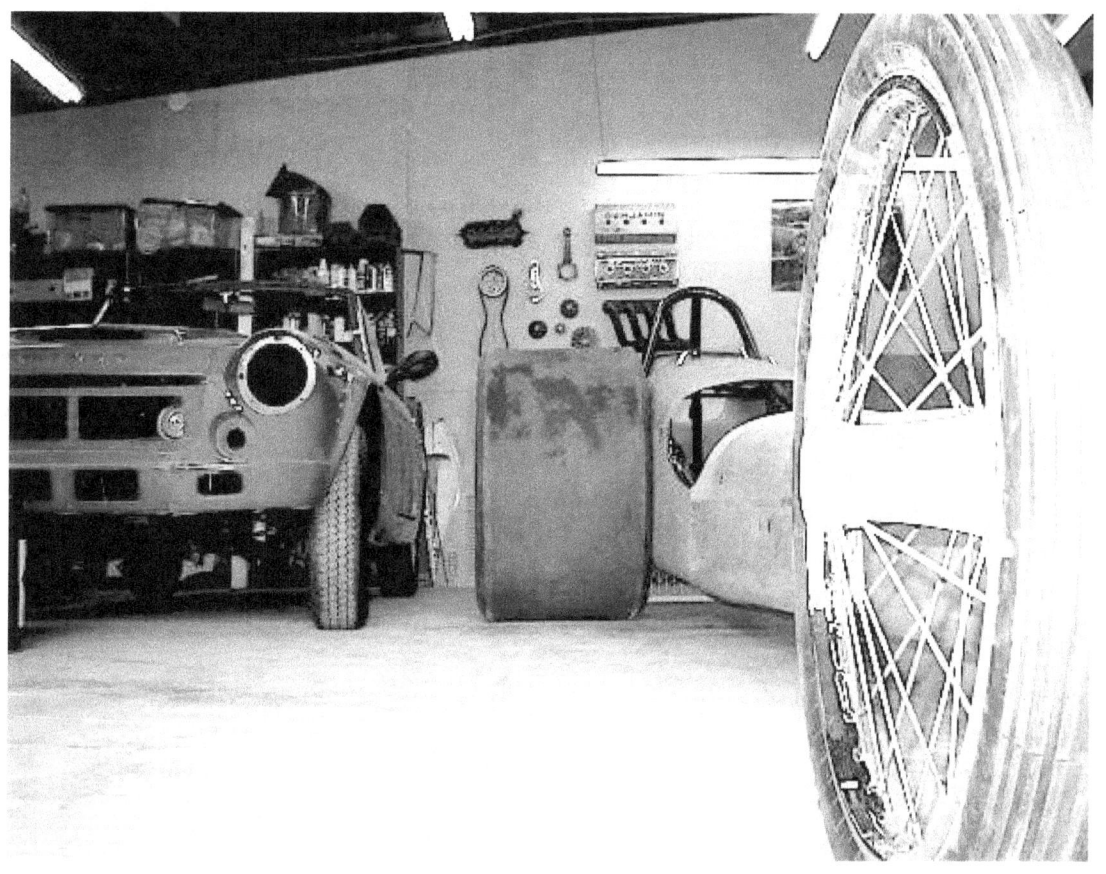

The Fuller closes off with a 'rice-burner' ... ... "Don't even need an engine for this", say's the Fuller, as he prepares to dust off his Asian friend...

An Evening At Home

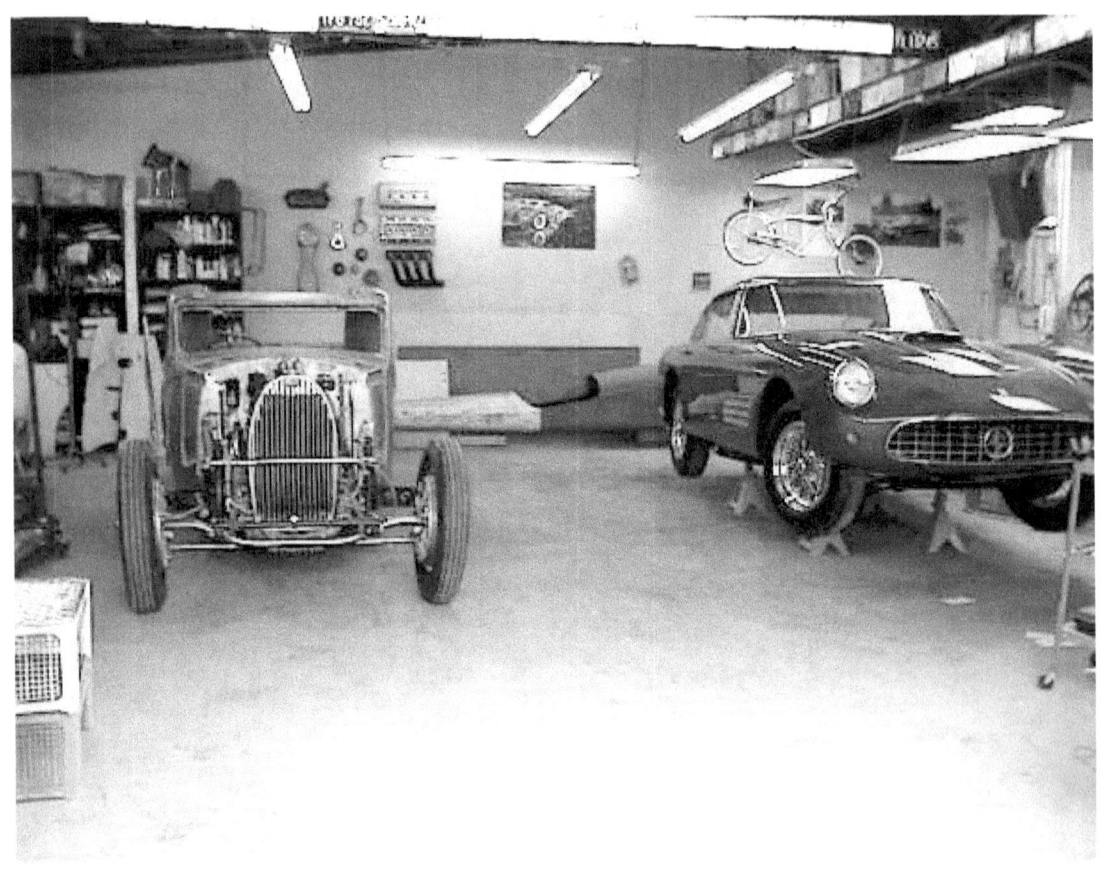

Here we see The Fuller and his girls spending a quite evening at home ... note The Fuller in the background - while the French chick seems to have removed most of her body parts, (how French) ... and Gina Ferrari is all dressed up and ready to come off the jack stands for a night on the town...

Before-N-After "Space Magic"

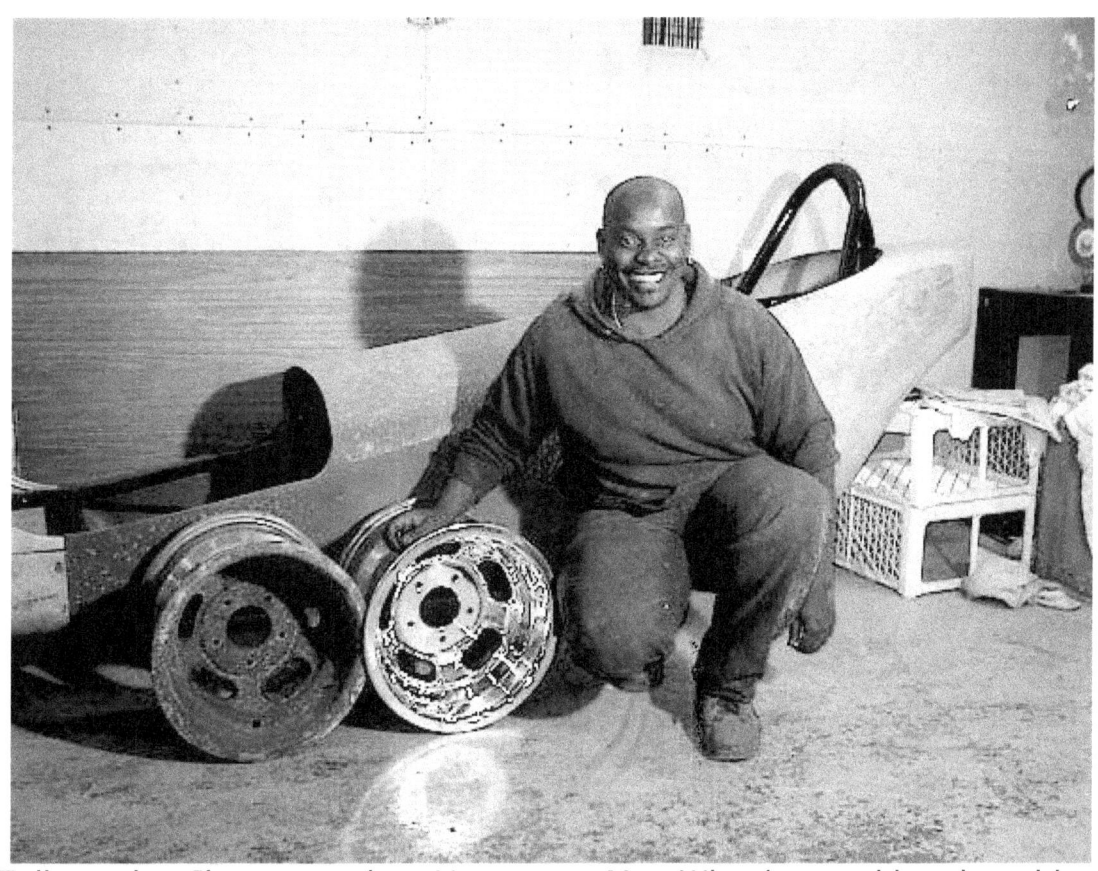

Tell ya what I'm gonna do... Ya say yer Mag Wheels are old and cruddy - Ya say they're gray and flaky... maybe they been settin' under the workbench in your shop for 35 years ... ... Well bring'em to Eric J Hayes - 'The Polishing Wizard' Hey!!! If ya need 'Super Polishing'... it's erichayes@bikesters.com (shameless plug)

See Ya'

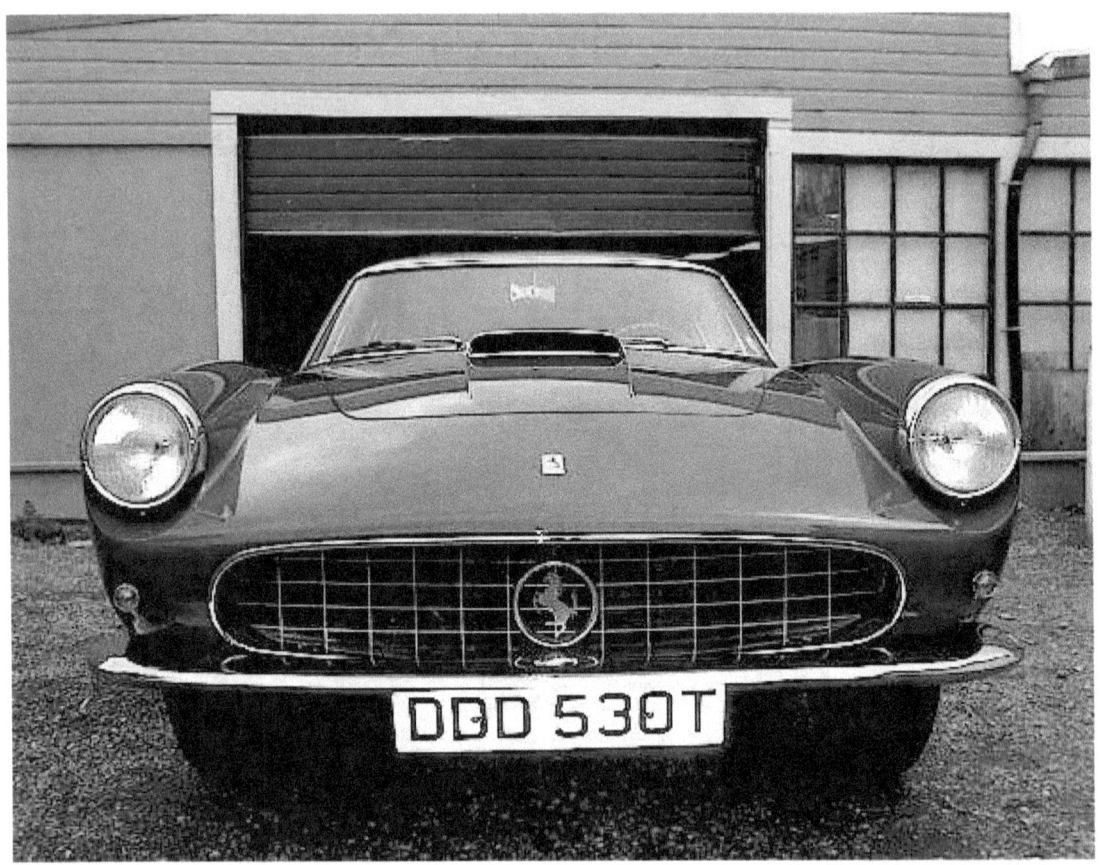

Don't let the door hit ya in the taillights - yells The Fuller as Gina storms out after a rather nasty tiff ... Geez, "all I asked her was to get me a beer" thinks The Fuller as he returns to staring at his newly polished wheels ... "Besides, I am not vain"!!!

"Don't Need None of Ya'"

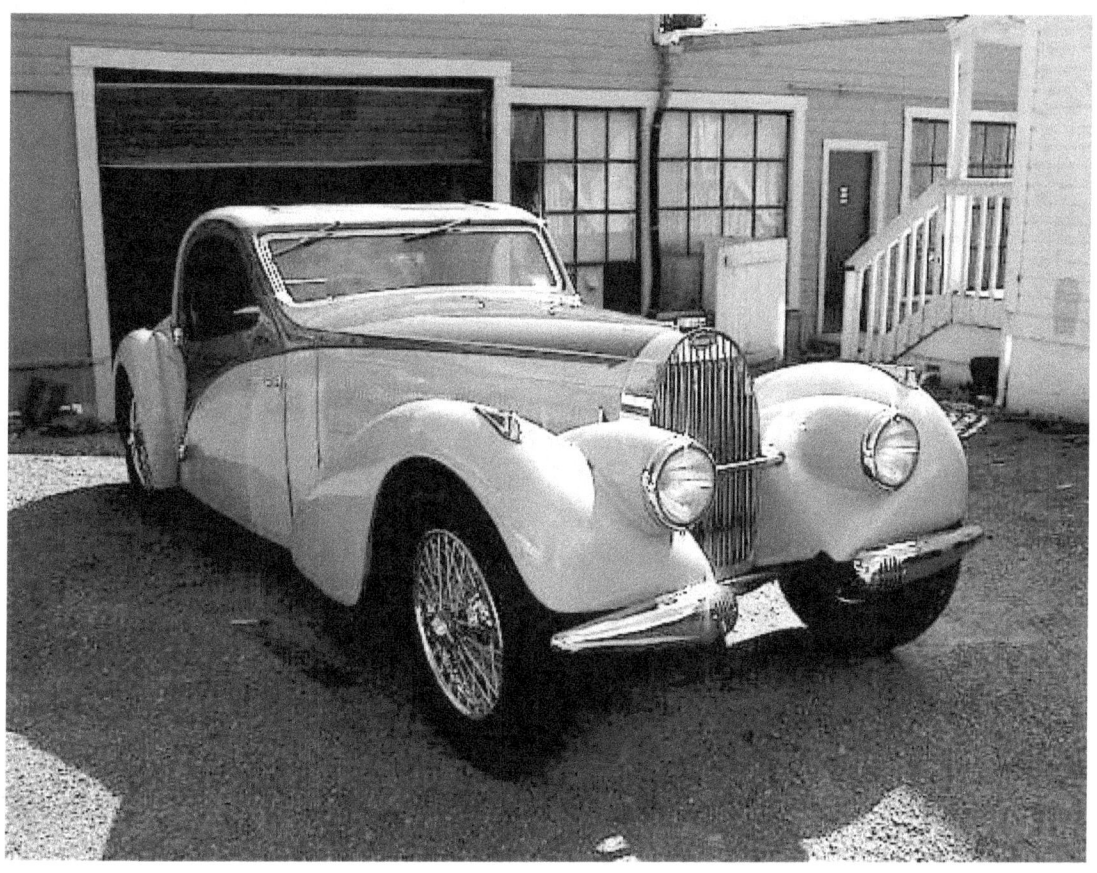

'The Fuller' turns to look ... and the French chick is headin' out the door
too - - goin' to LA to party with the 'Bigs' ... "Go ahead" say's The Fuller
... I don't need you guys any way ... ya' ain't even Drag Racers.........

Gone But Not Forgotten

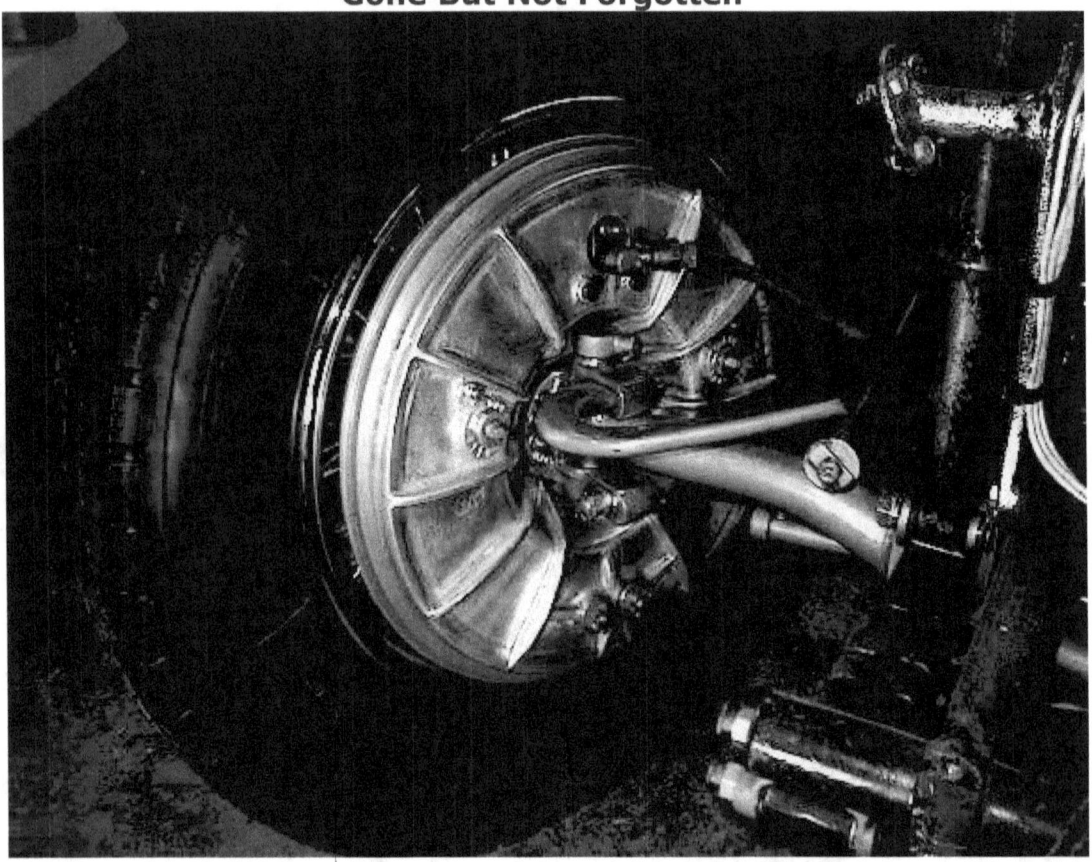

All Frenchie left him with was a picture of her backing plate.... She did have a nice Backing Plate - - sigh's The Fuller

"Party Down"

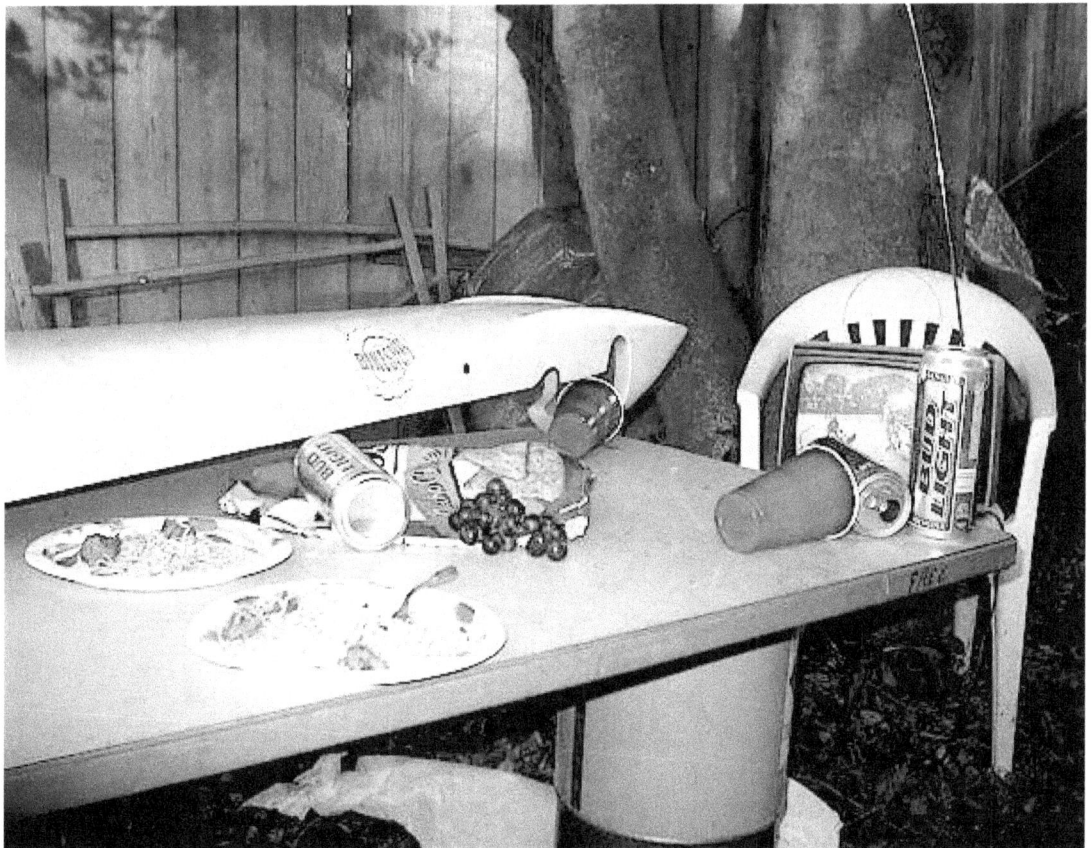

"Taking time out to drink a little beer and watch the ball game will help me forget those 'third world' chicks", thinks The Fuller

New Roomie

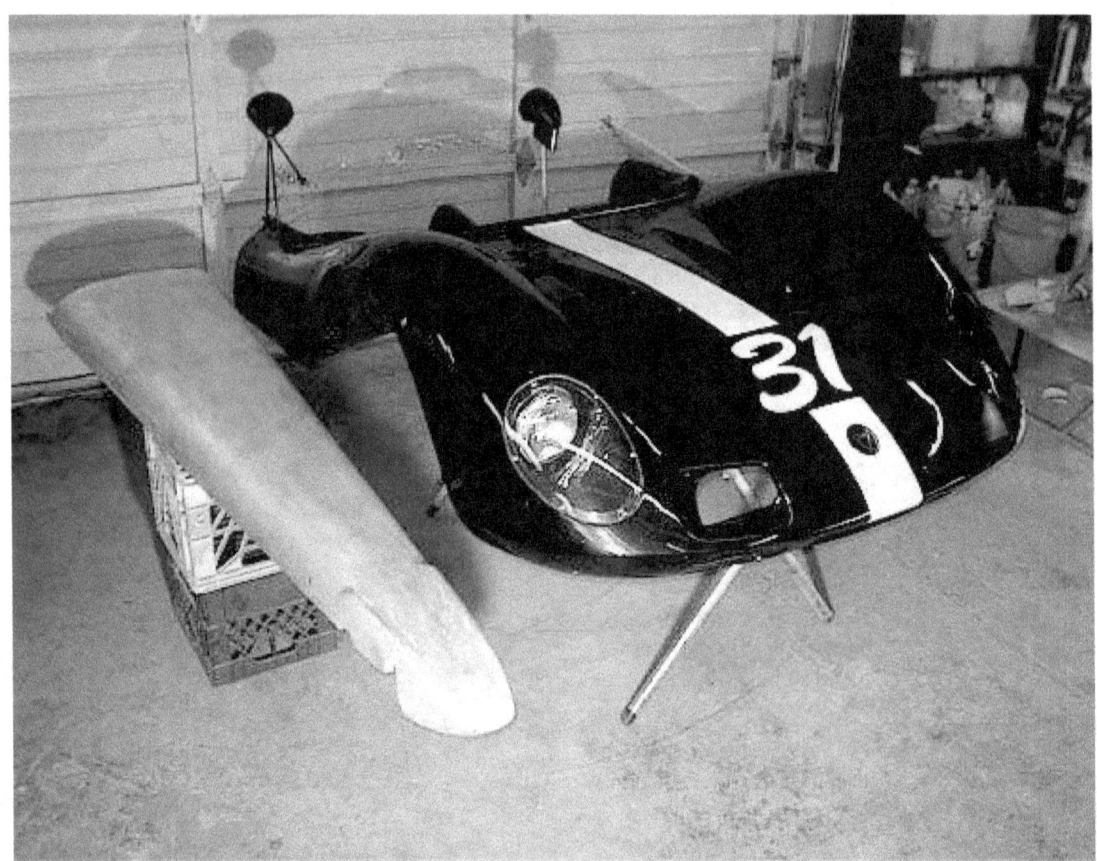

The Fuller compares noses with new room mate Elvira ELVA ... After putting up with the volatile Gina Ferrari, and having the French chick take off for LA ... It's nice to have another racer around ... and she's English - They speak the same language, (sorta) ... Hey! at least she's gotta V8 ... even if it is just one of those little 215 deals - - and ya know - I don't care what those 'limey's say - - it's a GM....

A Bugatti Bedtime Story

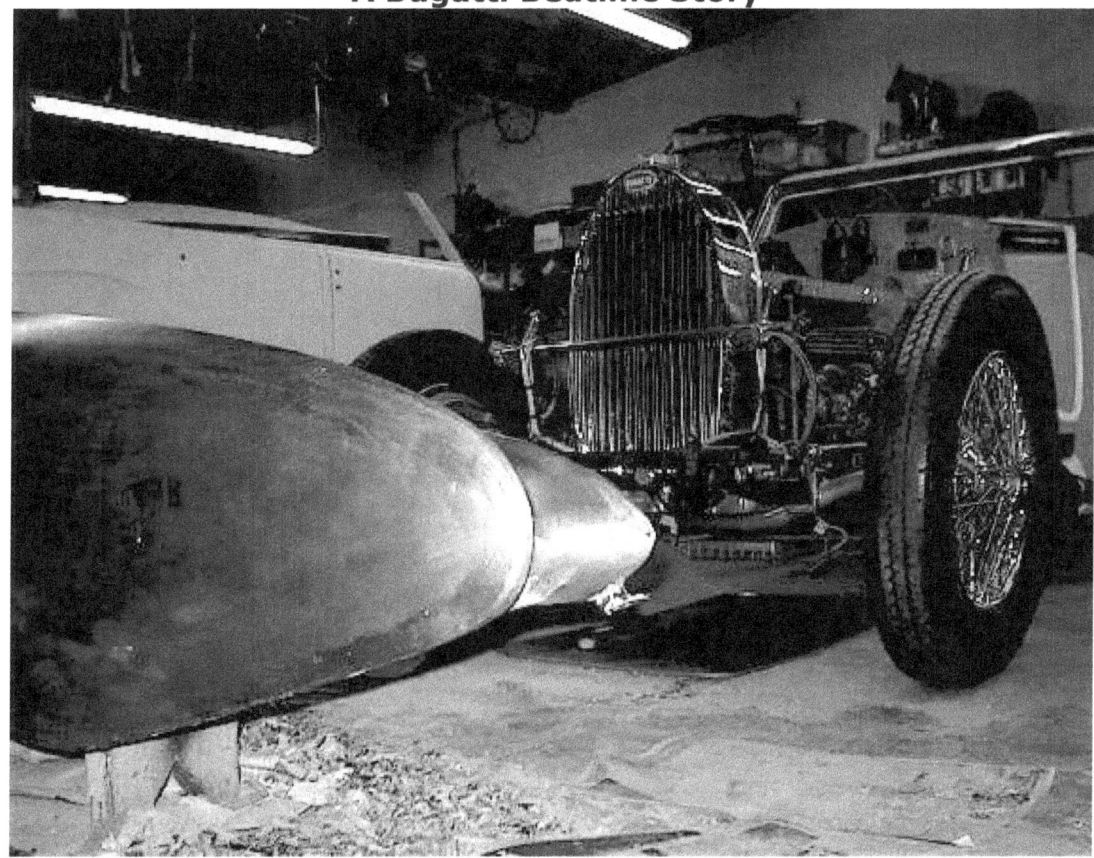

Barbra Bugatti, (38 Bugatti Atlanti), has a very interesting history. Besides being a unique car in the fact that it's one of the few Bugatti's ever built with hydraulic brakes and shocks... The old man (Ettore Bugatti) didn't believe in such things... most of the cars had these strange adjustable with cables (from inside the car) friction shocks... and of course, good old mechanical brakes. But for a very brief period, Bugatti's son ran the engineering department and went modern... His son was killed in a testing accident - trying out some of his new-fangled ideas... and Bugatti quickly went back to the old ways, and stuck with them... It's also the only Atlanti with 'Vintu' fenders, (Pontoon style)... However the real story comes after the car was created. When the Germans over ran France in the war... one of the first things they did was begin gathering up art and trucking it off - back to the 'Fatherland', (spoils of war, ya know). Bugatti's are, (and always have been) considered works of art by the French Government; you still have to get government permission to take one out of the country. The French may have pretty much rolled over for the Germans, but they went to great lengths to hide their art... especially the Bugatti's... this particular car has perhaps the best story of all. The people of the village where this car was... disassembled the body, wrapped all the pieces in oil cloth... and buried them in several different farm yards... Then they put a beat up old truck body on the chassis and used it as a farm truck all through the war... If you've ever heard a blown Bugatti run ... you can imagine them trying to pass that deal off - make a great movie. They pulled it off... And after the war, they dug up the body pieces... put 'em in the back of the beat up farm truck... and drove the whole works back to the Bugatti Factory, where it was restored, and reassembled... The original front fenders were the only things lost in the war... so they built the 'Vintu' fenders at the factory - just for this car, (far better looking then the originals... The car lived in a private museum in France since the mid 50's... and was brought over here last year by the present owner who is having her restored. The guy who owns it is kinda interesting too ... besides having made a whole bunch of bucks in the semi-conductor business... He's an old time hot-rodder went to high school with M/T and worked for Evans Equipment in the early 50's building flatheads ... was a Drag Racer ... and held the overall record for a couple of days with a car that he built with Potvin. He's gonna dig in his old stuff... he's pretty sure there's pictures from those days in there someplace, Fred. Here's a shot of the car apart that fender is a killer piece of metal work - eh? Guess maybe those French guy's aren't all bad...

Nose in DP

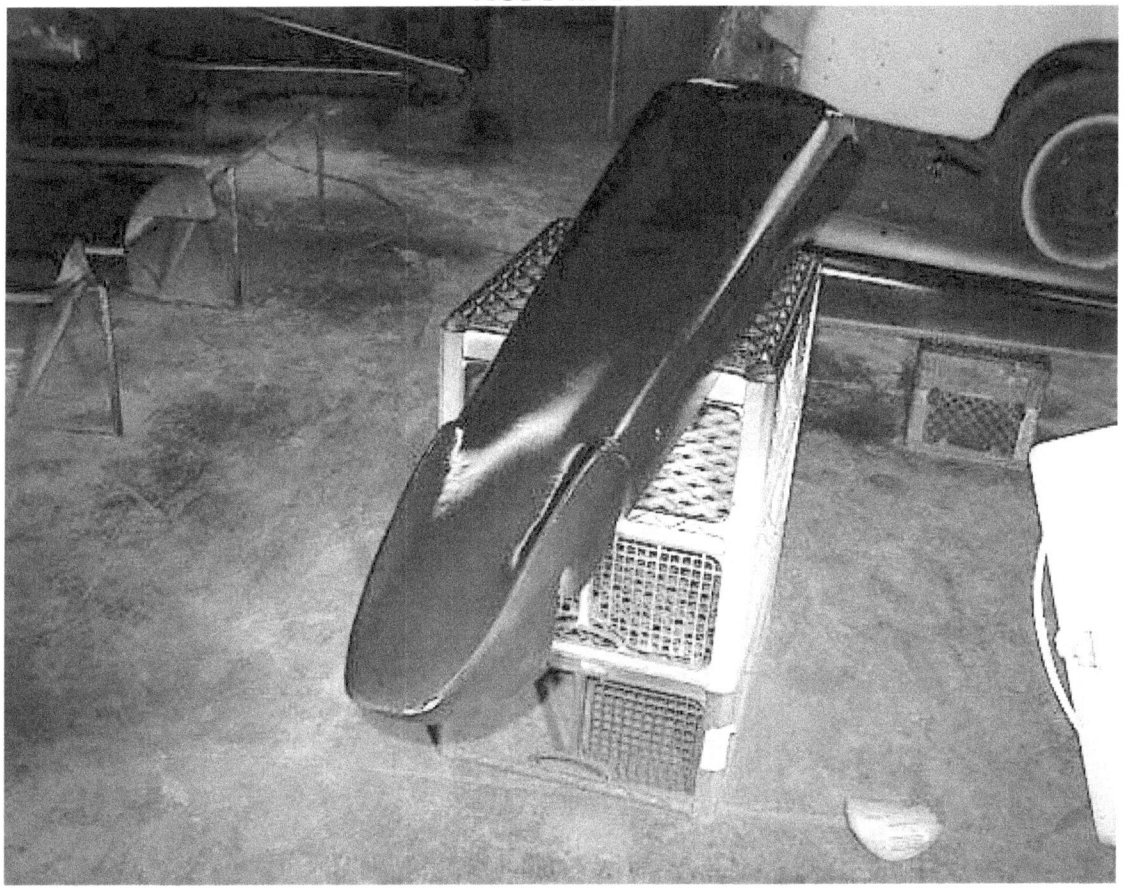

after taking any paint off the body pieces with chemical stripper, then sanding and cleaning the aluminum to the freak out point - - as in - you could eat off it' - (if FULLER would make you a chrome-molly knife and fork), they get a coat of Zink-Chromate ... and then a couple of heavy coats of DP (epoxy primer) ... looks sorta bad in black - huh?

Yellow Fellow

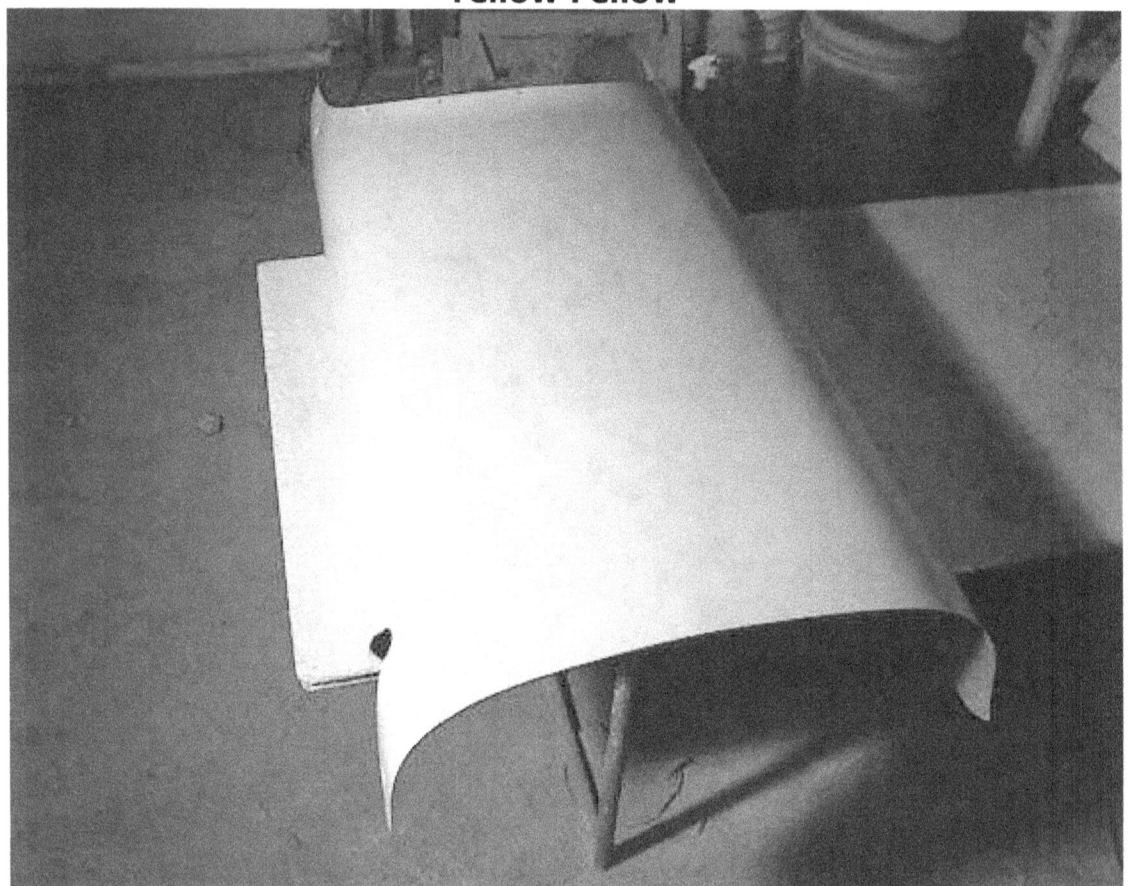

Let the DP catalyze good (dry) and pile on a bunch of urethane primer, (lotsa brands to chose from). I always go over the DP with one of those scotch-brite scrubber things just to make sure the primer sticks.... I learned to paint back in the 'olden' (Lacquer) days - and I find that these catalyzing type paints sometimes don't stick to each other - where as with Lacquer the coats just melt into each other - - I like Lacquer – sorry

Block it

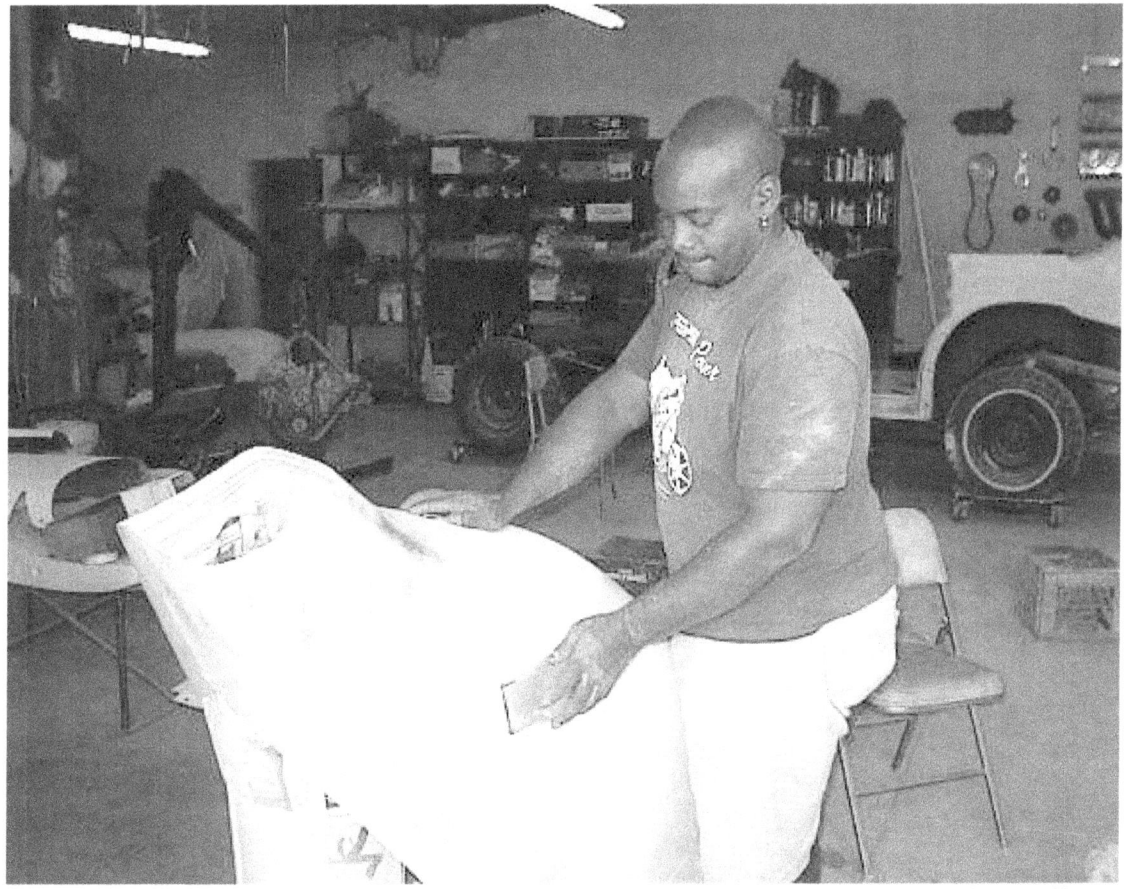

Here we see Eric in the 'block sanding mode'... the primer on The Fullers tail is that yellow urethane stuff. The camera just decided to make it look white), the black speckles are a guide coat to show the low areas We use all different sizes and hardness of blocks... it's pretty much - what works best for the area your doing at the moment

The Never-ending Blocking

Ugh!! This block sanding deal goes on for ever - - and ya' gotta' do every piece two or three times to get it just right... Here's Mr. Hayes using a thin block that he can bend to the contour of the nose... 'The Fuller' will settle for nothing less then 'The Perfect Look'!!!

Blocking Done Captain

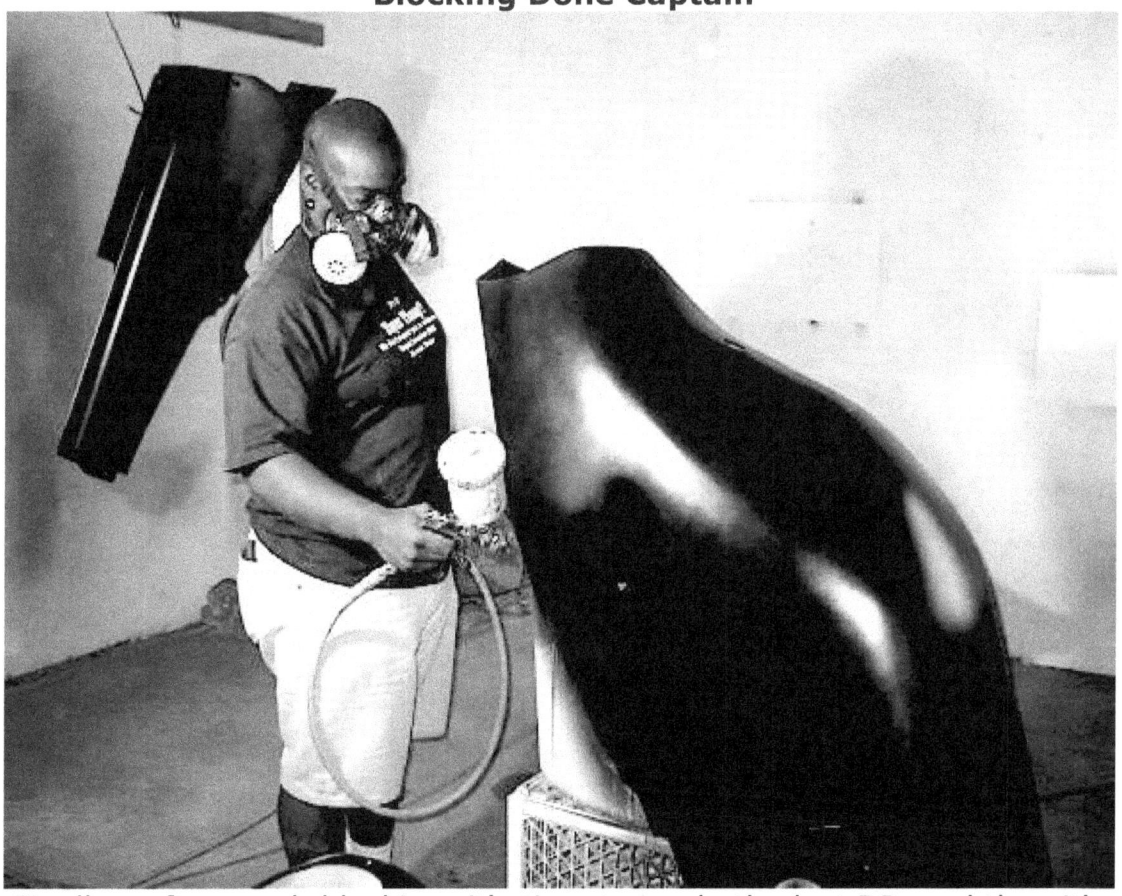

Finally - after much blocking, it's time to apply the last DP, and then it's onward - - to color... "Bout time" say's Eric...

"Badder in Black"

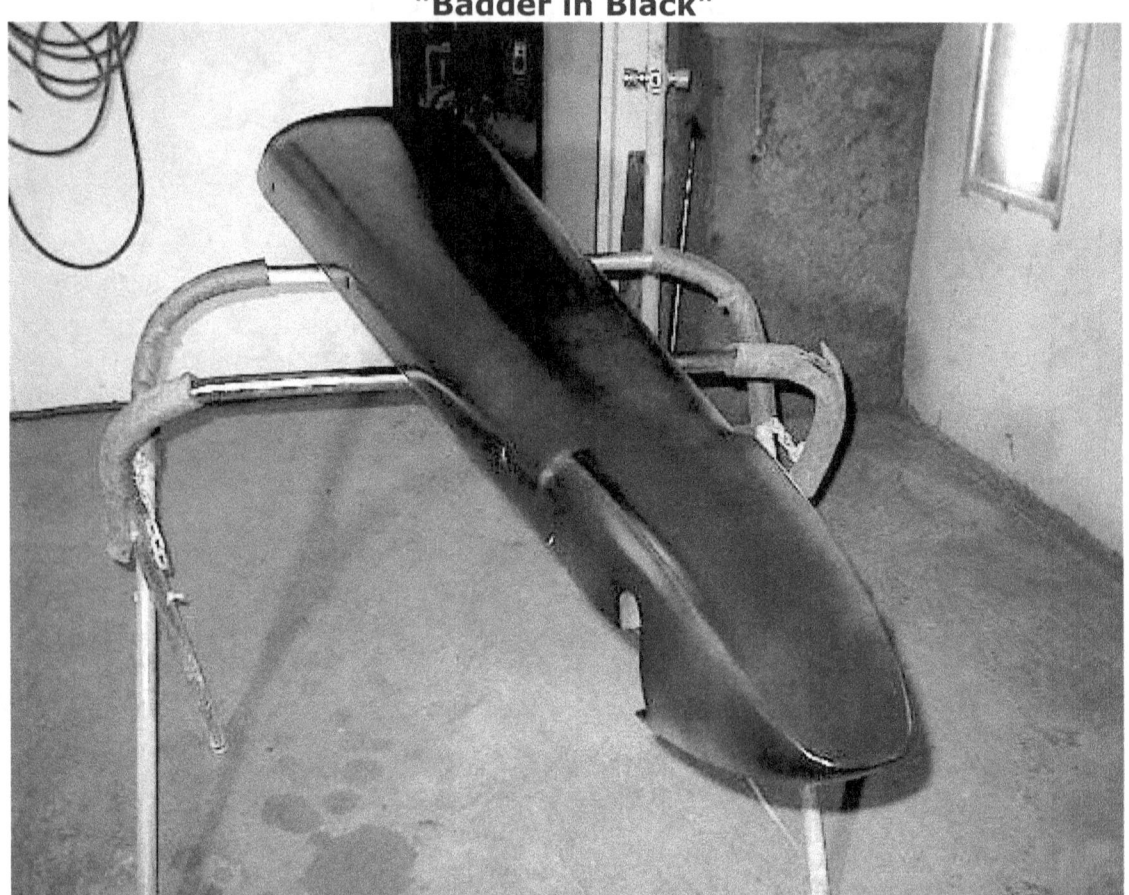

The nose is lookin' pretty crisp... and ready for color...

"Hi-ho Silver"

Nose in silver base coat - - still lookin' pretty Bad! ... (That's BAD - - as in good 'n' BAD!!!)

"Flake it"

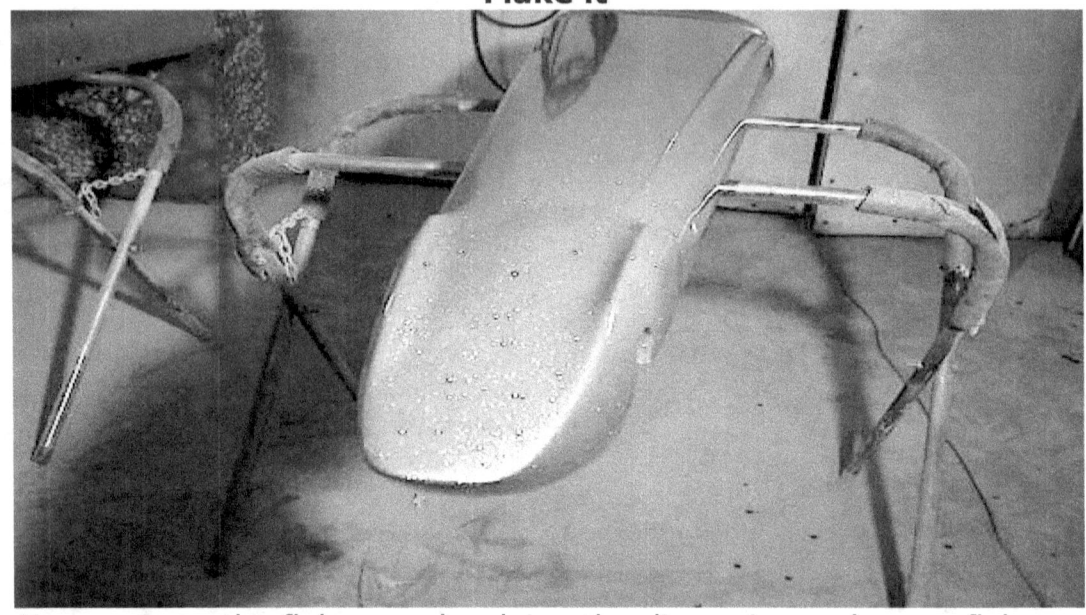

Now on goes the flake... we're doing the digger in candy over flake so we're just using silver, no colored flake... I like to start out with a couple coats of fine flake - Then a coat or two of the coarsest (biggest) stuff possible, then a bit of Diamond Dust, (cut glass), on the top to give it that extra kick. Hey if ya' wanna be subtle what are ya' doin' with Metal Flake! Immediately get all the clear over the flake that you can Do Not touch or sand, ect. the flake ... We just use a clear that's part of the Base coat - Clear coat system - - (we use PPG) ... after the clear has dried (catalyzed) completely ... sand it fairly smooth - and clear it again - and again , giving it plenty of time in between times to do all it's shrinking always being very careful not to sand down to the flake that'll leave spots... Lotta work Huh!... This is of course with 'REAL' Metal Flake (saved a bunch of it since the 60's) ... it's not that coarse metallic crap the sell at the paint store and call Metal Flake... Anyway, after a bunch of clearing and sanding - you'll end up with perfect finish (like glass) Metal Flake

One Last Look

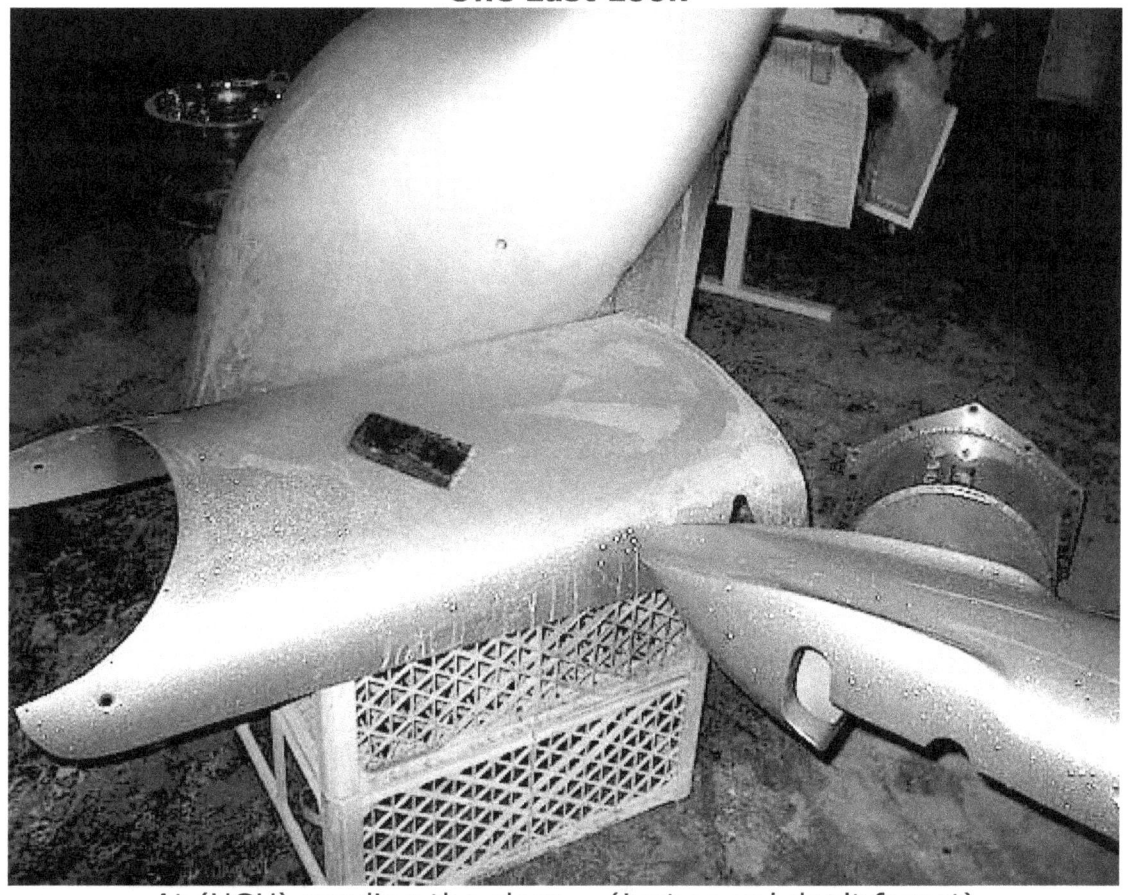

At (UGH) sanding the clear... (just so ya' don't forget)

Graduation Day

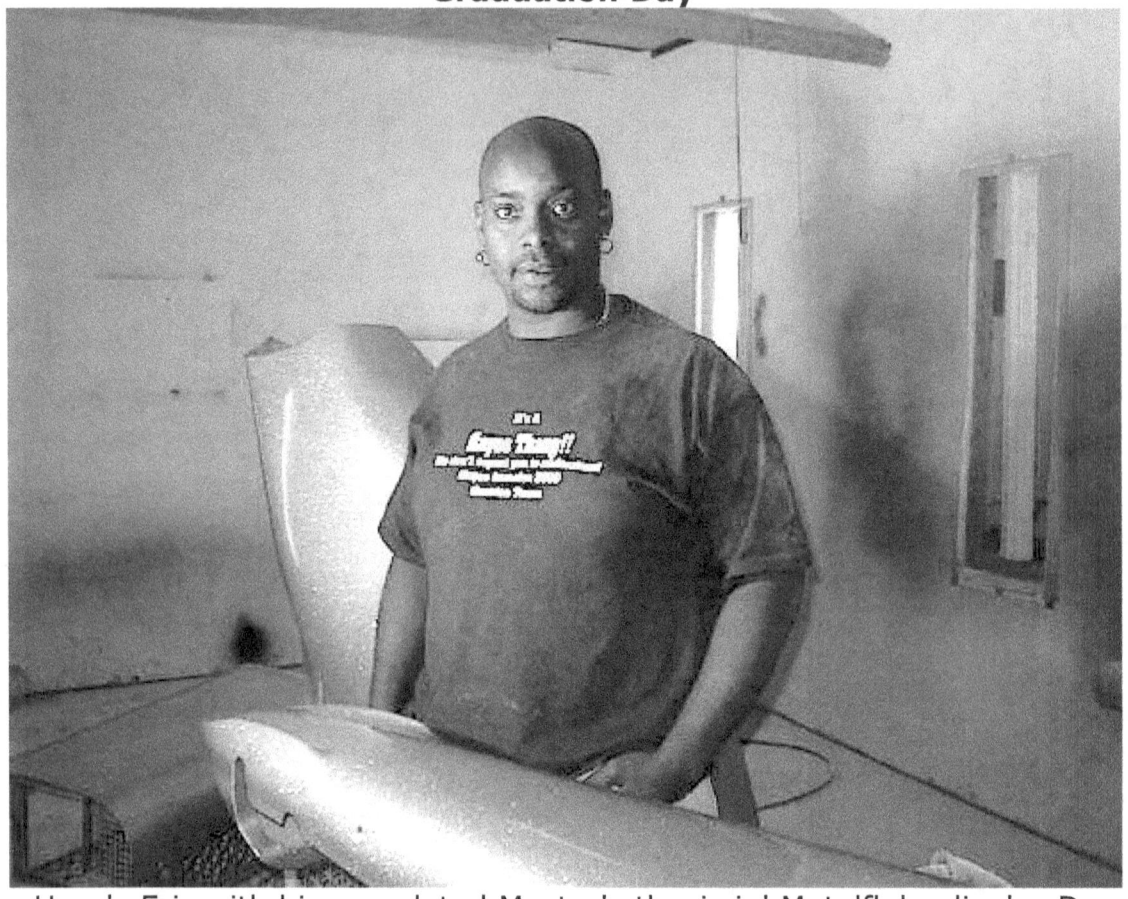

Here's Eric with his completed Master's thesis in' Metalflakeoligy'... Do these pieces look slick - or What!!! Now their ready for a light sanding #600 grit ... and taping out the graphics (design).

I "Donno"

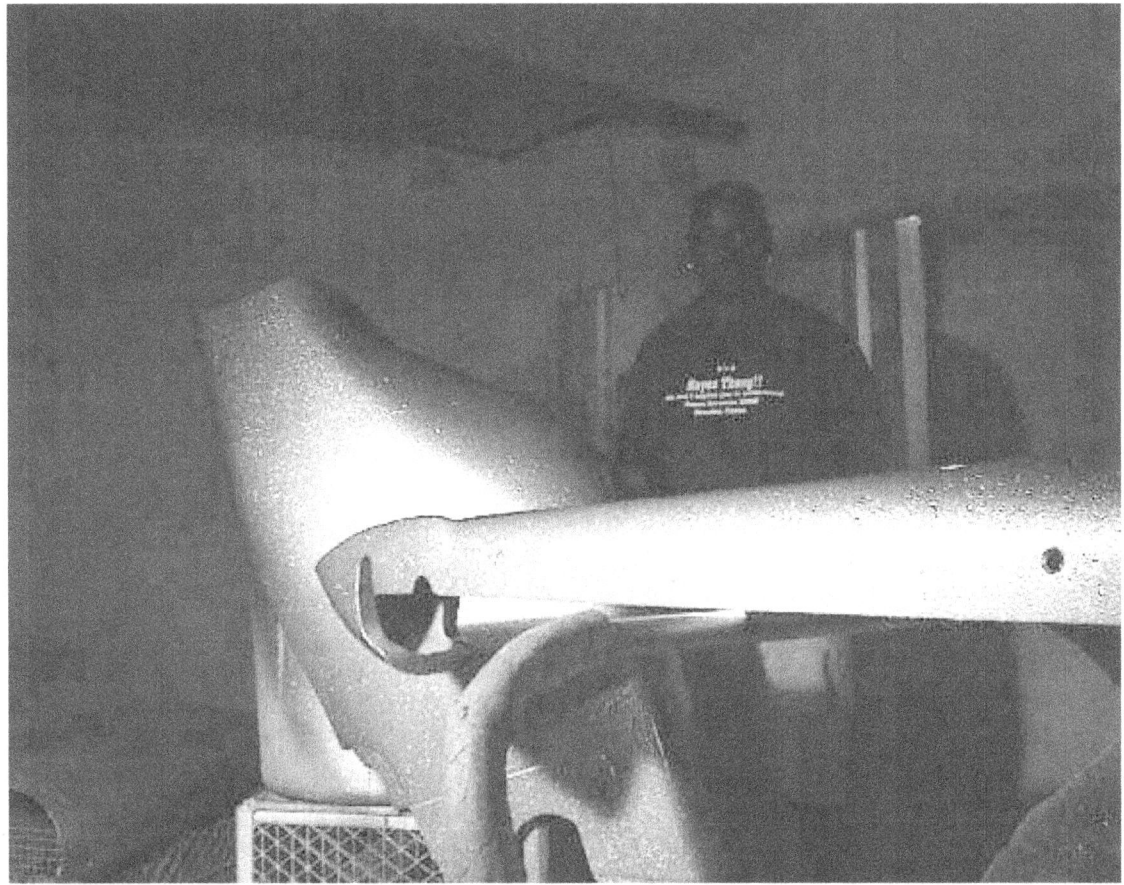

I just like this shot... FULLER ... thanks for creating the shapes that all this is ... I've been painting these things since 60 and still marvell at it ... ... Actually Eric Hayes did all the painting on this one ... I'm just helping him out, (kinda teaching Metal Flake 101)... ... The kids are OK. - - Eric's a natural...

Tapen'it Up

Pullin' tape ... A man's job.......... yeah

Gotta' Get Loose-man

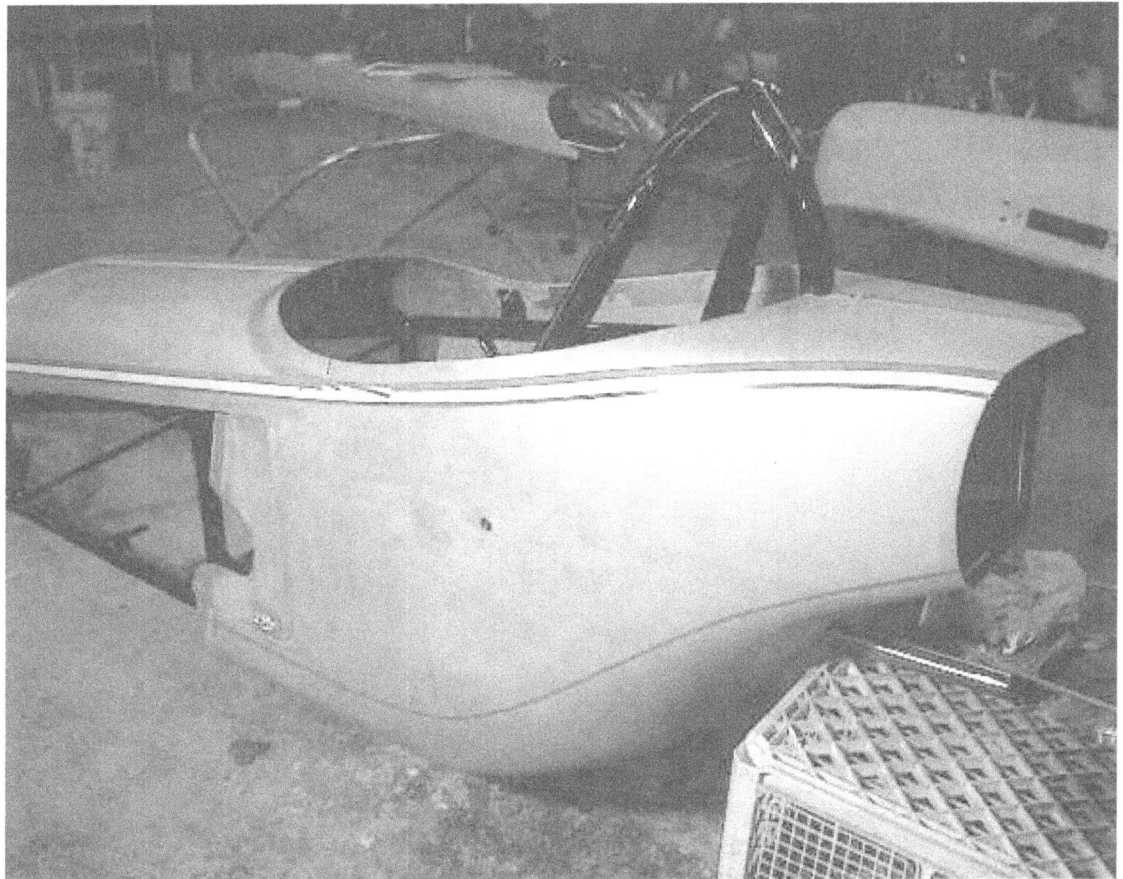

Pete say's that bottom line is just a little to fancy ... huh! Racers!!! To tell ya the truth - this whole deal of putting a design that's already been done once on a piece - leaves me sorta cold - - I kinda like to wing it ... every thing should be different then before - - move ahead, that's the deal ... I lost most of my interest in painting race cars the first time somebody showed up at my shop with a digger and a set of drawings from their sponsor's PR department of the paint design ... I said Hey! Take it down the street to the body shop - they can paint inside the lines. I sure can't. When I paint a racecar - the only thing I ask the owner is, "What color do you not like - and ya only get one." Then I get half the money up front, (like a hit man), and he goes away till it's done, but this one was for Pete and for FULLER, so I bit the bullet...

Pals'n'Paint

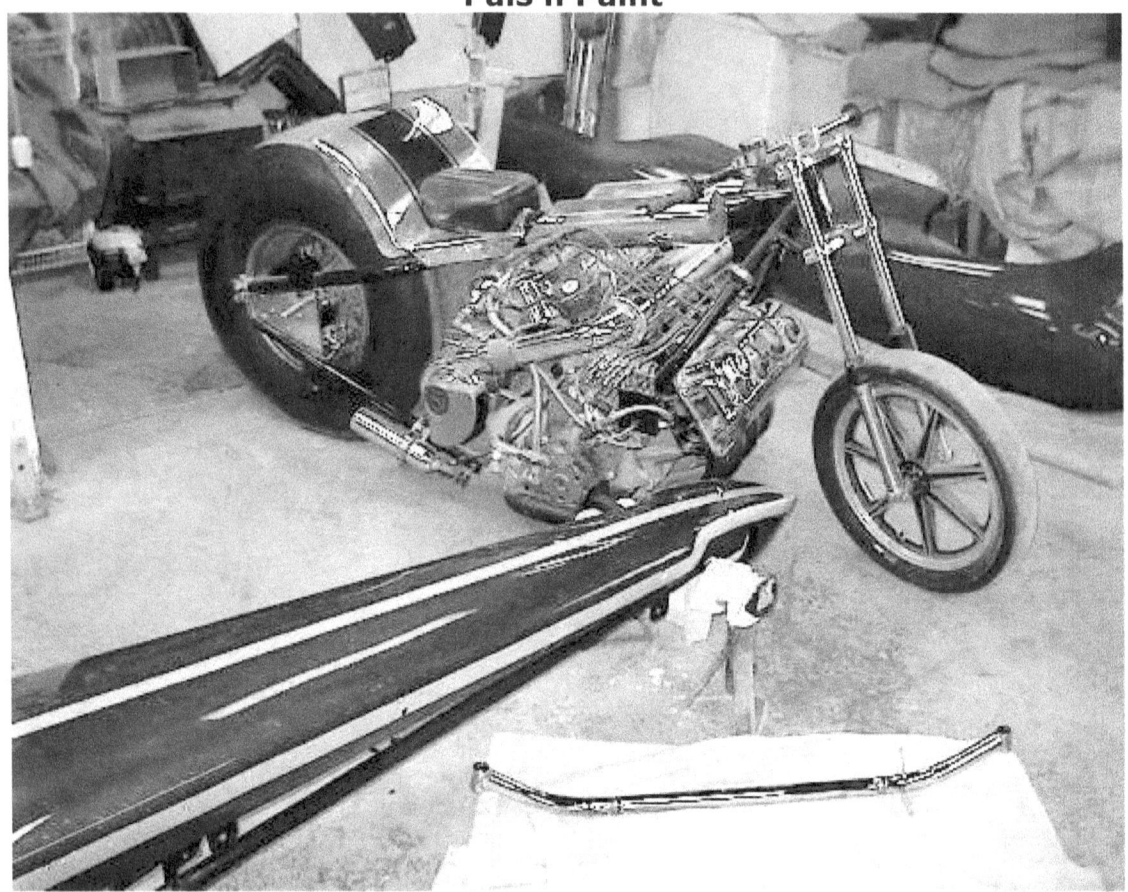

OK so we jump ahead now what can I say, Battery's went dead in the digi-thing? Dog ate the camera? Took a buncha pics, but I was holding the thing backwards? None a that, I just forgot to take pics, so we rejoin the gang with the paint finished. The process I went for on this one being the paint is urethane, was to do the candy just like it was Lacquer so rather then using any of that pre mixed junk at the paint store, or that pre packaged Joe Komiskiwe stuff that he calls 'candy' we did it the old way, Sent Pete to the paint store where he looked at the mixing toners, and found the color he thought it should be, mixed a little toner with some real thin clear and sprayed it on a coat at a time, till the color was right Eric did the spraying and hit it right on, a perfect transparent Candy Red. The red toner we used is Deltron DMD 669 we use PPG DAU 82 clear it's an Acrylic Urethane which is what I prefer it's a softer clear and gives a nice deep luster more like the quality you get from Lacquer, but any clear in the base coat, clear coat urethane systems will work. Here's the Fullers Nose showing off his new look to his 'bud' SuperBike. Hmmmmm, looks like 'Axle Rose' fresh from the chrome shop, in the picture too....

"School's Out"

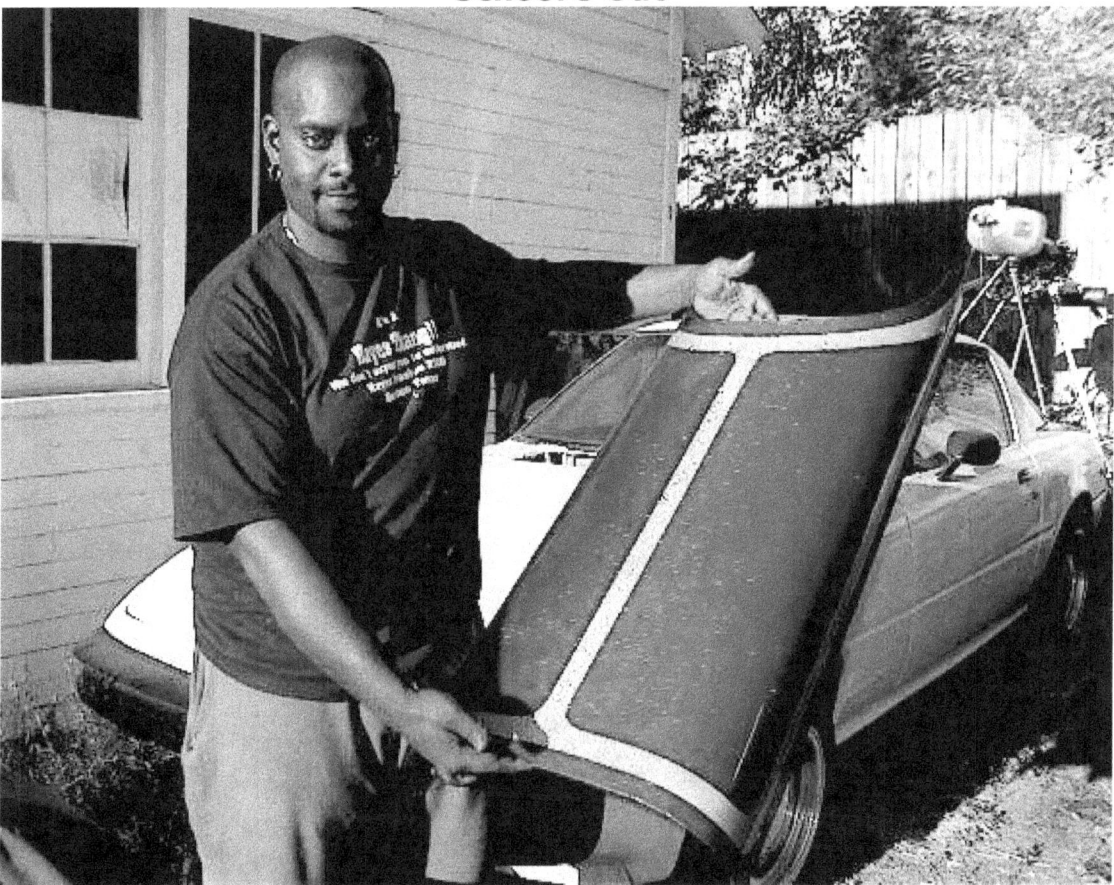

Here's Eric holding up his Doctoral thesis in candy painting - which went on to win best paint at 'The Grand National Roadster Show', (the show formaly known as 'Oakland'), among many other wins ... I told Eric, "you don't wanna paint any more - it's all downhill from here" - - take it from me

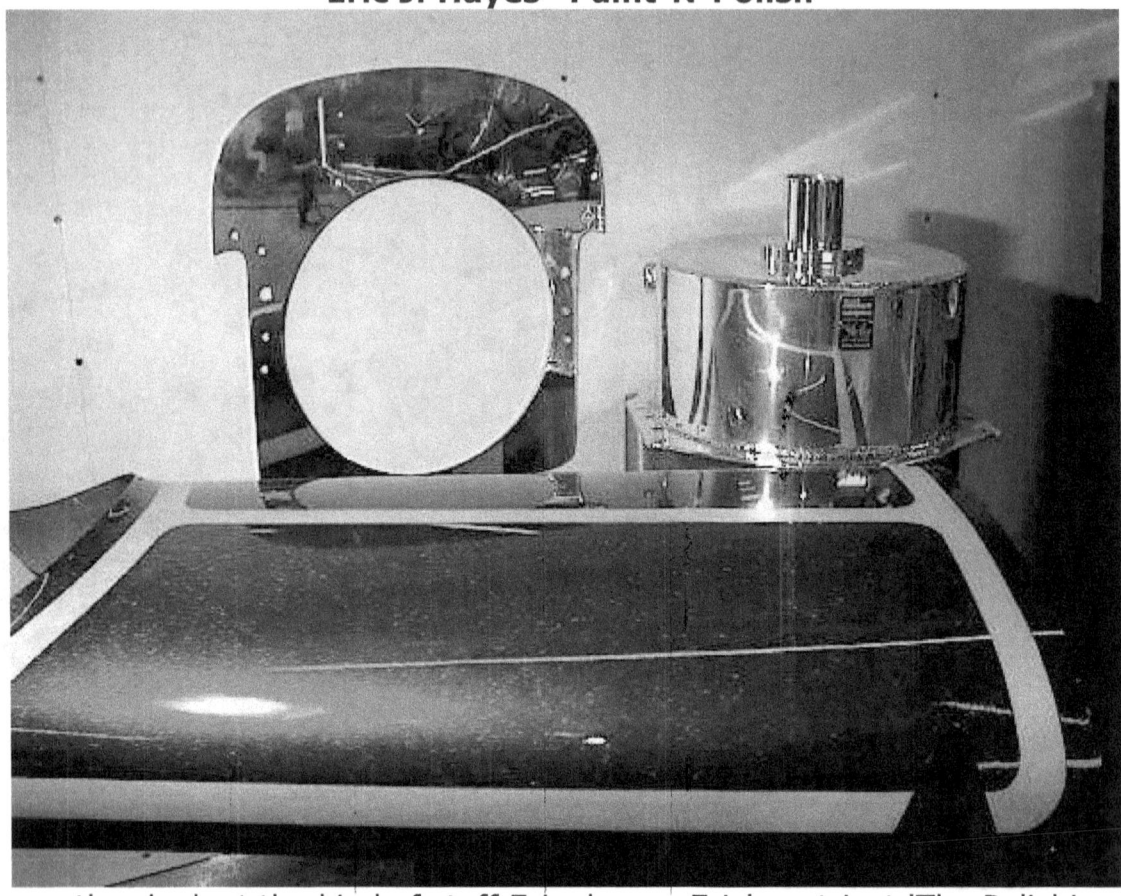

another look at the kind of stuff Eric does... Eric's not just 'The Polishing Guy' now ... ... We just call him ... 'Da CandyMan'

Pete's Baby

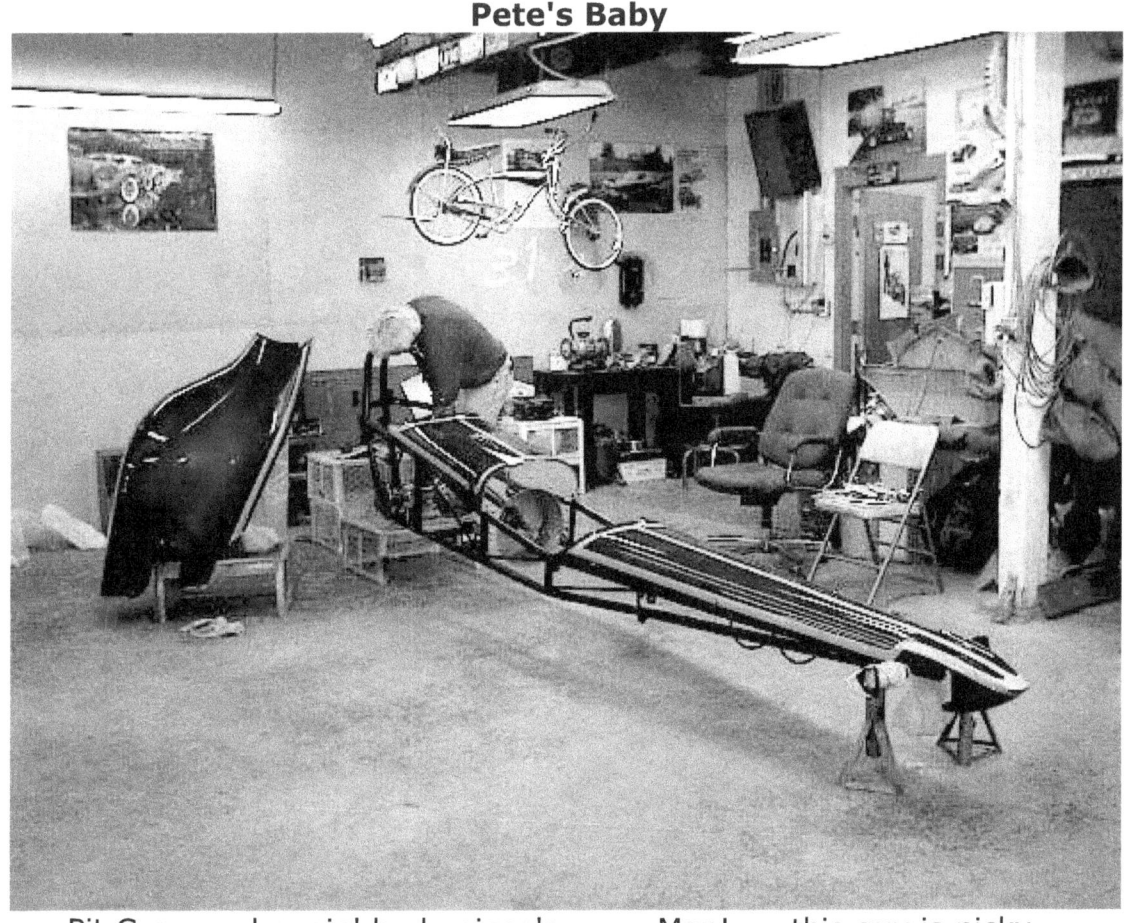

Pit Crew - - hangin' body piece's ... ... Man! - - this guy is picky...

"Nose in the Sun"

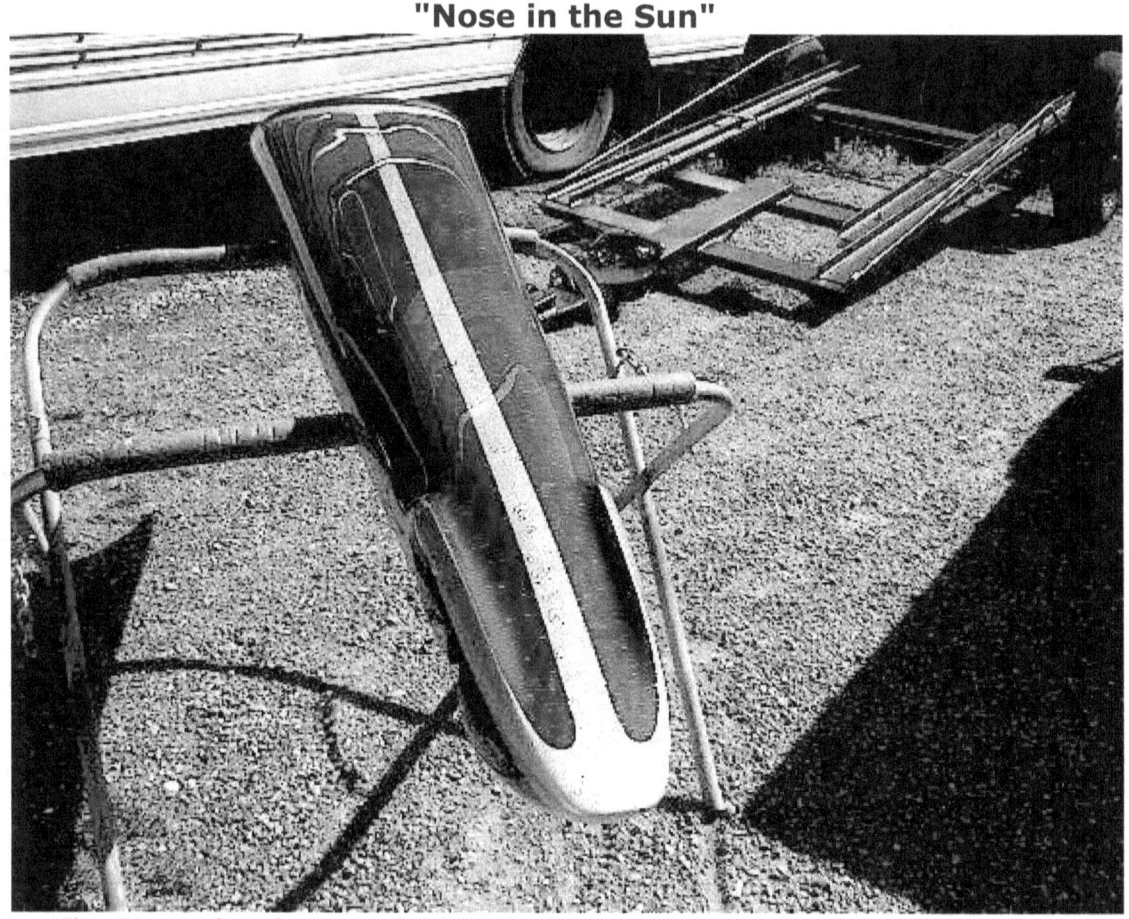

The Nose decides to take in a little sun ... note the 'original' FULLER Trailer in the background...

Get Outta the Way

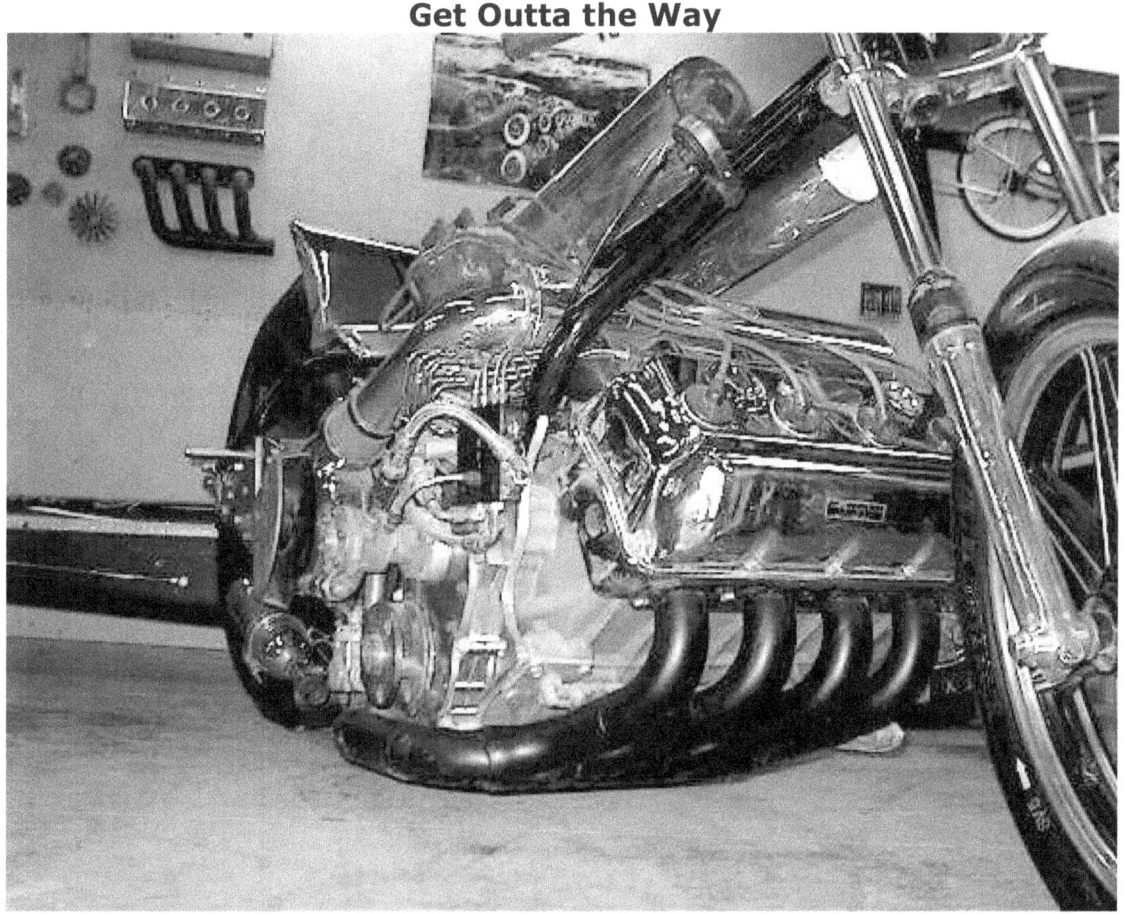

Growls 'the fuller as 'Supe' gets in the middle of a profile shot...

"Shapin' Up"

It's about time to call the pin striping - lettering guy I think...

Hanging-Out with "Crazy Rick"

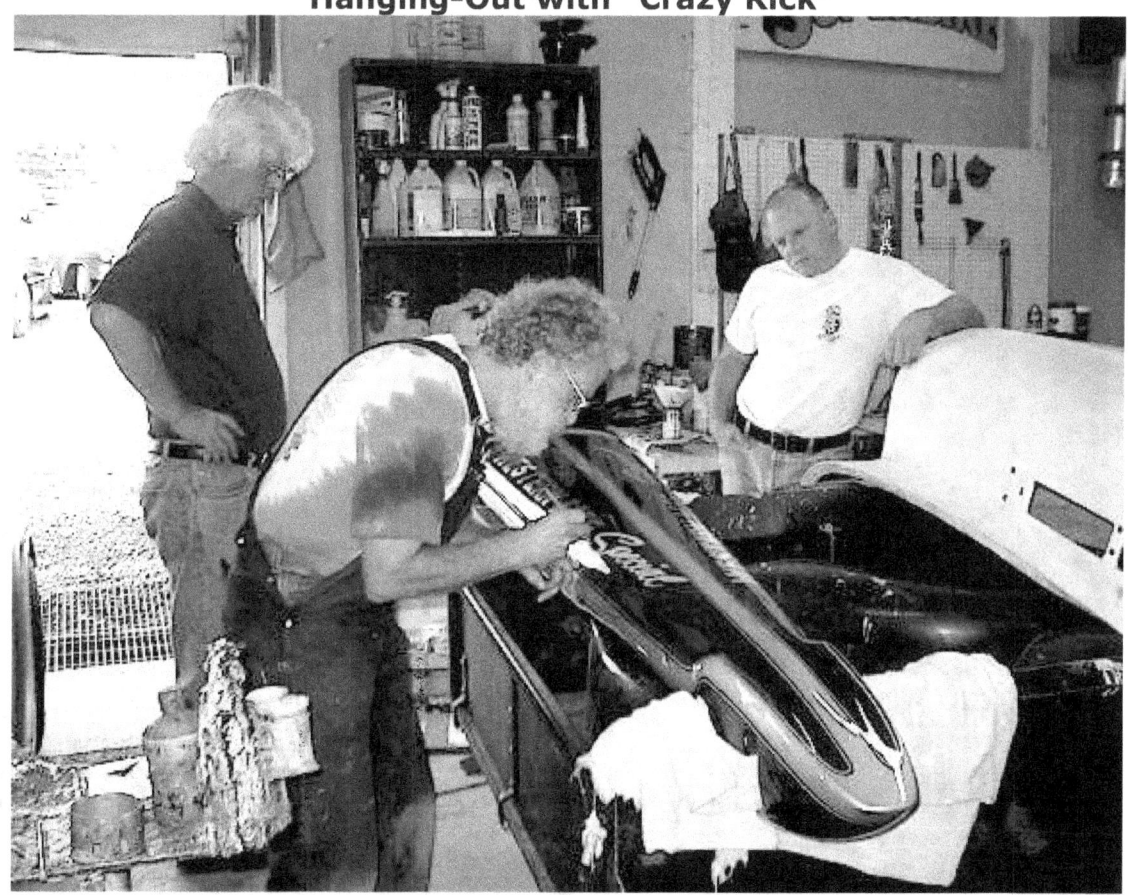

Weird Rick the sign painter works on the silver leaf while Pete and Tim Conder kibitz... Tim's the guy from up the street who's got the two Ogden AA/FD's... BAD!

"SWEET"

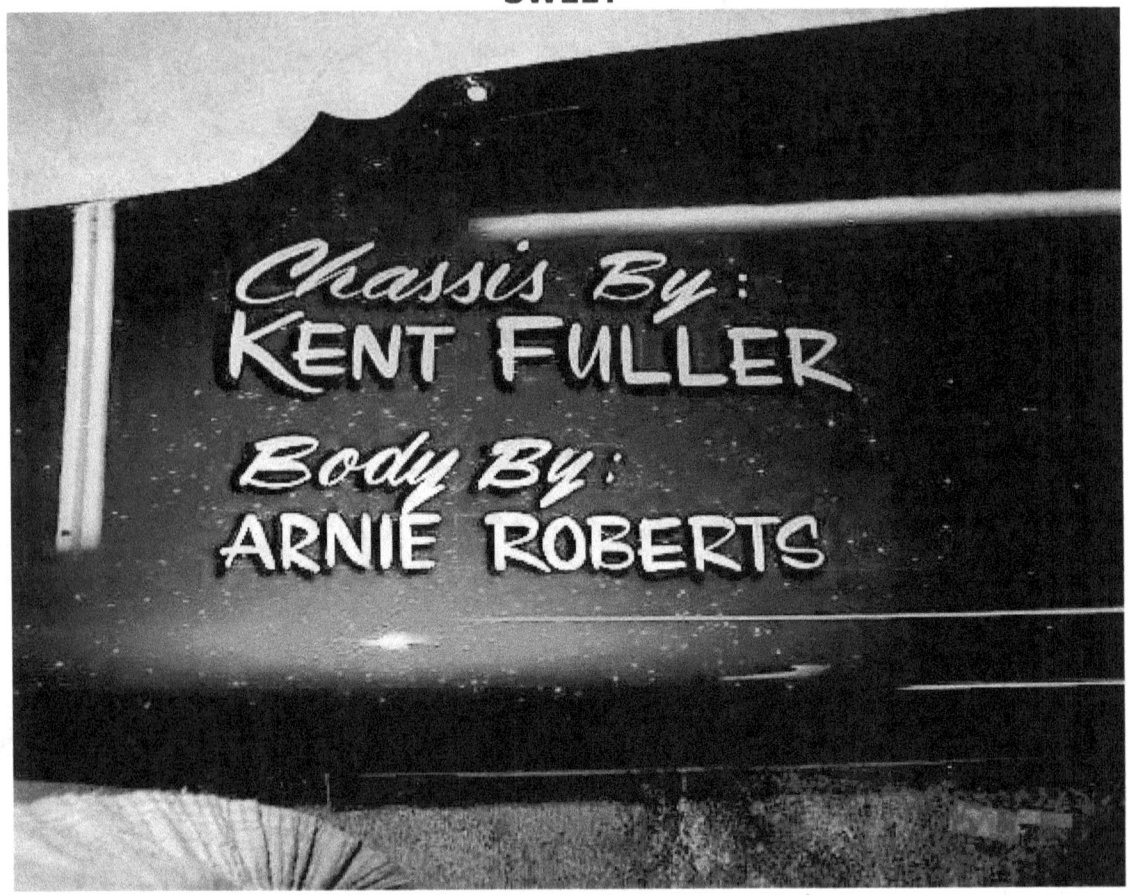

Chassis By:
KENT FULLER

Body By:
ARNIE ROBERTS

This Rick Evans guy does nice work...

"The Visitor"

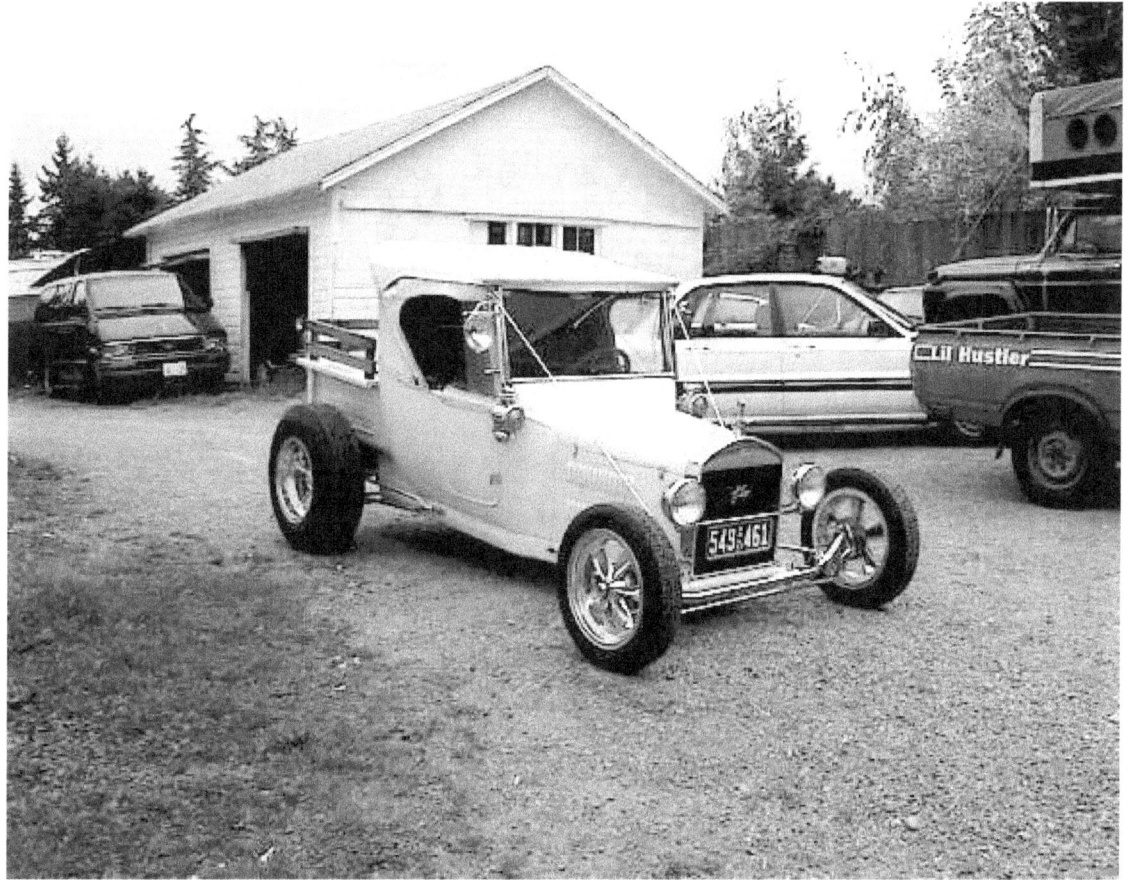

Hearing the gravel crunch in the driveway and peeking out the window - - 'The Fuller' thinks, "now who could this be ... Hmmmm..... that little car looks somehow familiar - I fcel this strange bond to it ... Like somehow we're related"...

"???????"

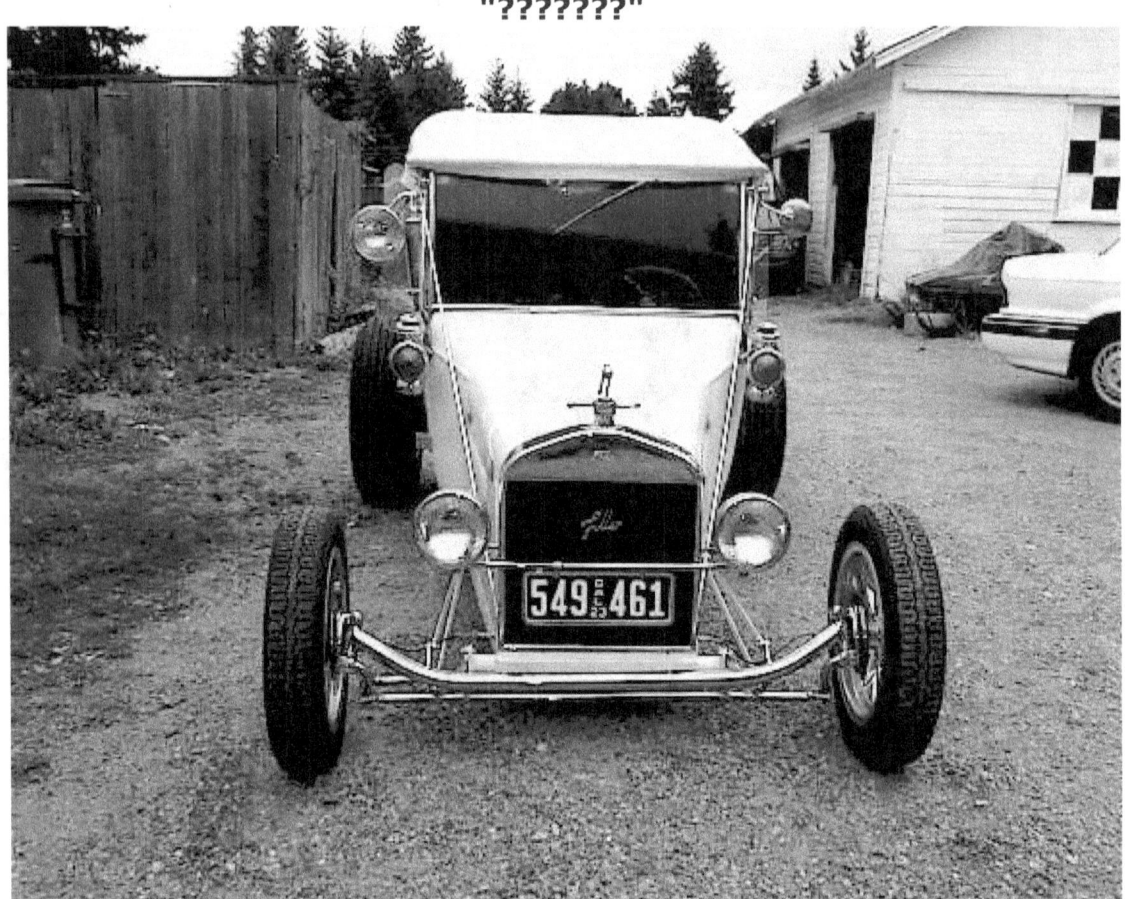

"Geez!" thinks The Fuller ... "this thing has the same front end as I do ...
Hey Man! this is race car stuff ... not for you streeties!!!

"Say What"

"it's ... It's.... "The Creator", at last... He's come to save me from these savages!!!"

"Fullers" in the House

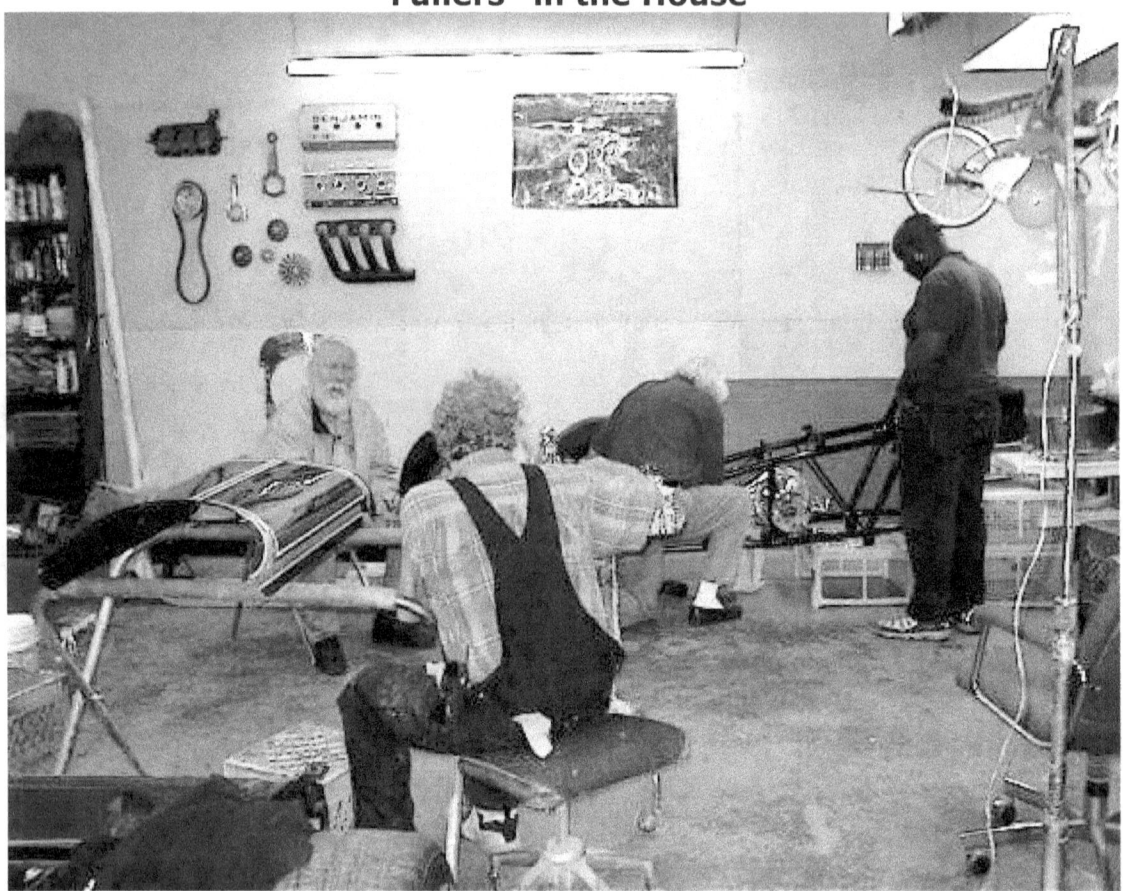

While Pete and Eric slave away on the car ... FULLER visits with 'weird Rick' ... the letterer guy ... who turns out to be from Fuller's old neighborhood in LA ...... Hmmmm.... going by weird Rick - - it musta been an interesting neighborhood.................

Arrrrrrr... Matey

Captain Fuller entertains us with tales of the sea - - 'n' stories of the Drag Races too...

Fuller's Words

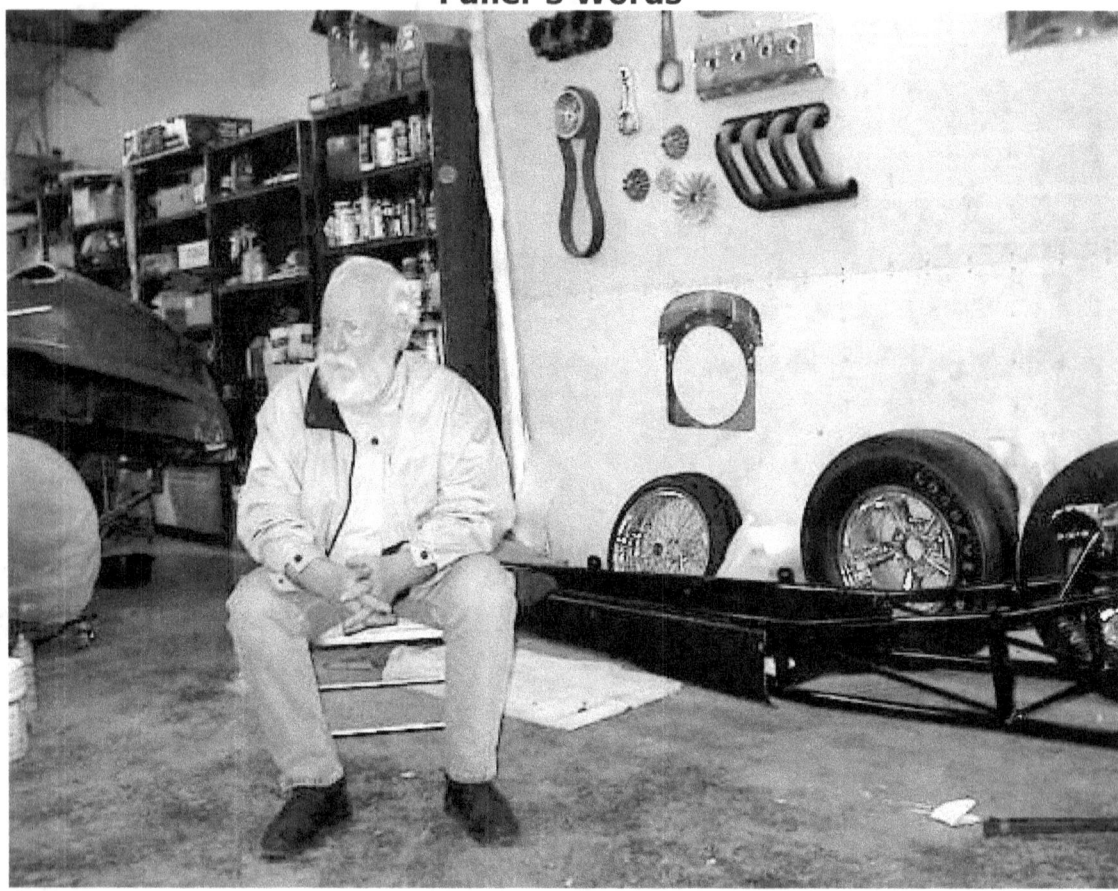

"Uh..... Pete", says Fuller ... "I thought you'd have this thing all together by now ... should be out running it this weekend!".... ... "Yeah, well you know, suppliers and things" stutter's Pete...

"Just Do It"

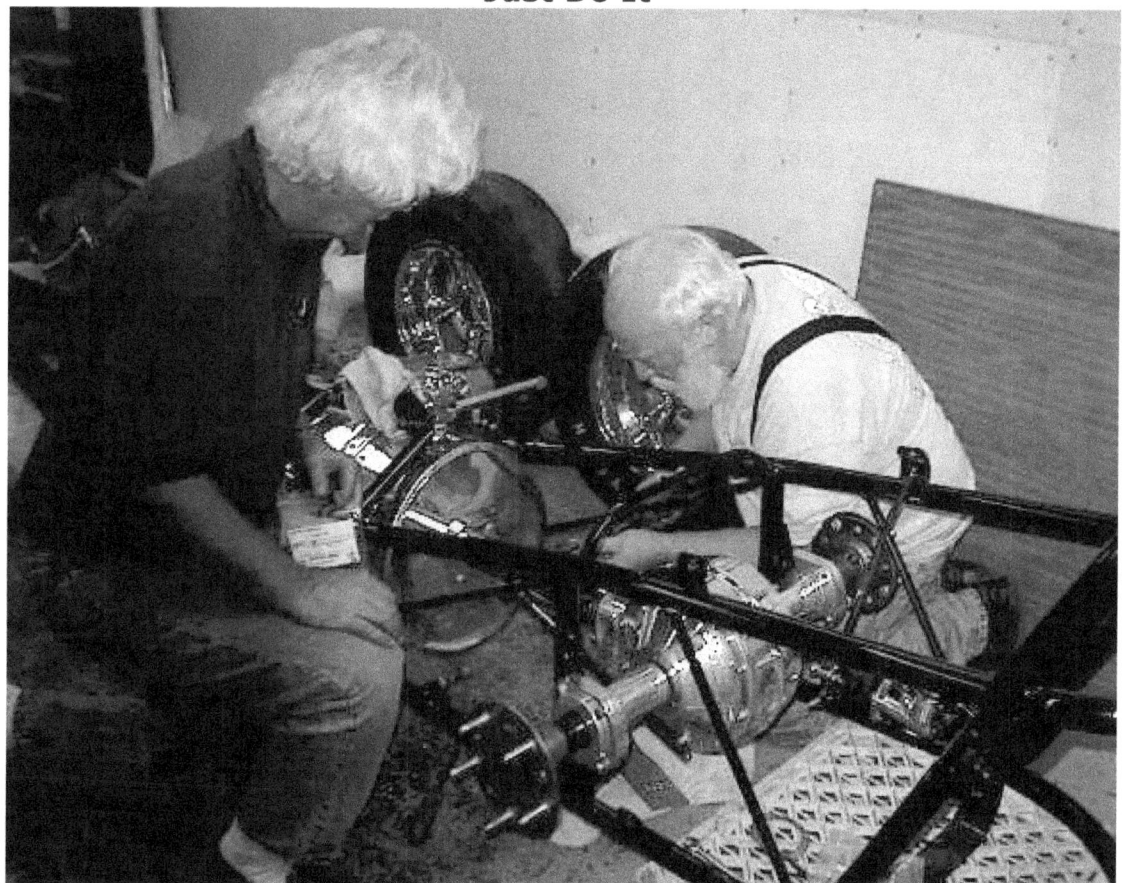

"Enough of this messing around ", say's Fuller, "here's how you make this fit ... hand me that grinder!!!"

Nothin' To It

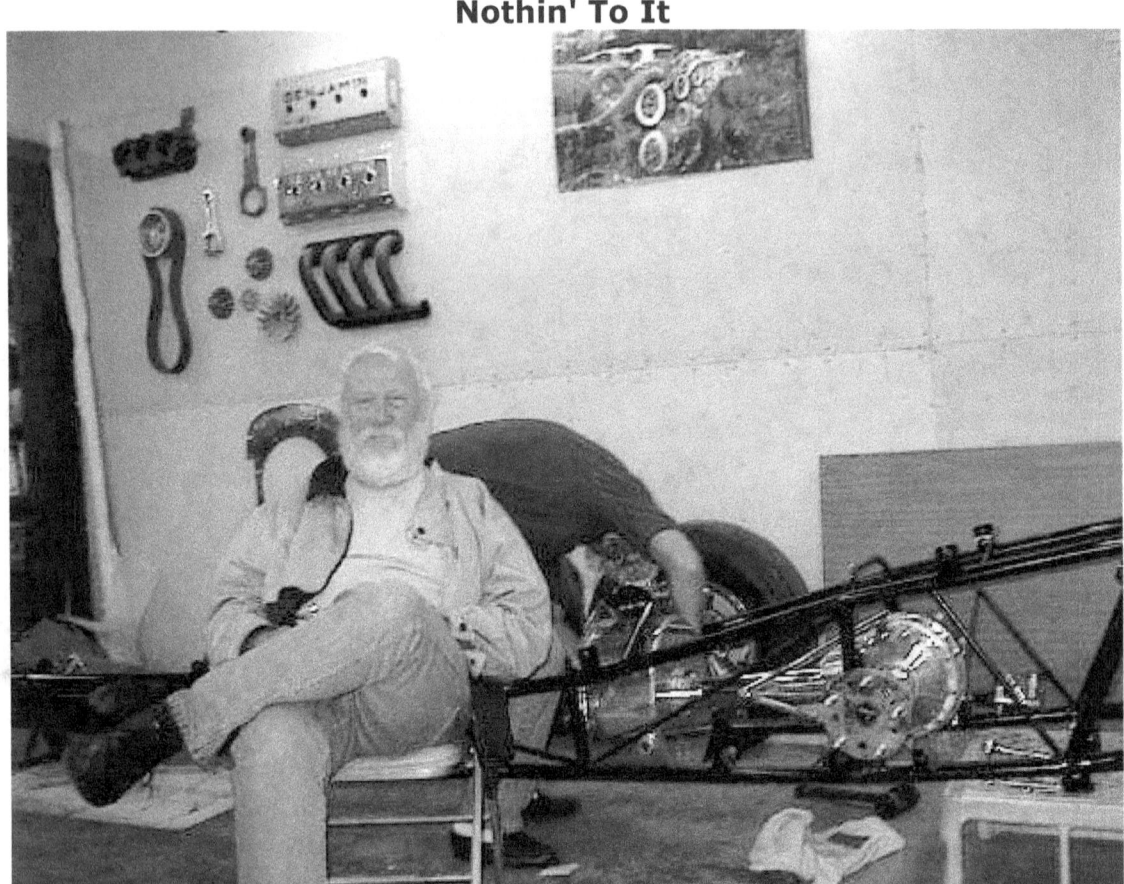

"There now", says Fuller, "That wasn't so hard, was it?".............

"Moving Along"

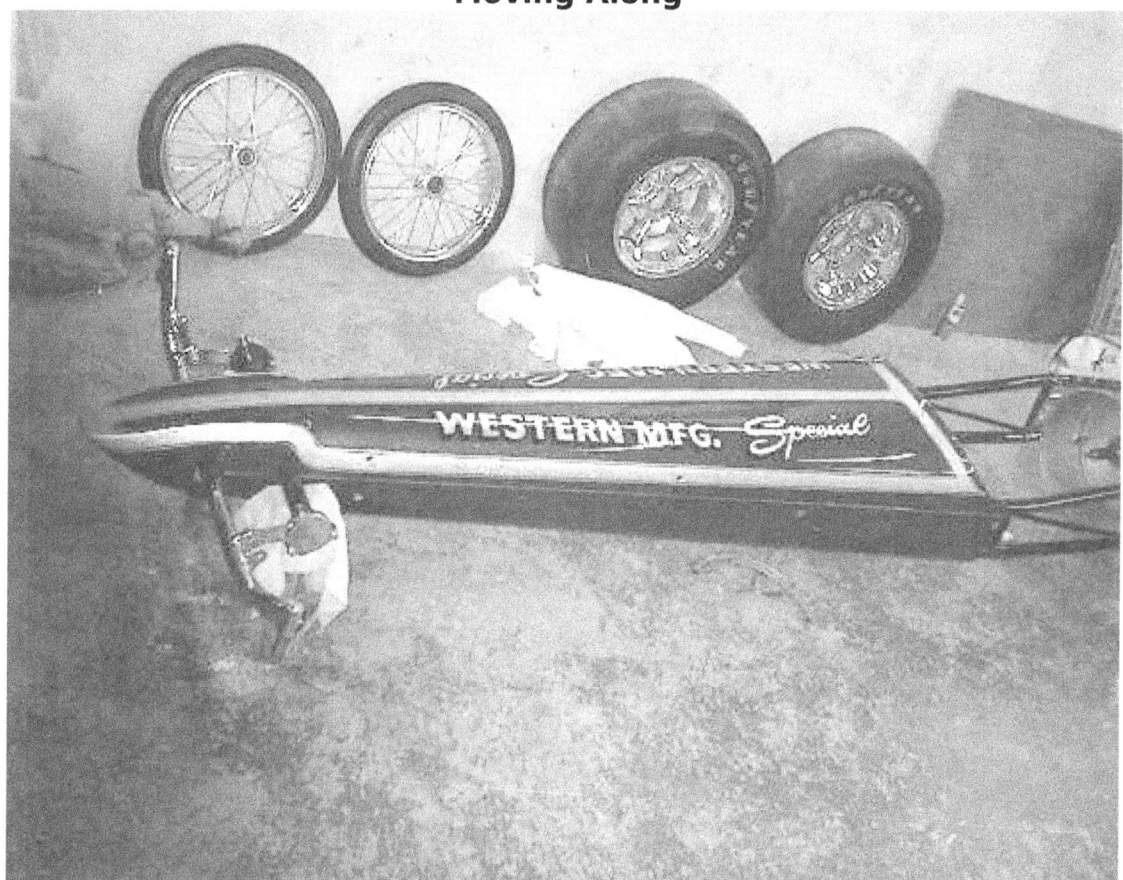

Well in the beginning of this saga we've seen chassis painting, and alloy body prep and painting even let loose some of the long held hidden secrets of the forgotten black arts of Metal Flake and candy, plus we learned a little about the secret lives of cool cars and bikes and what they do and say when nobody's around. Now we move on to assembly. Here's where you really get to see the brilliance of KENT FULLER. He is perhaps the father of the ART of chassis/racecar building for maximum acceleration, before FULLER, dragsters were little more then engine stands with big tires on the back and little ones on the front. Take a good look at these next photo's this is a car that was built 42 years ago in it's AA/Gas form, as it has been restored to, it weighed about 900 pounds and probably had 6 or 700 horse power a very efficient perfectly balanced, one purpose vehicle. FULLER didn't put anything on these cars that didn't need to be there for that one purpose, which was to get to the end of the quarter mile as quickly as possible and safely! Each bracket is a work of finesse and efficiency many of the brackets do two or three jobs. Yes Fuller is a practical man - but a crafty one. The word was you didn't have to steer a Fuller car down the strip it just worked... Fred Vosk

"Christmas in Kirkland"

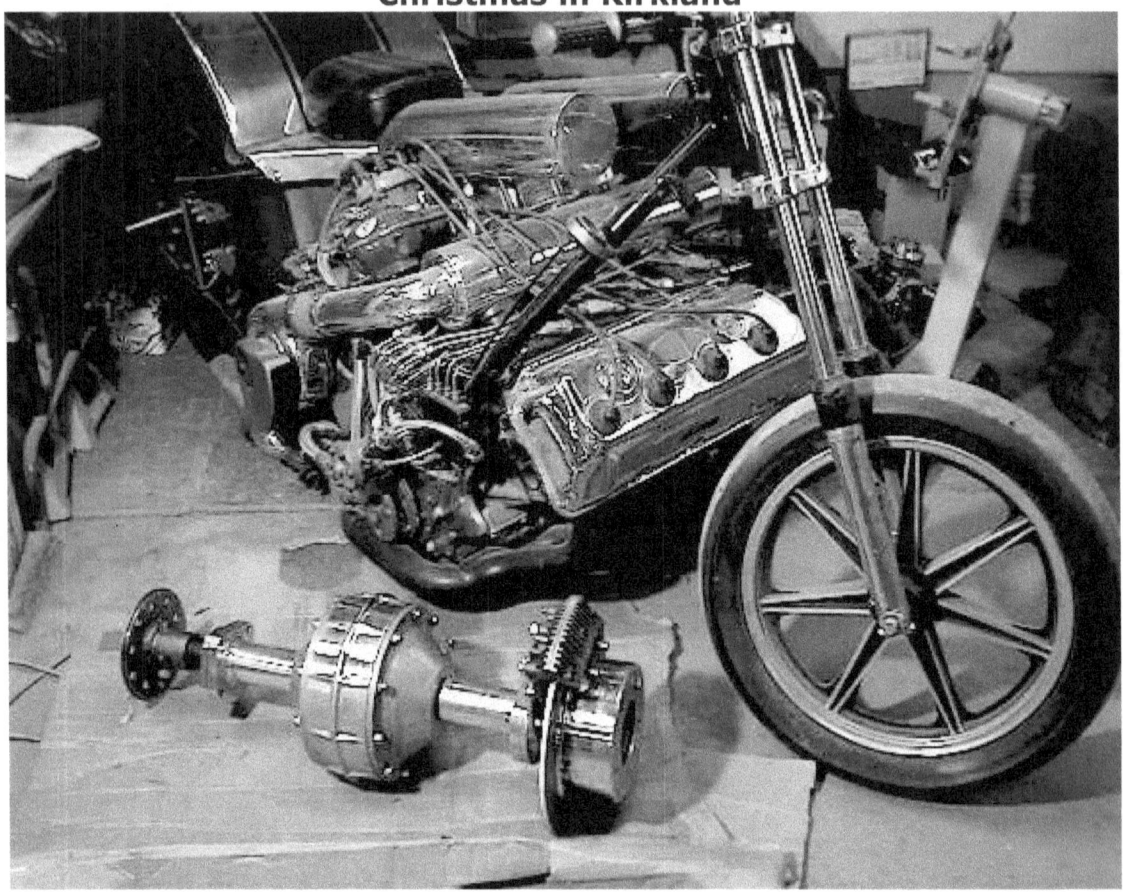

SuperBike looks on excitedly as the package is opened, thinking, "finally my new stroker crank has come ... only been waiting for years"... BUT NOOOO!... it's something else for the new guy ... whats worse - new guy gets neater stuff... Its 'The Fullers' super trick 'ultralite' rear end... 74 pounds ready to bolt in, brake and all, this is most likely the lightest rear end ever in a blown V8 car, it'd based on a 'mag' Halibrand center section - live (chrome molly tube) axle - (so it only needs one brake)... it was originally built by Dave Jeffers... and was down at FULLERS shop being freshened - - FULLER say's it's ready to go now...

"Still in Shape"

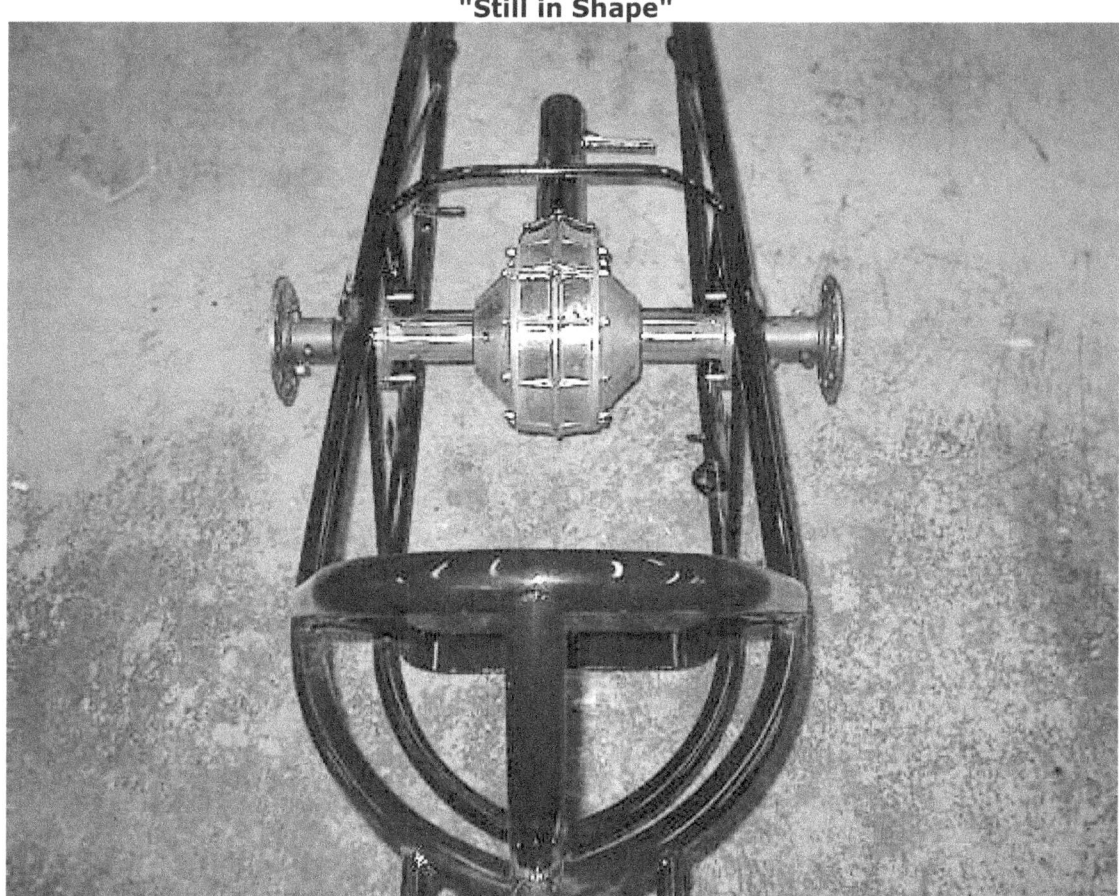

"Hmmmm," say's the Fuller, "35 years and it still fits and they say I've let myself go…"

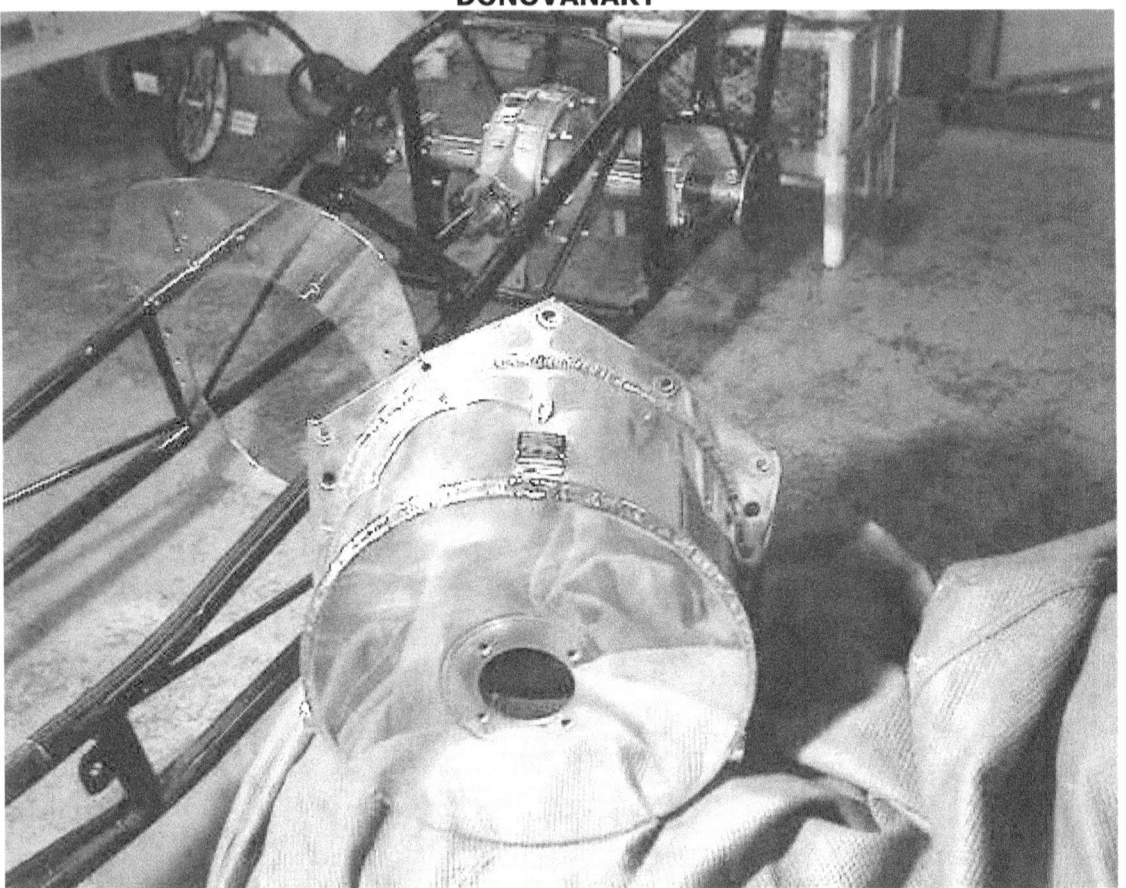

Hmmmmmm............. kinda weird reflections huh! Rear end in - - motor plate in - - now let's see if the can still fit's...

"Oh Yeah"

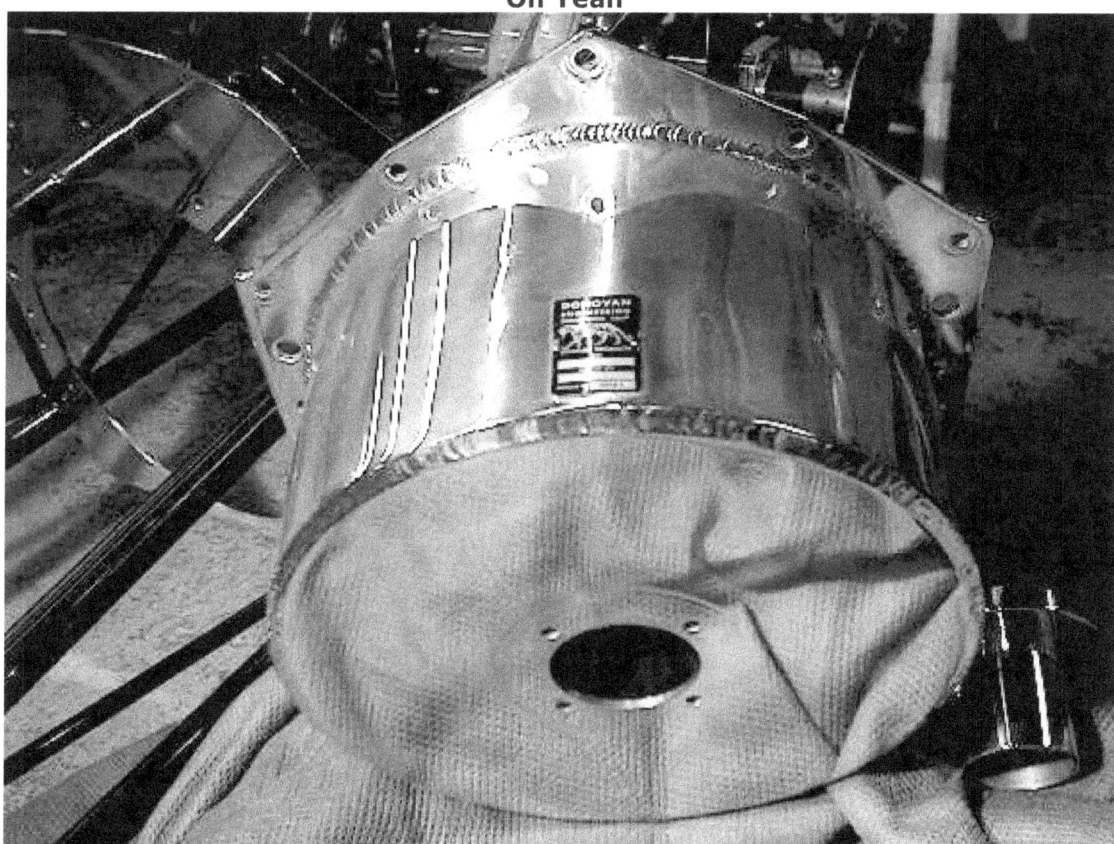

The Mole

"Drive Line In"

Driveline in ... so where's that motor? All 'of course' polished by Eric Hayes... remember
if ya' want to play the game at this level, it's erichayes@bikesters.com

"Hey"

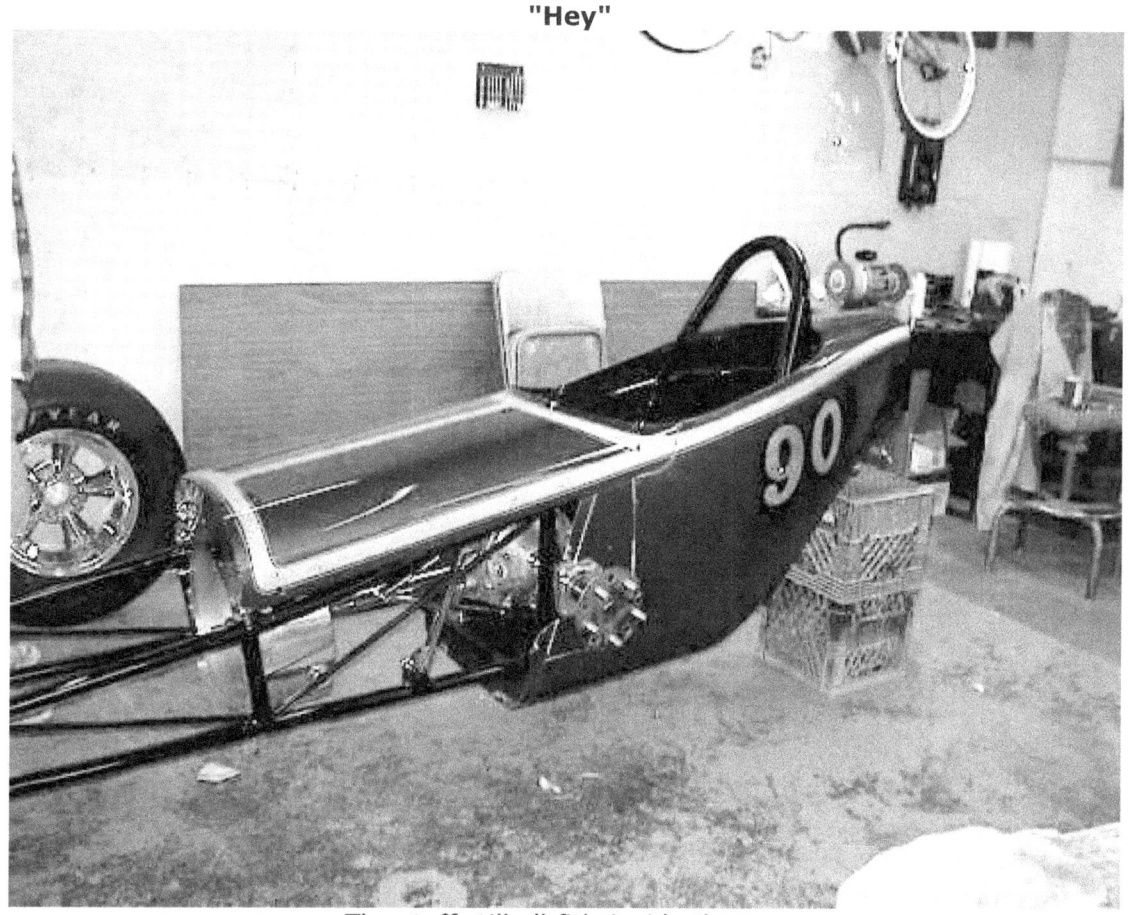

The stuff still all fit's inside there...

"Pete 'N' Doug"

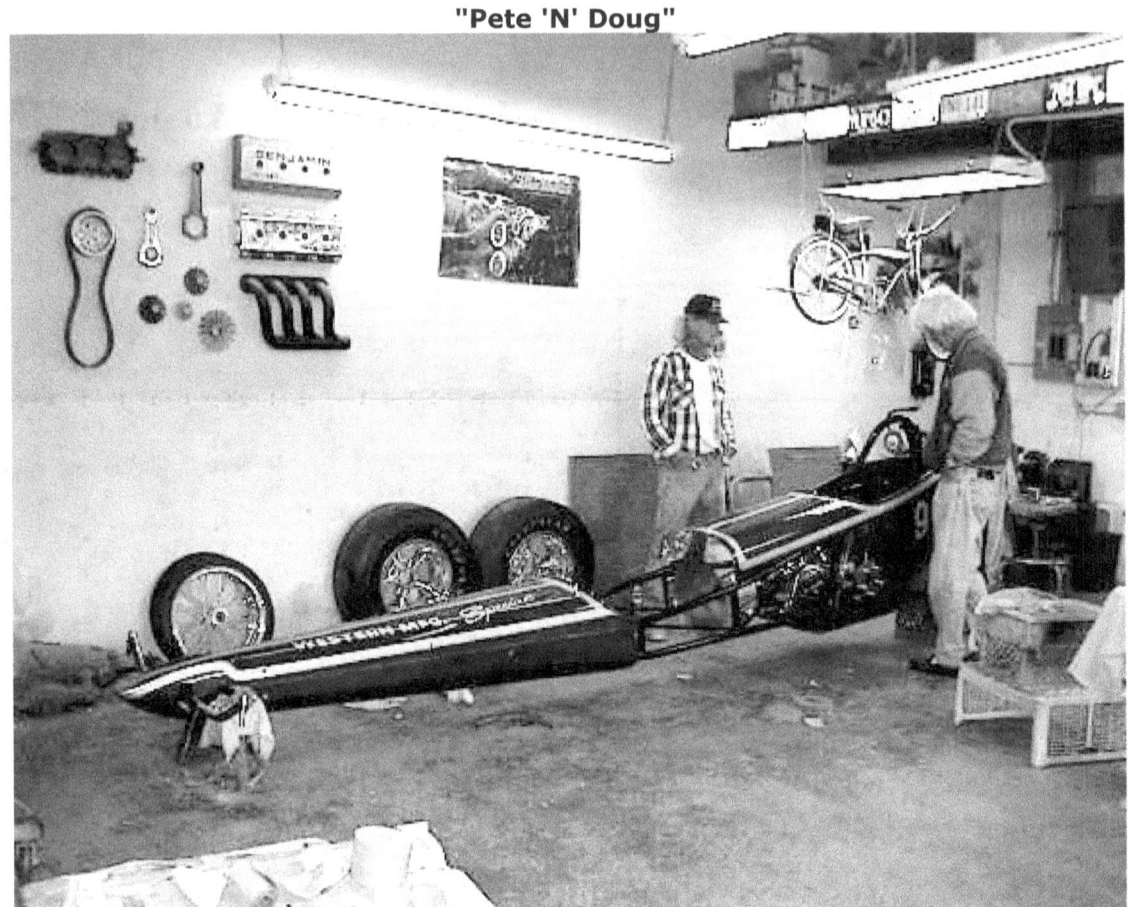

Pit Crew and 'Boat Racer Doug', (our next door neighbor) , check out things while waiting for the engine to be finished ... Doug (Pratt) put in a bunch of hours on this project ... and he does super nice work - - couldn't a done it without him............

"For ME?????"

The Fuller ask's ... but he already knows the answer...

"YUP!!!"

The Fuller guessed right........... Man ... does that Eric put a polish on stuff - - or what!

"Under the Polish"

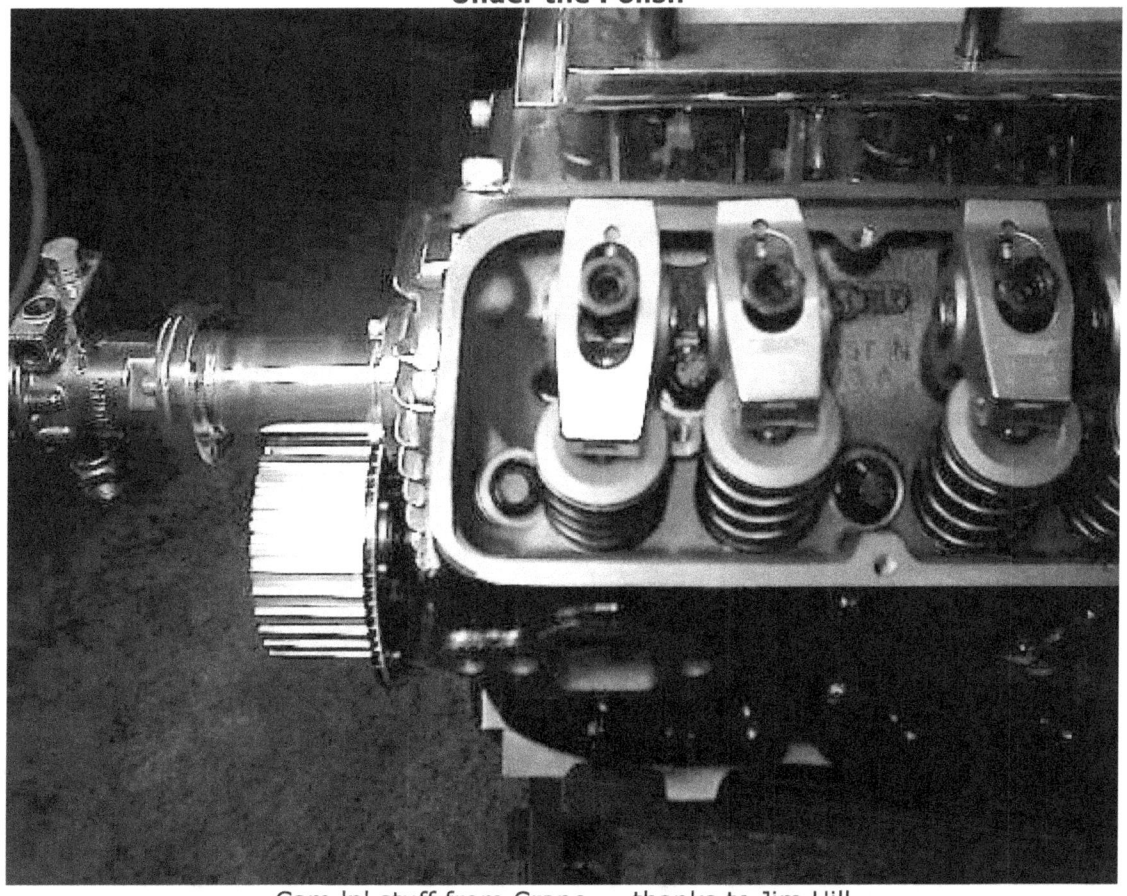

Cam 'n' stuff from Crane ... thanks to Jim Hill

"The Clutch Wizard"

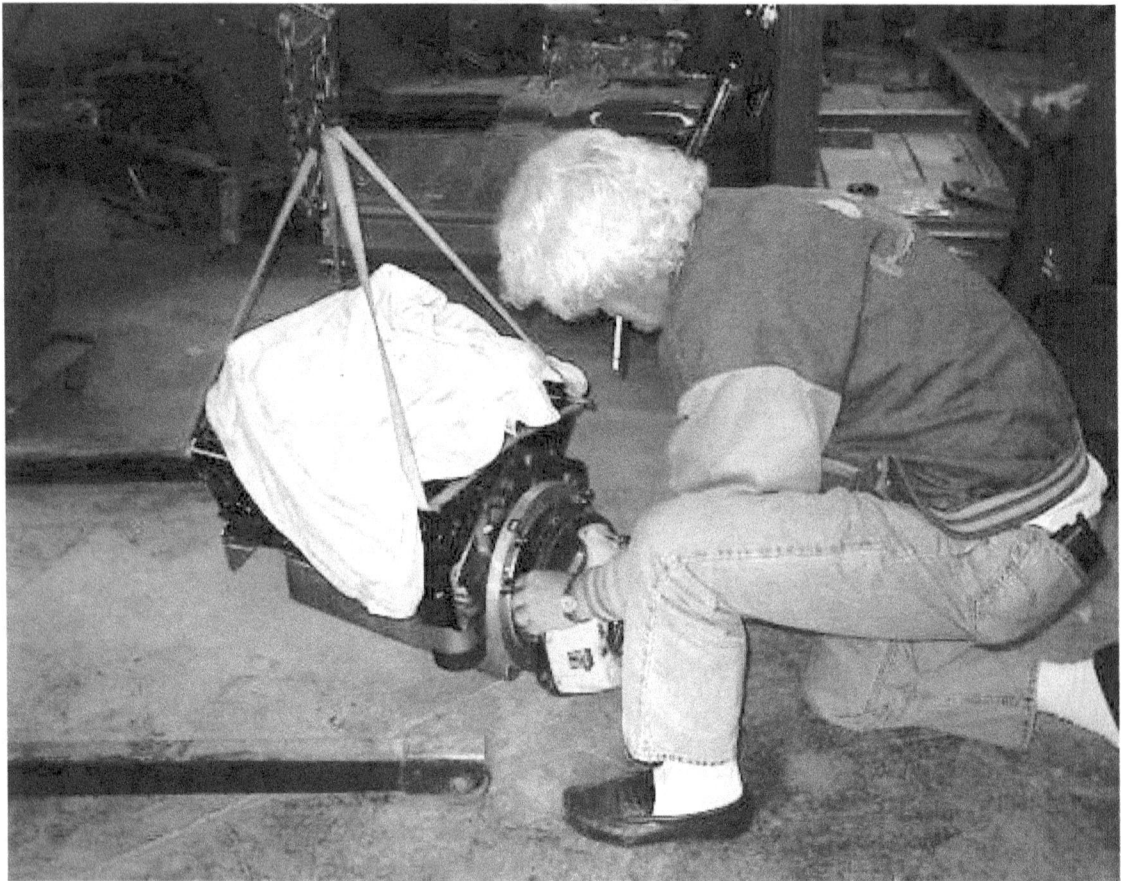

Hmmm.... sounds like something from 'Tommy' ... ... Looks like a course in pre-101 clutch pack's and management system's......

"Yellow Fever"

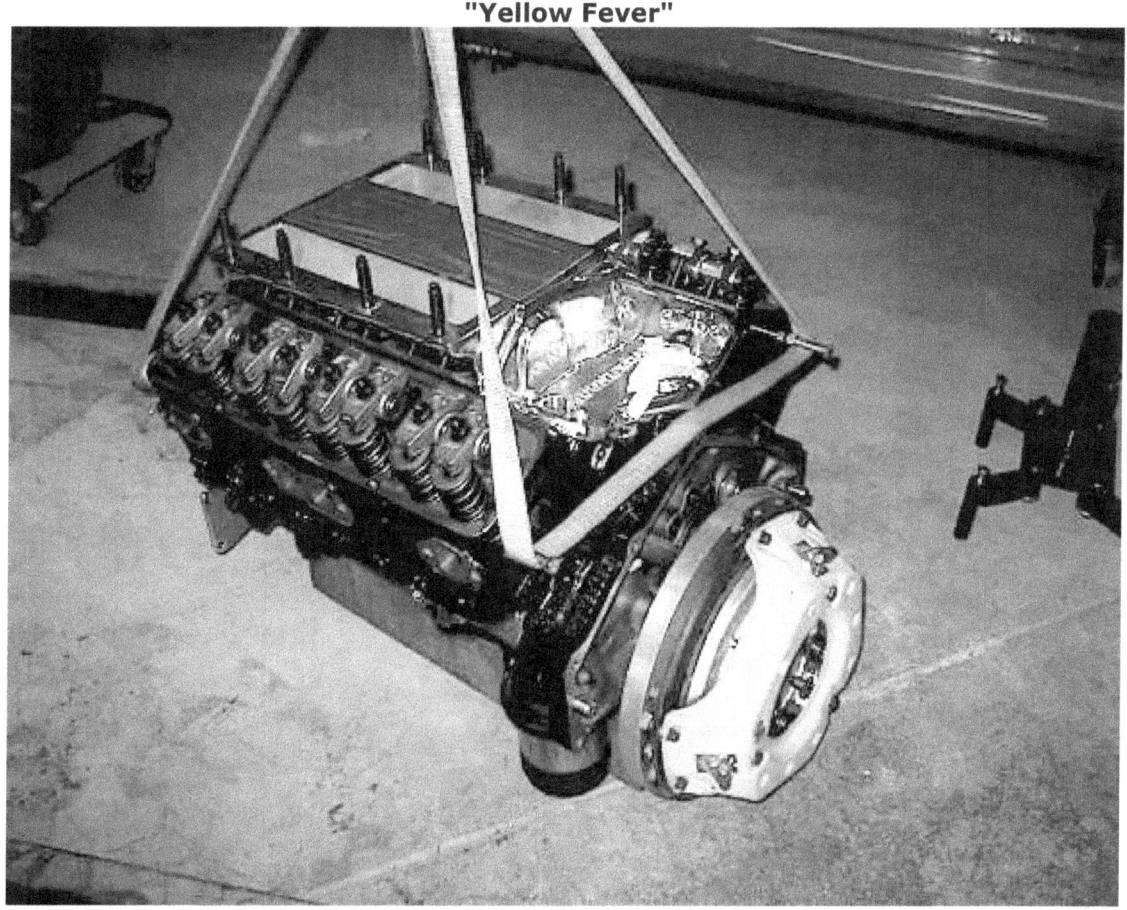

There it is ... the latest thing in double disc set up's, (in 1965) ... I won't even tell ya how much lookin' Pete did to find the exact right (65) shade of Schiefer Yellow for this deal ... like I said - - this guy's picky..........

"Plate 'N' Can"

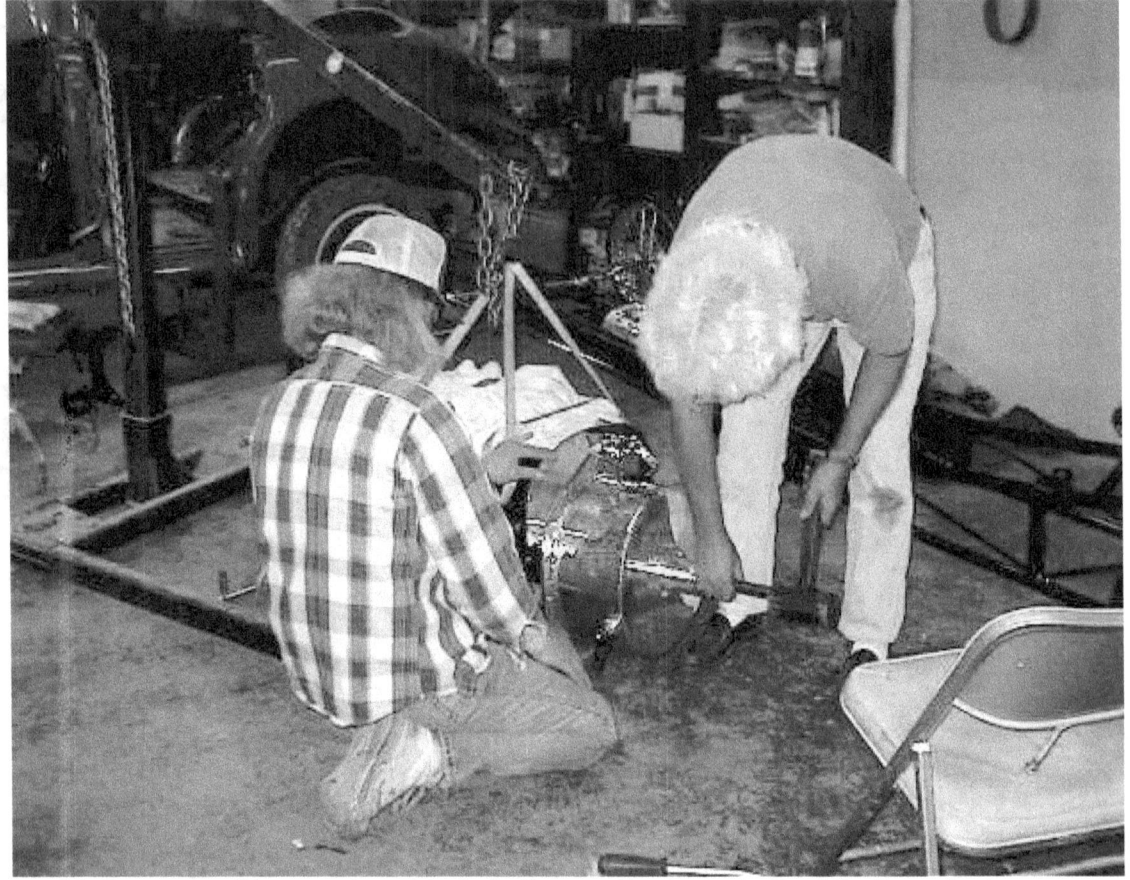

Pit Crew uses 'the convincer' to help line up the jack shaft while Doug looks on...

"Mouse"

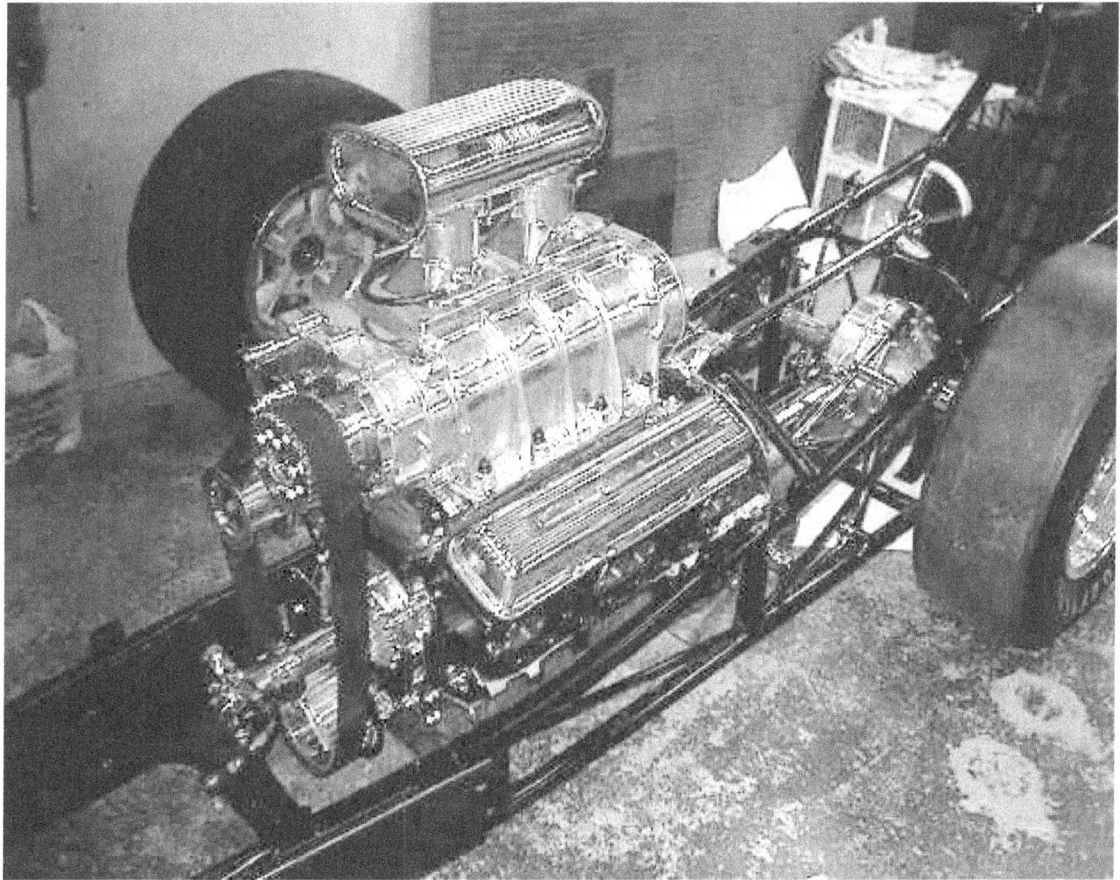

And sure enough - just snap your fingers - - and there it is - - Blower and injector on ... ready to go - almost...

"Tall Mouse"

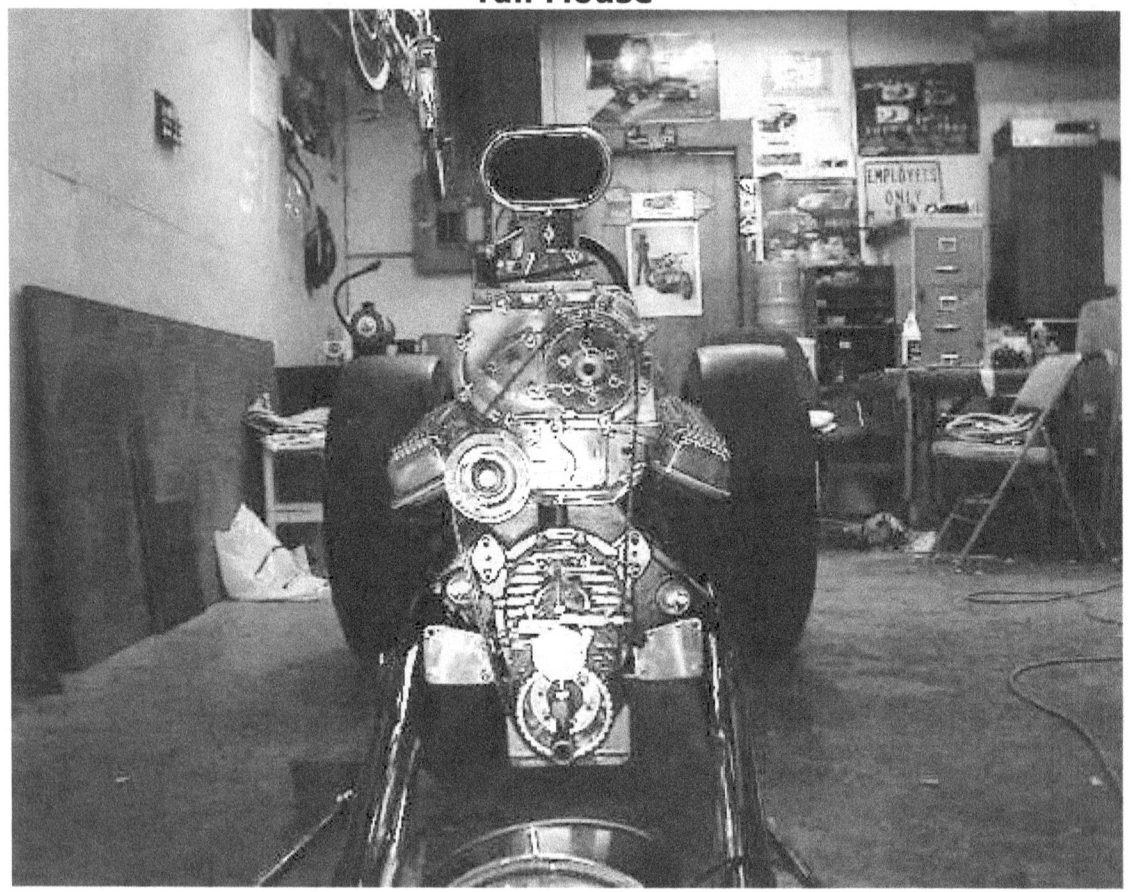

Yeah ! ... pretty cool alright........

"Can't Wait"

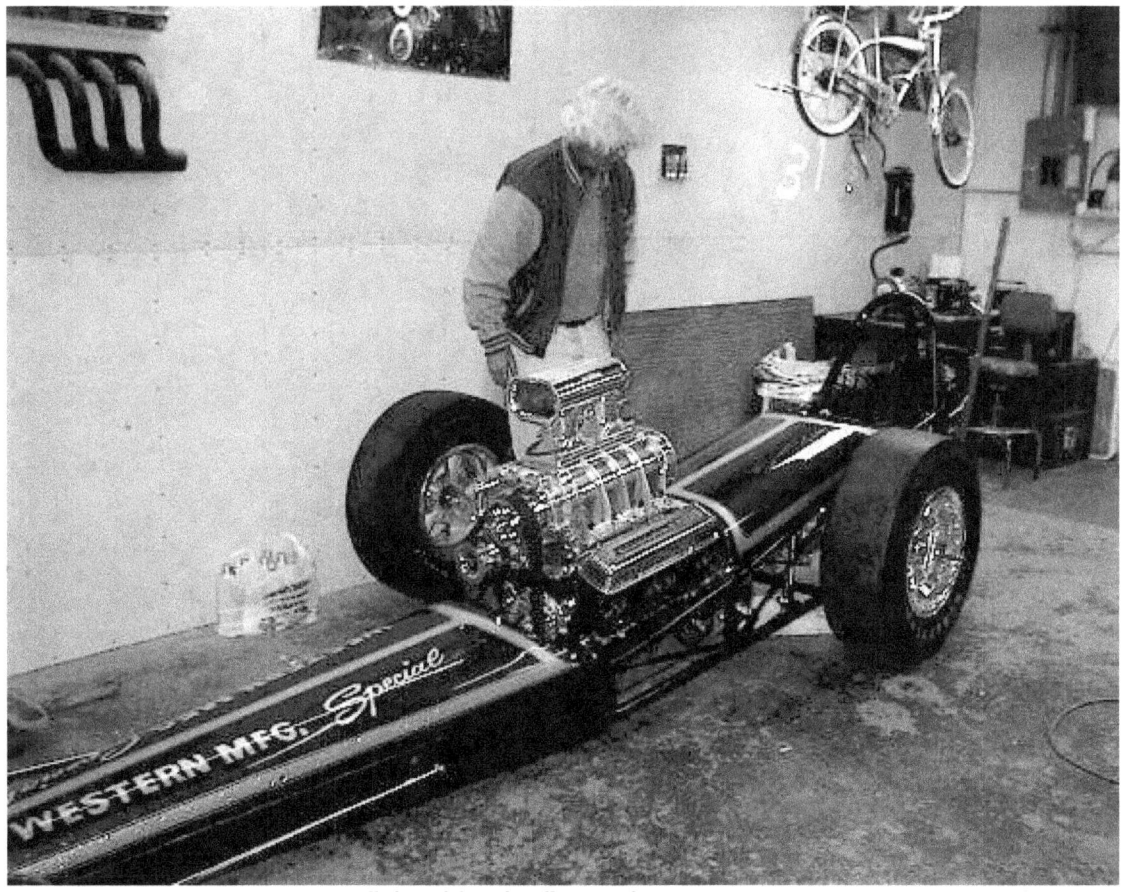

"I'm likin' it", say's Pete...

"But First"

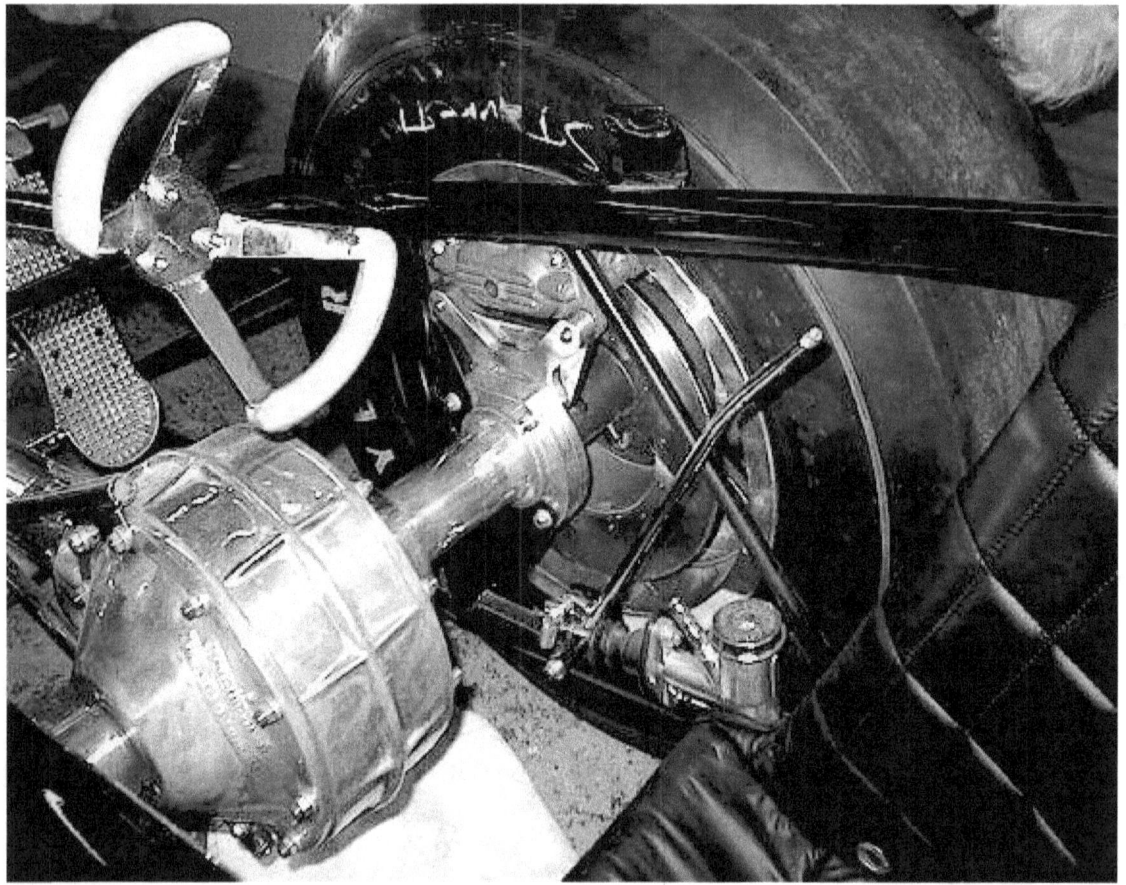

The very trick, (fresh off the CNC) ... Dave Benjamin brake caliper
bracket... ... (still gotta polish that airhart)........

"Thats the Brakes"

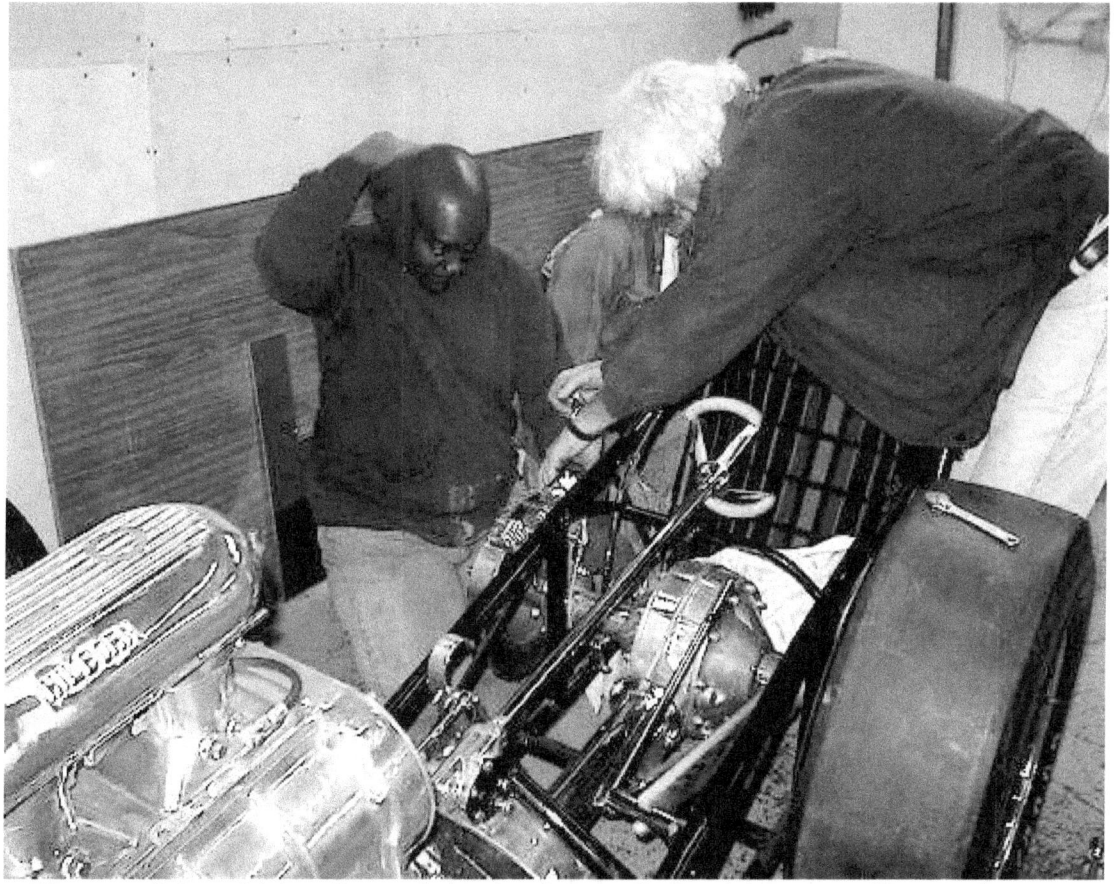

The traditional bleeding of the brakes... Or in this case, (live axle rear end) - - brake...

"HUH?????"

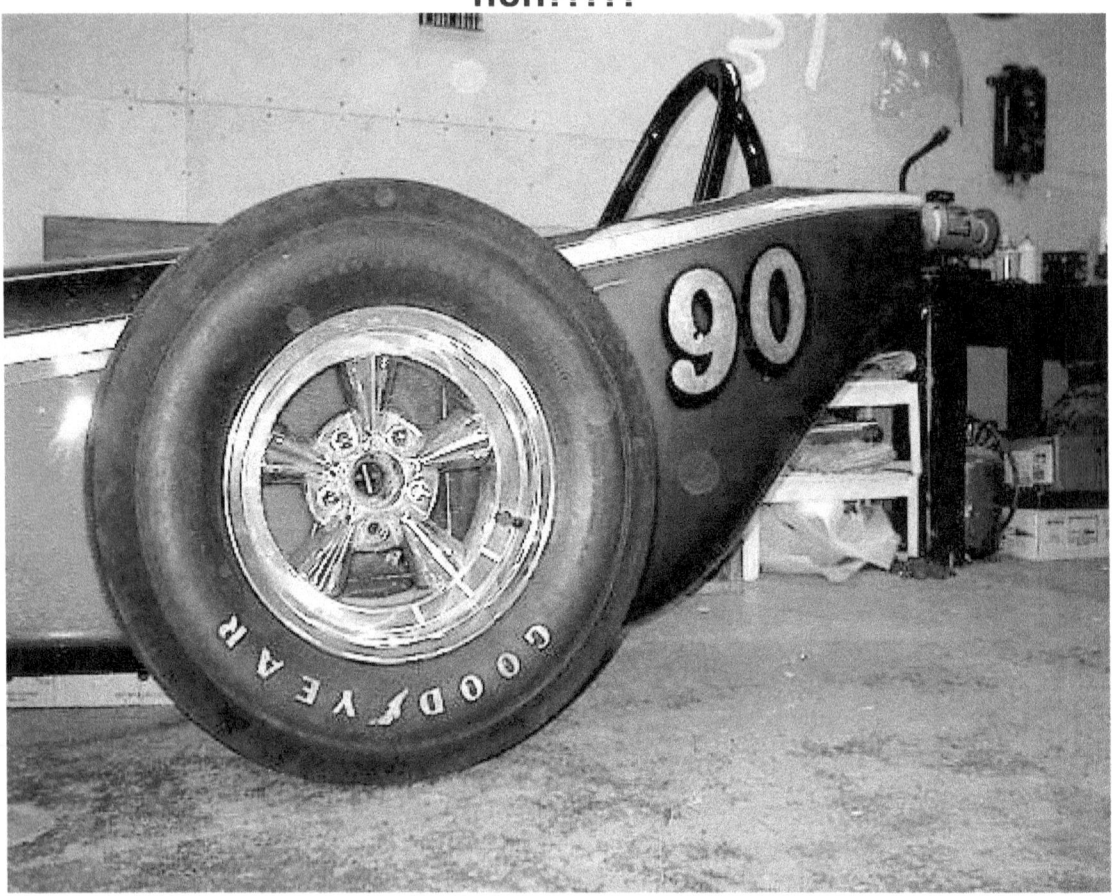

Yeah ... after Eric polished that super set of Halibrands ... it's decided to switch to American's - - forced by the avalibility of the right size slicks - ect. ... ... So it's back to the polishing room for Eric...

"MANNNN"

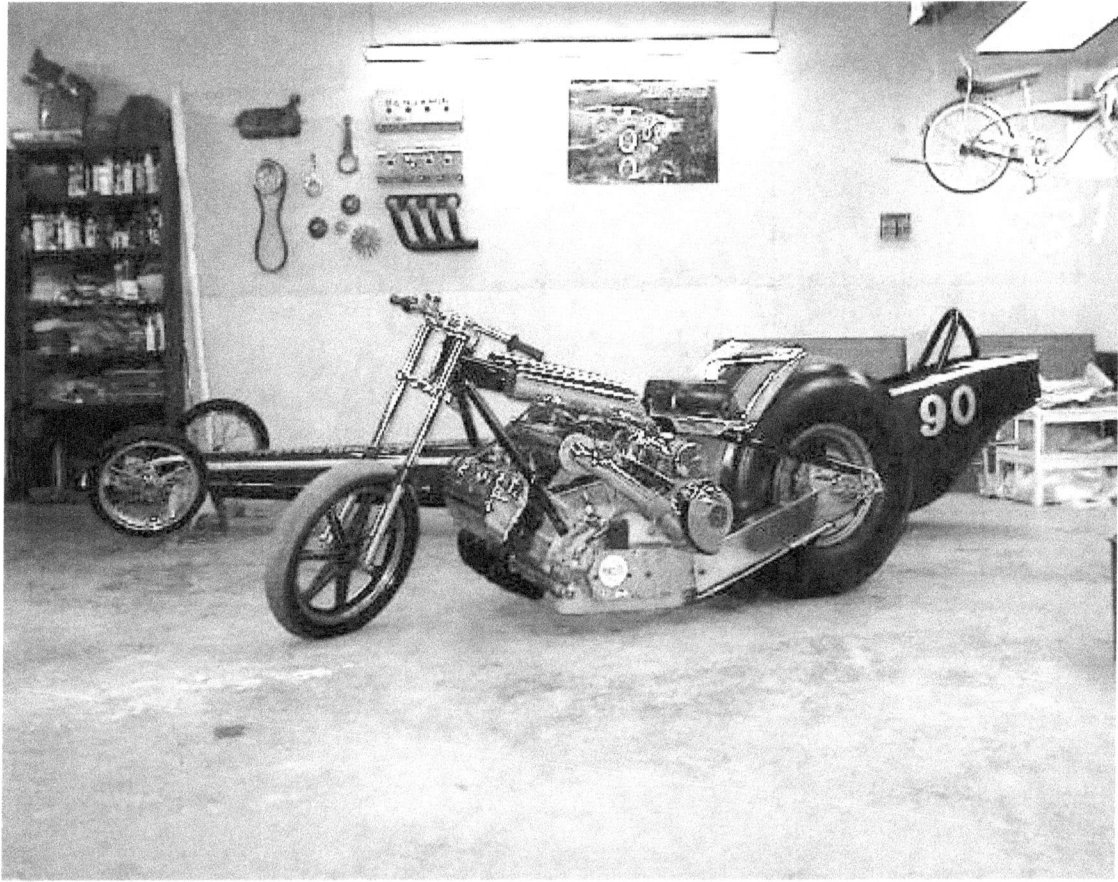

"Yer in the way again!", yells The Fuller ... "They came here to see me"
"Besides - - your kinda a short little sucker"..........

"Who's Da' Man??????"

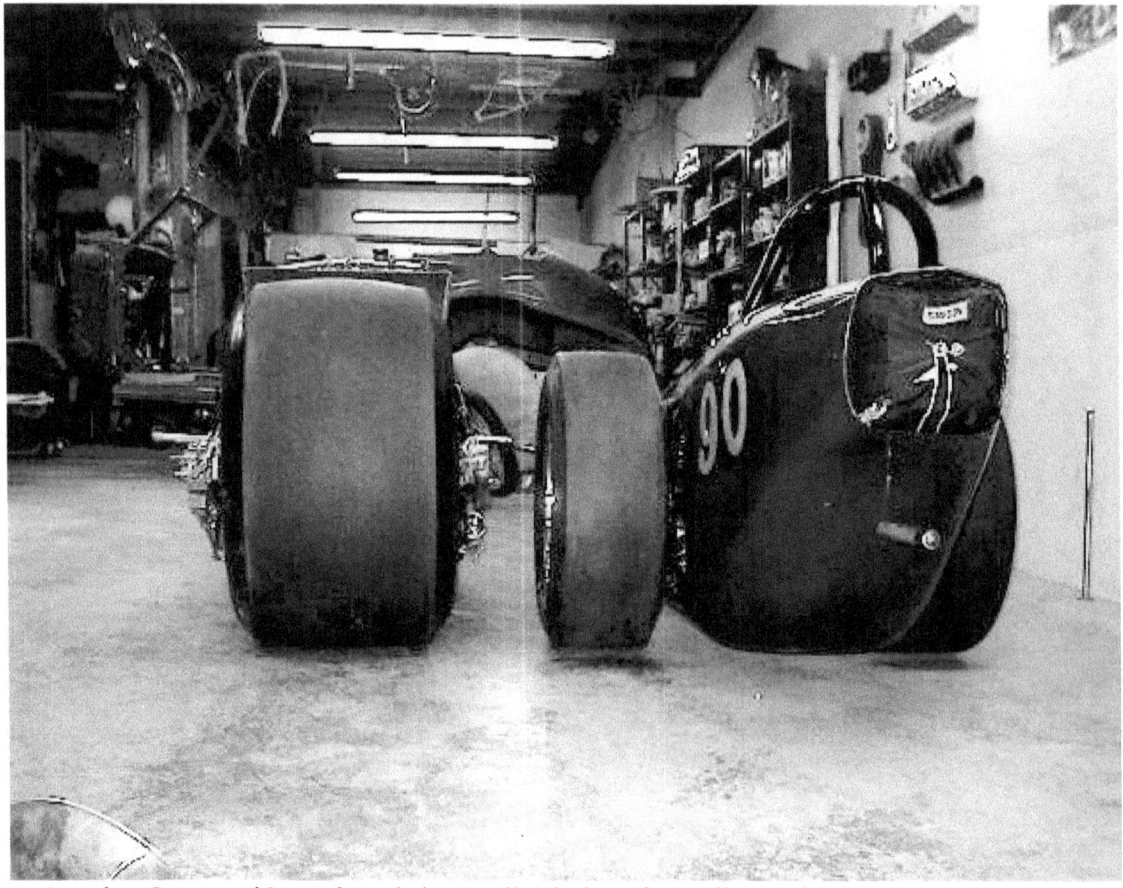

Pardon? says 'Supe' to 'The Fuller', but how 'bout hides ... ..." mine's bigger then yours - for sure!" ... "Yeah", answers The Fuller ... "But I got two!!!" ....

"The Nose Knows"

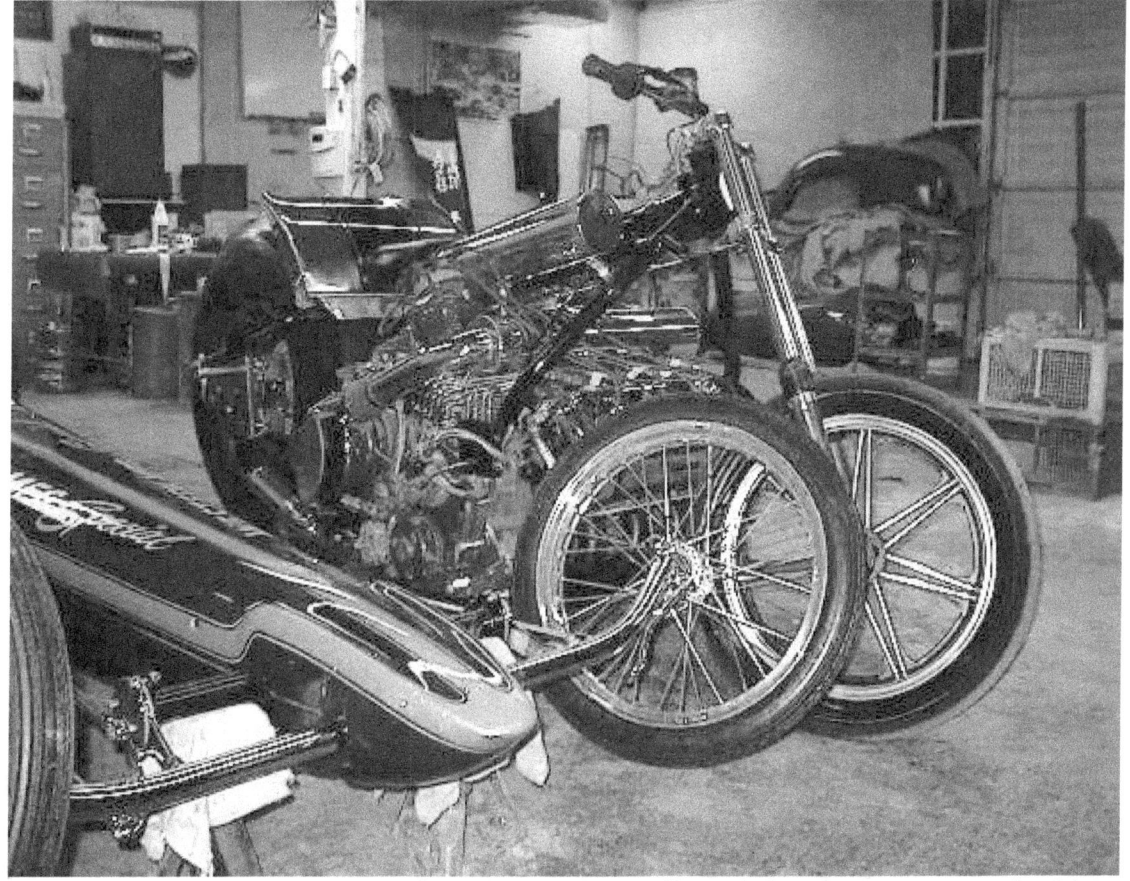

"I say 'Noses' at 20, paces" ... says The Fuller, (always very proud of his nose)...

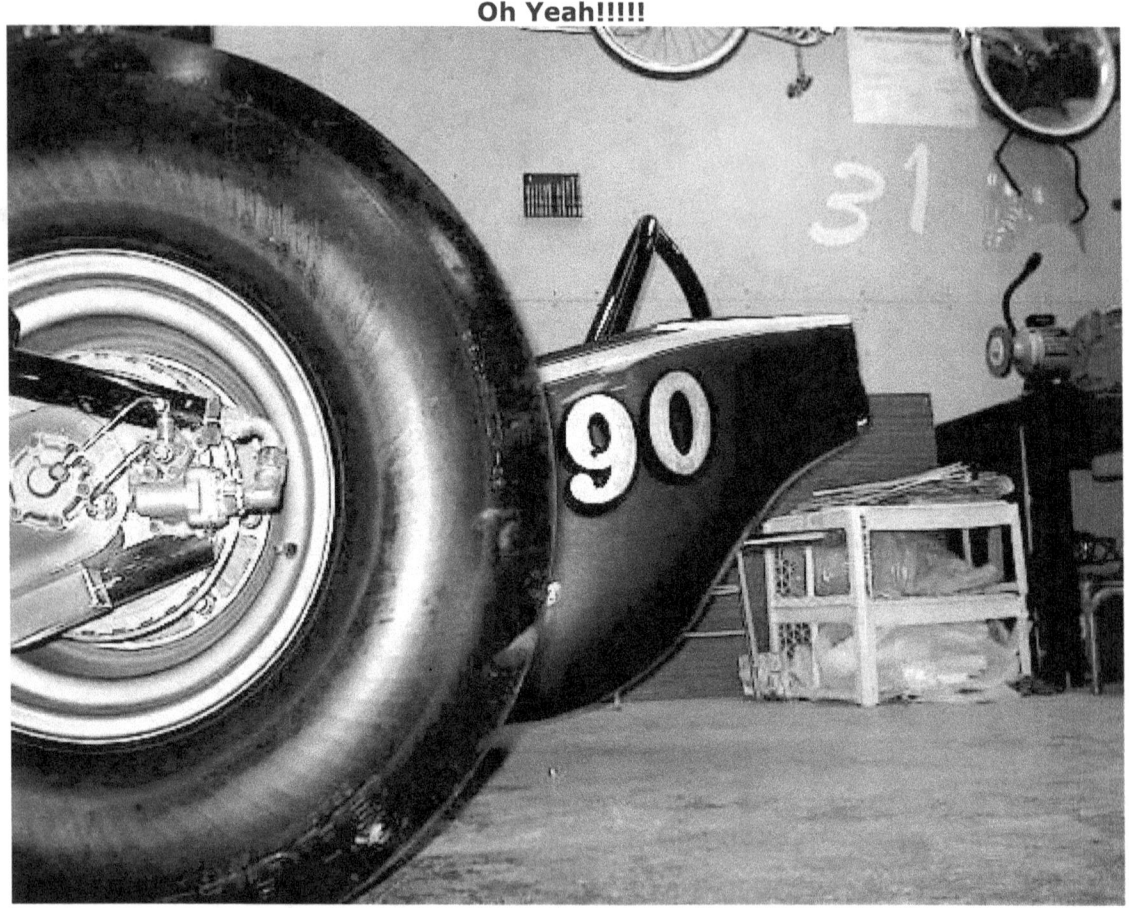

"I'd say I got ya' beat bootie wise too" say's The Fuller ... "Maybe we can combine our talents ... and rule the world", says SuperBike.................

"Ya Know Supe"

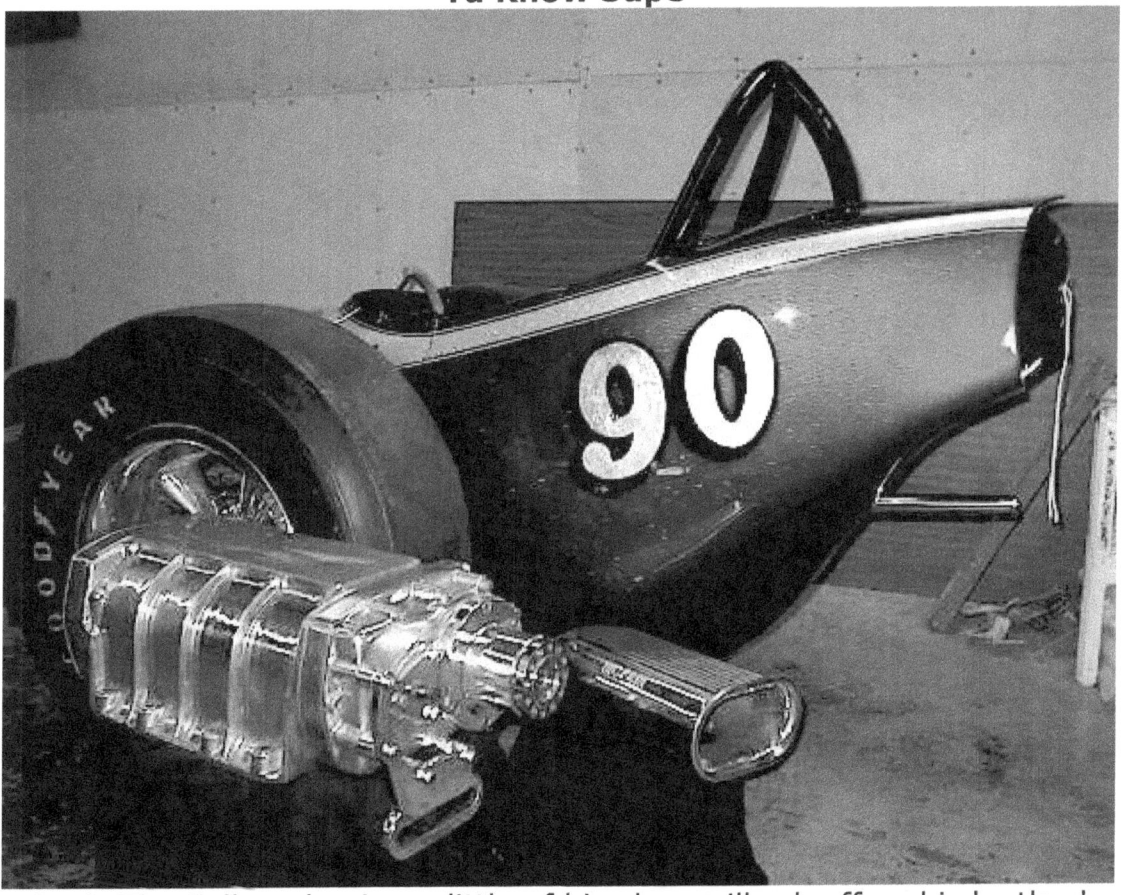

Say's The Fuller - hoping a little of his class will rub off on his 'outlaw' friend ... "The secret is to accessorize correctly"...

"Pit Crew" Pete

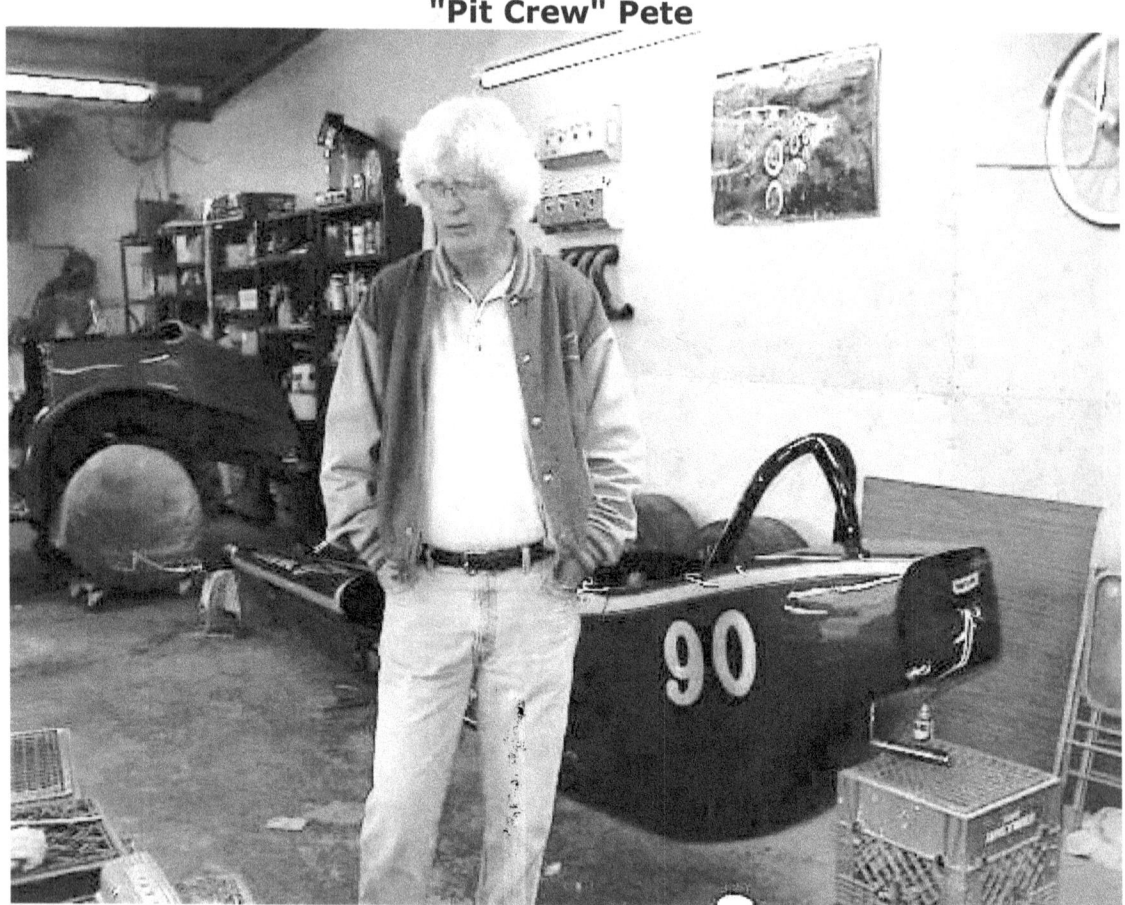

Pete say's, "My hair turned white about half way thru this deal"...

"Fuller Outside"

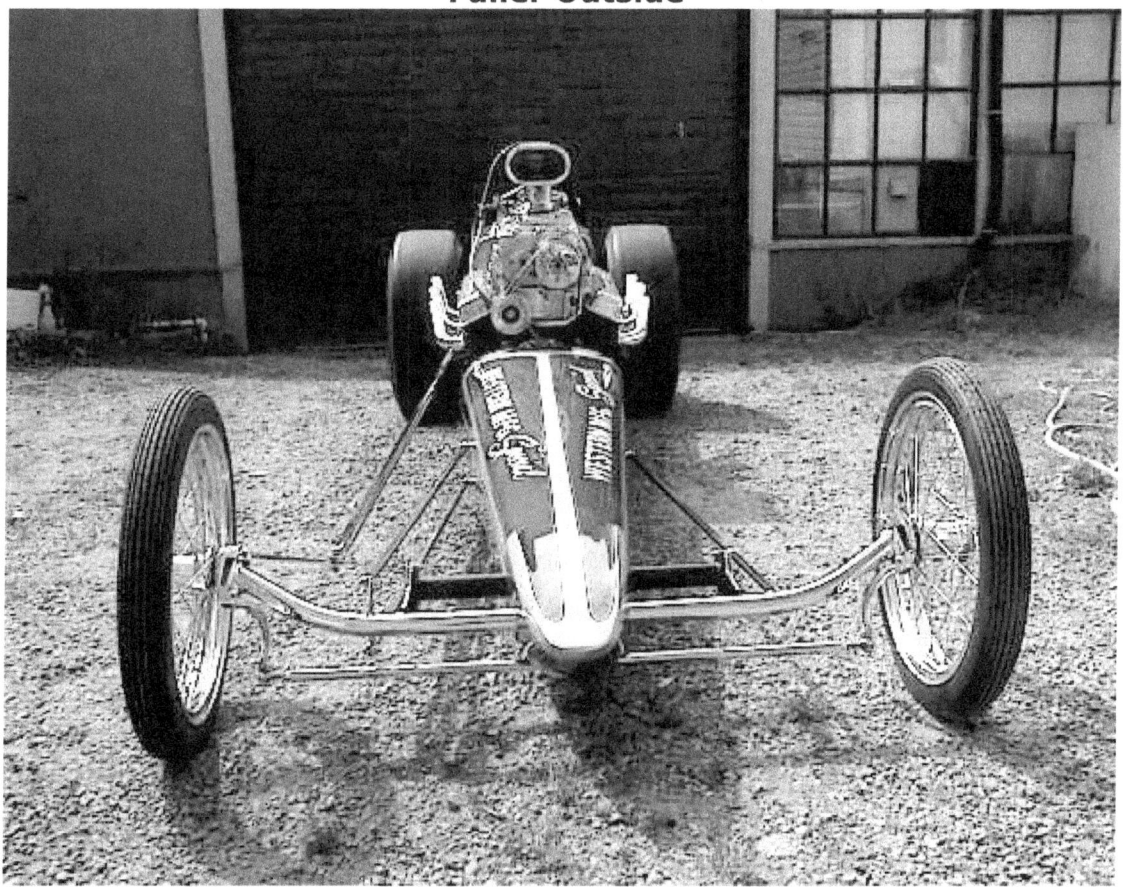

The Fuller ventures out into the sun... "Man", he thinks - do I look good -
- or what!

"Smooth Lines"

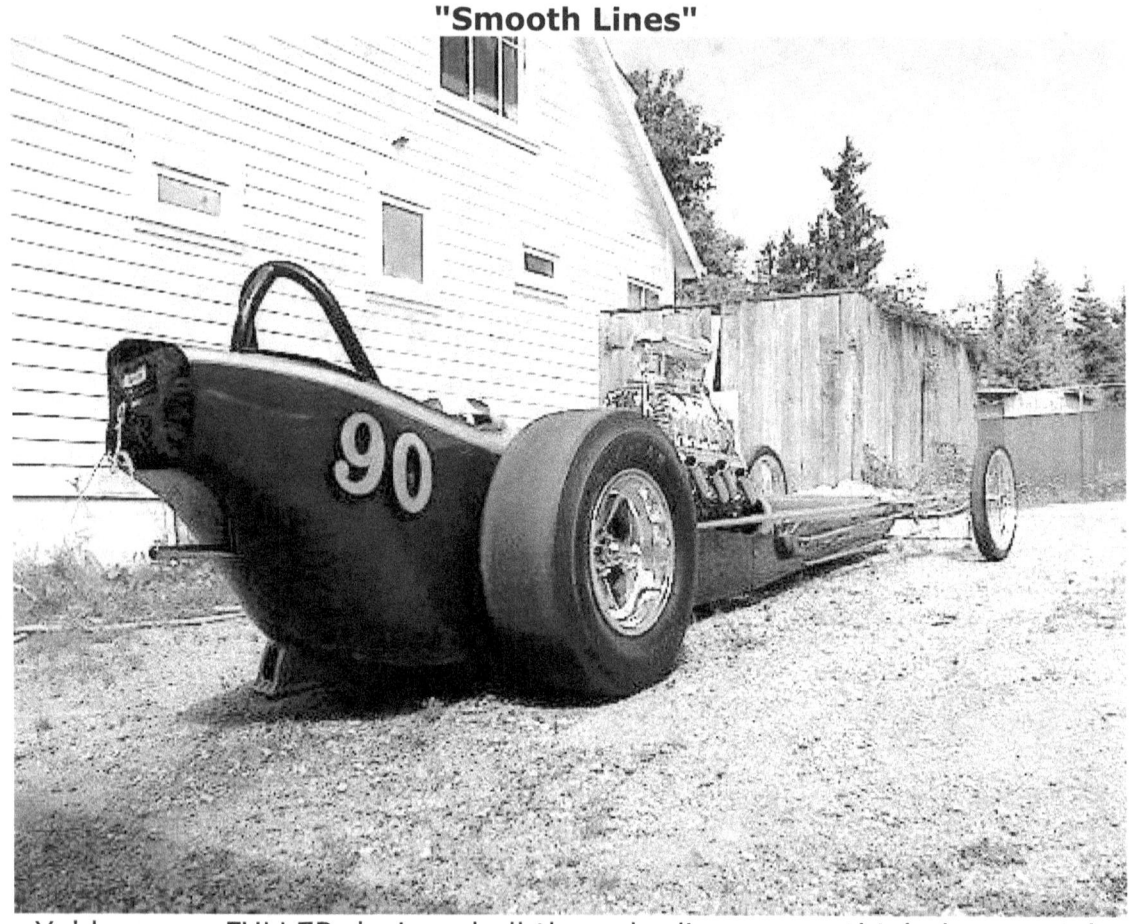

Ya' know ... FULLER designed all these bodies ... sumthin' else - - ain't they...!!! And the guy is still doin' stuff like this...

"Dig It"

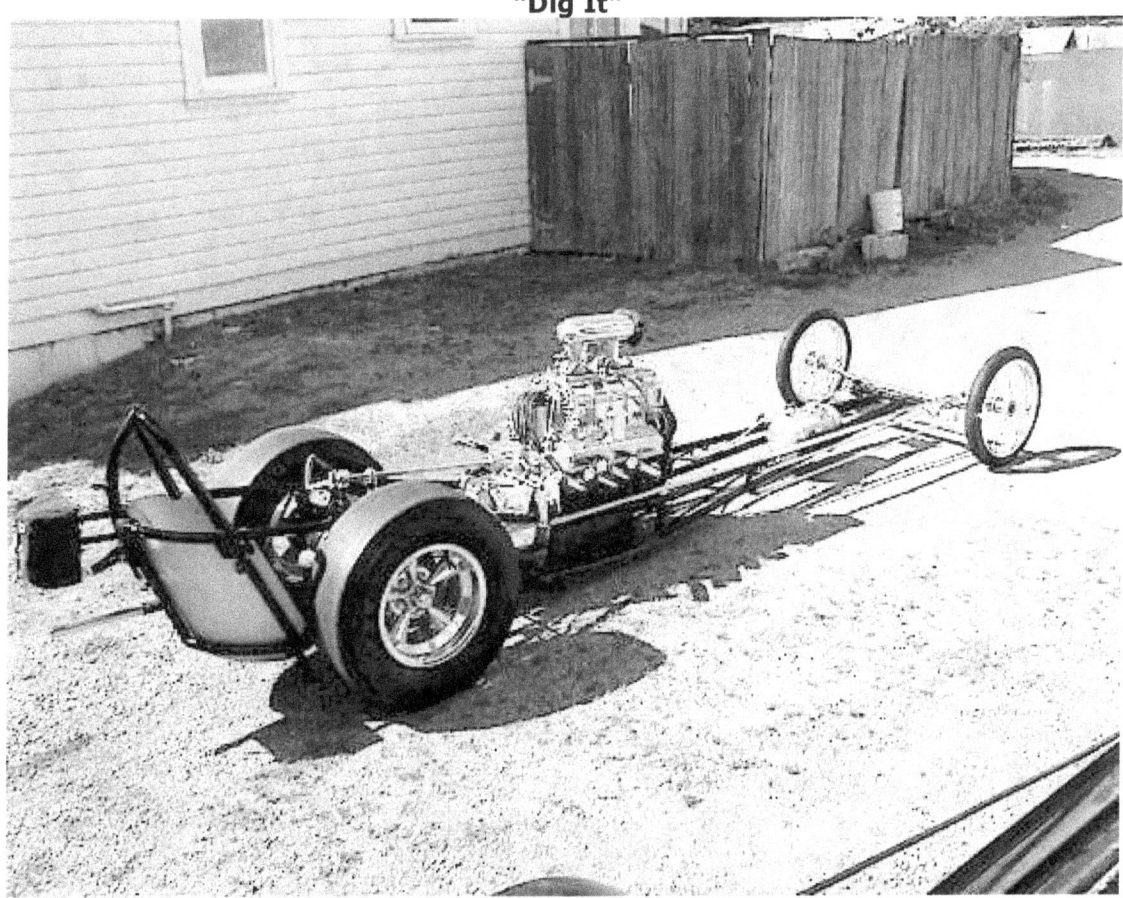

It's so nice out - The Fuller desides to take off his body panels and go for a tan... You really can appreciate the FULLER chassis - - eveything there for a purpose... no extra baggage...

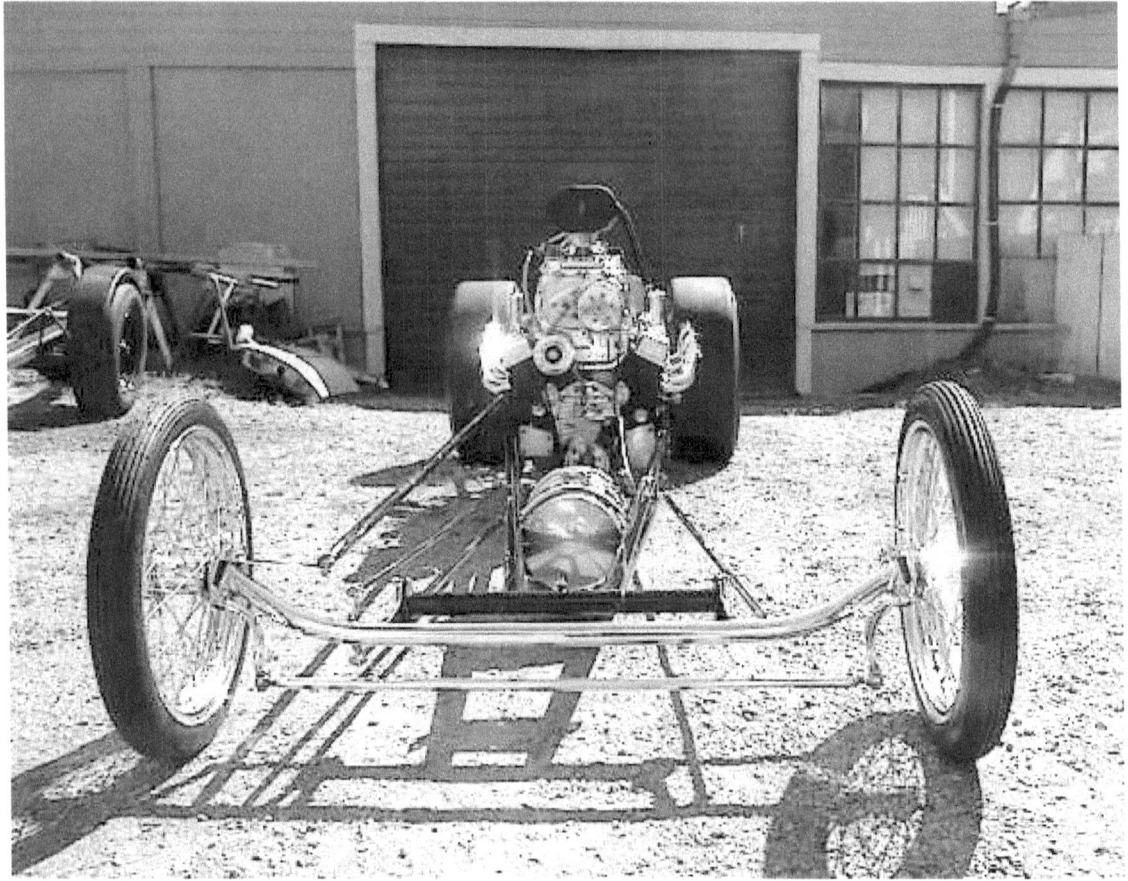

"This is the life", thinks The Fuller, "now where is that sun block?" ... "don't wanna tarnish my chrome"...

"Backyard Bakin"

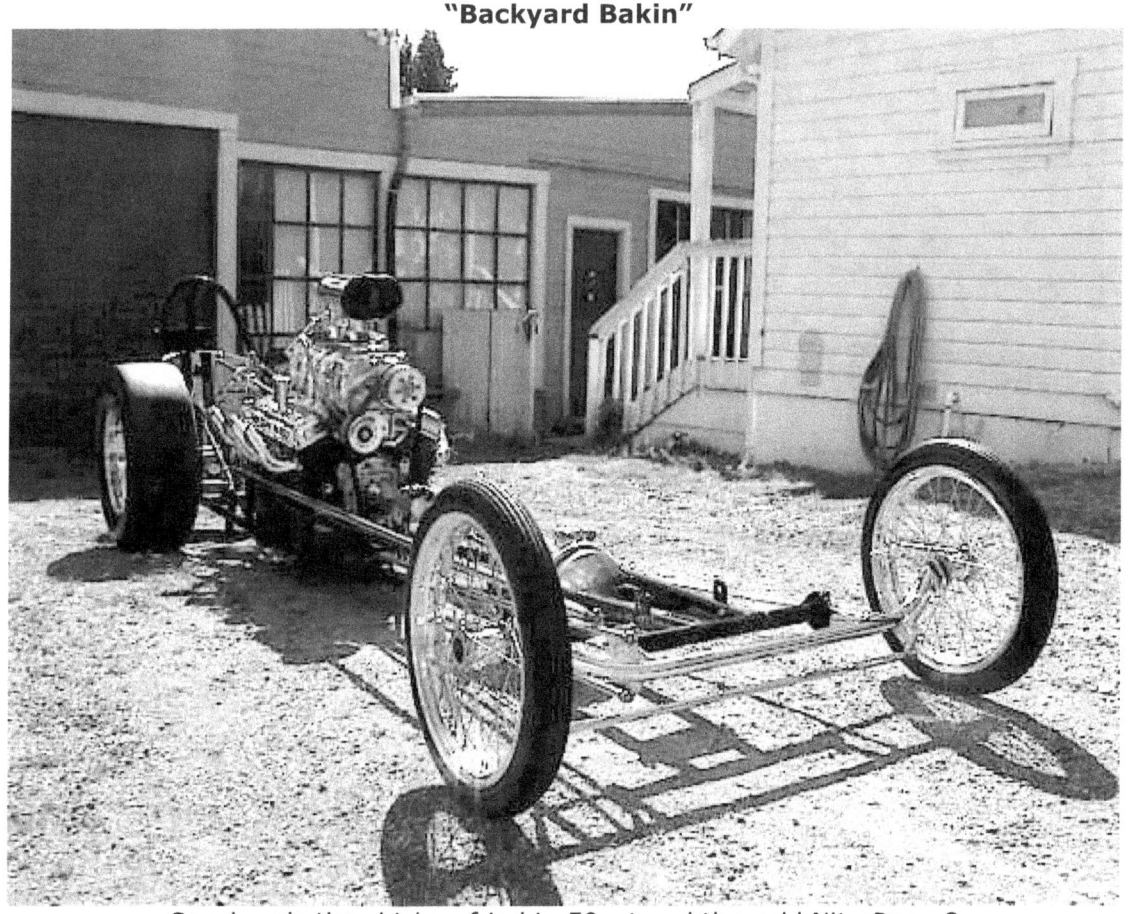

So where's the chicken fried in 50 wt and the cold NitroPop...?

"What Can I Say"

"I'm really a piece - ain't I", thinks The Fuller

"Time to go in"

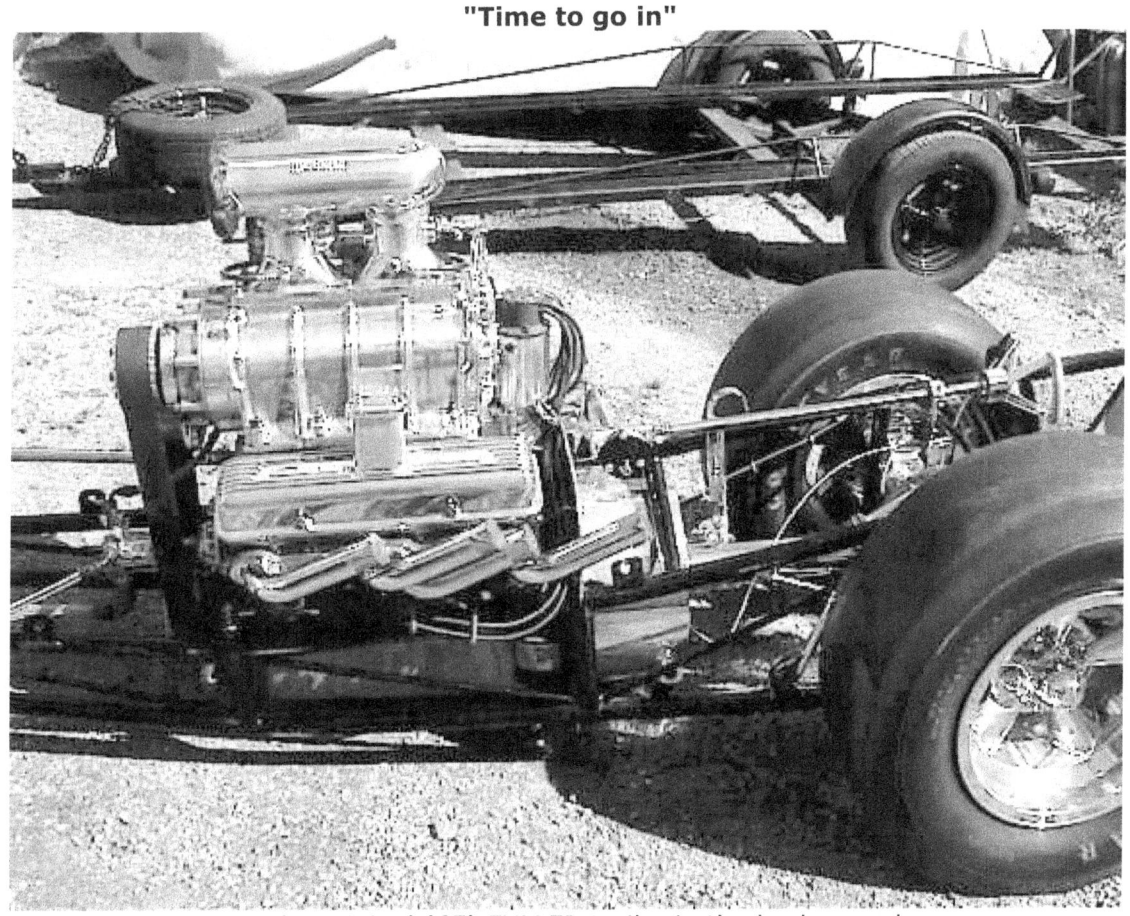

Note the original (65) FULLER trailer in the background...

"The Fuller and The Rocket"

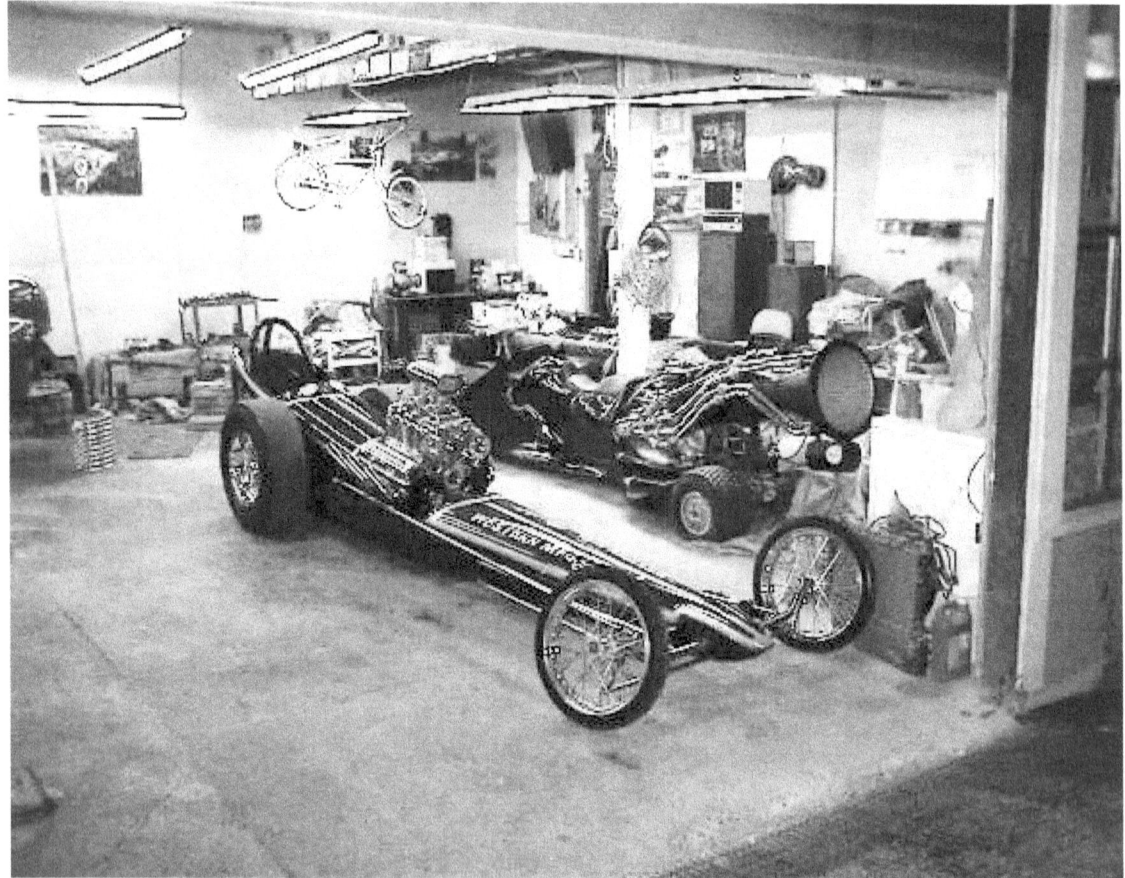

The FULLER puts his body back on - - and hangs out with RocketBike for the evening ...
The Rocket's a lot easier to get along with then SuperBike - who can be a
handful...........

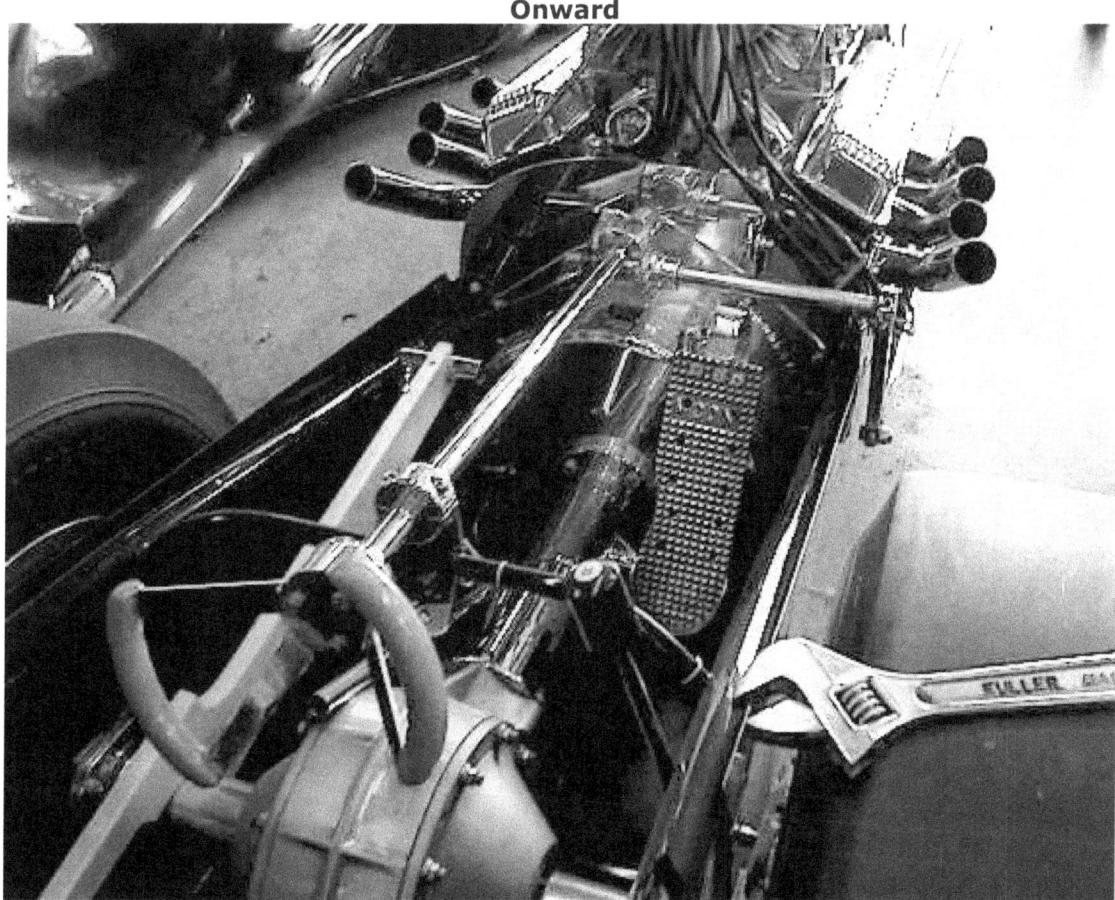

Hey! ... I think maybe we're approaching the finish of this opus ... as you can affirm in the photo - only the period correct FULLER tools were used during this project ... ... So now we move on - to 'The Public Fuller' ... a few photo's of the digger 'out and about' at shows and such ... We've had a lot of fun with this last side of the project - - the car brings back memories of the past for a lot of folks who see the car and grew up in the 60's - - I mean, everybody, (everybody who was young at least), during those times - knew what Drag Racing was... And many were obsessed by it - (Hey, there's worse things) ... Lotta old guy's, show their kids - - and (gulp) grandkids, the car, and explain to them how it works - to let them know what it was like in the 'Olden' Days'. And it brings back the art and beauty of a bygone era for people to once again marvel over ... ... Stimulate the Mind - - Entertain and Educate ... that's what we're here for......... Fred Vosk

Pete 'N' Pam

'The Fuller' allows a few last photo's before loading up to head for Bakersfield for his public debut at the Califorina Hot Rod Reunion. Here you see him posing with 'Pit Crew Pete' and 'Pit Crew Pam'...

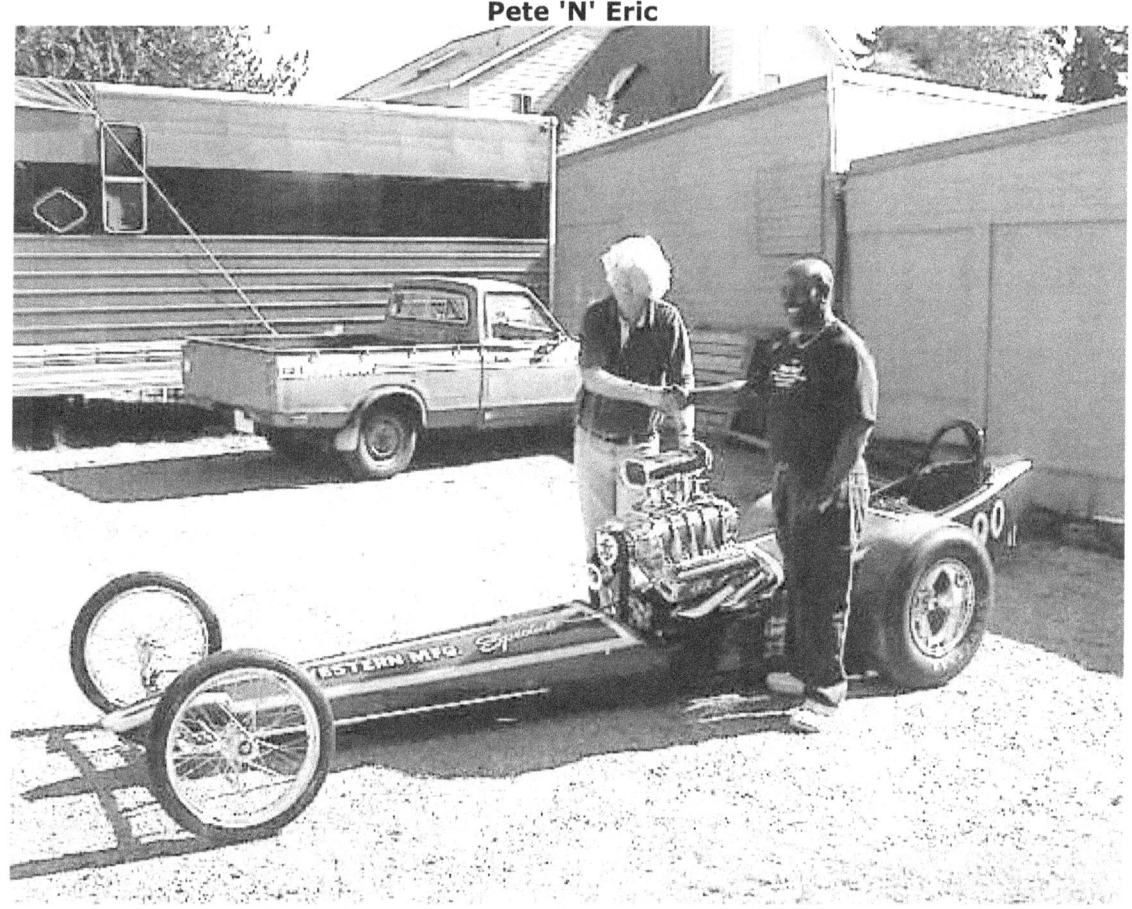

Eric tells everybody ... "Pete's my Dad"............

See Ya 'round

Supe' and good bud 'The Fuller', talk about old times while Pete frets over last minute details........

"Mouse & Elephant"

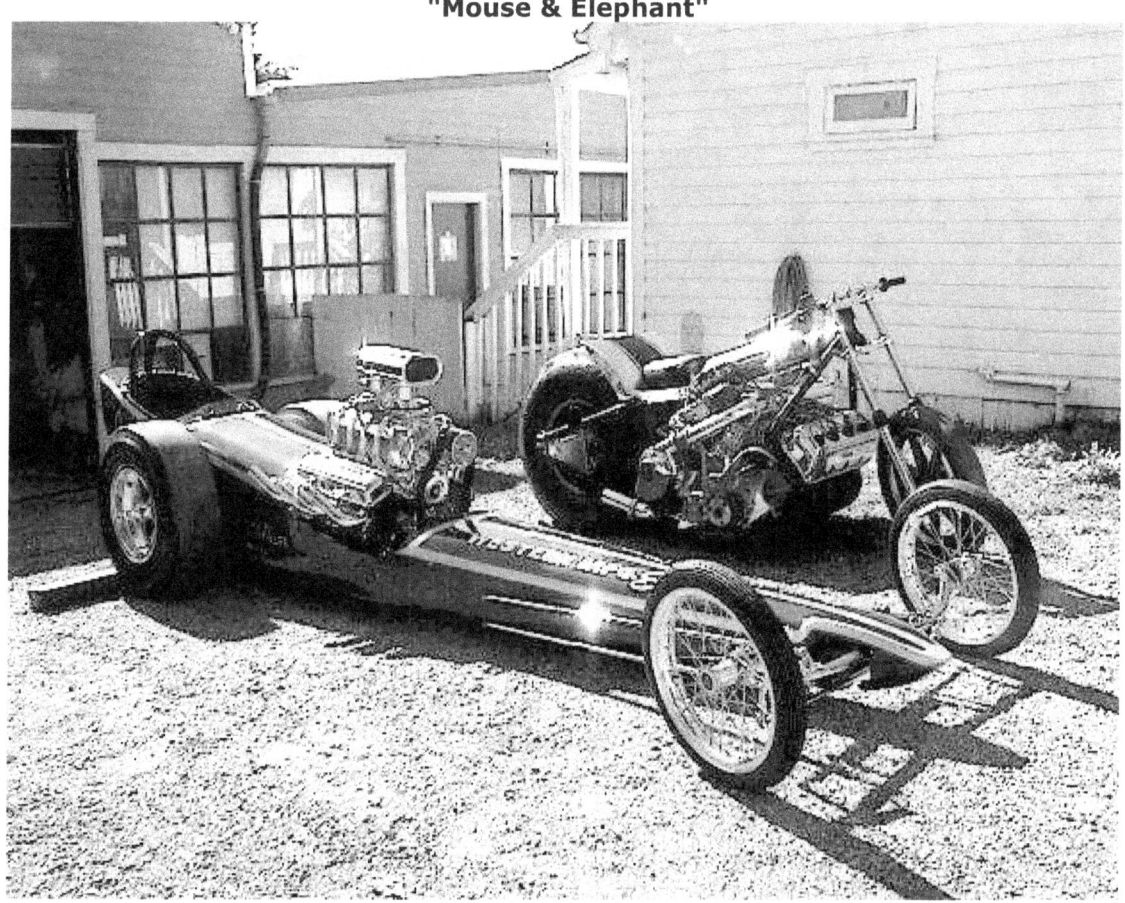

SuperBike says 'later' to his shop buddy The Fuller'

"One Last"

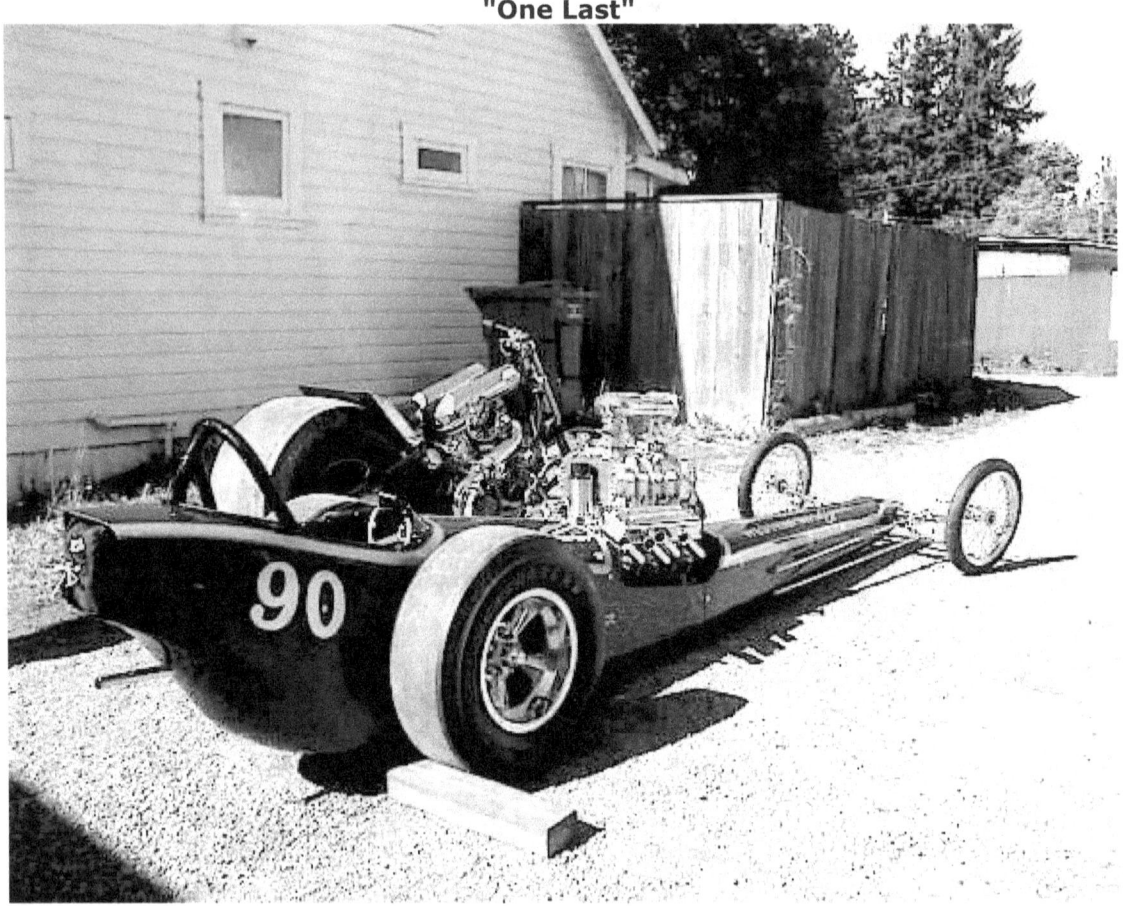

race around the block - - for 'old times sake...

Last Night at Home

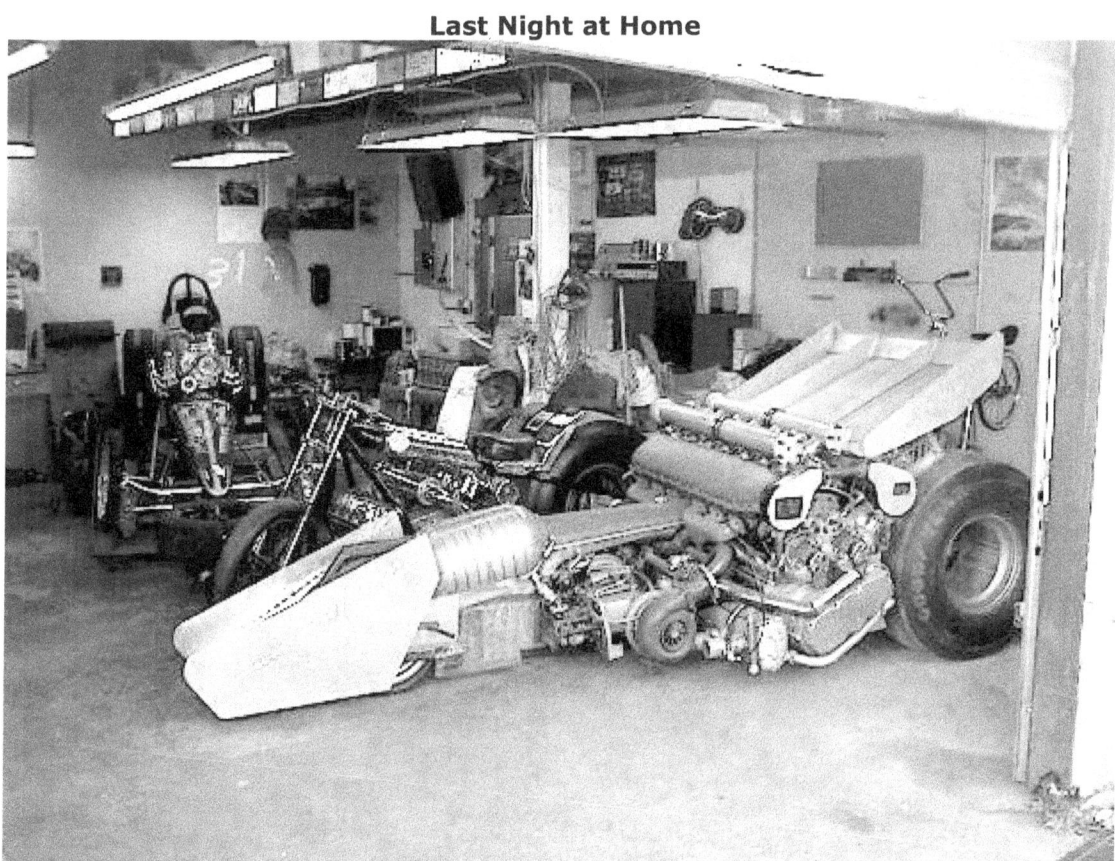

The Fuller spends his last night at the shop swapping 'road' stories with SuperBike ...
and being a little grouchy about the fact that a new guy has already moved into his
room ... It's Supe's cousin, 'MegaBike' ... or as the 'family' just calls him - 'BIG AL' ...
he's a bit of an animal (to say the least) - - and to tell ya the truth, The Fuller doesn't
feel real bad about having to leave town tomorrow...

"Big Day Tomorrow"

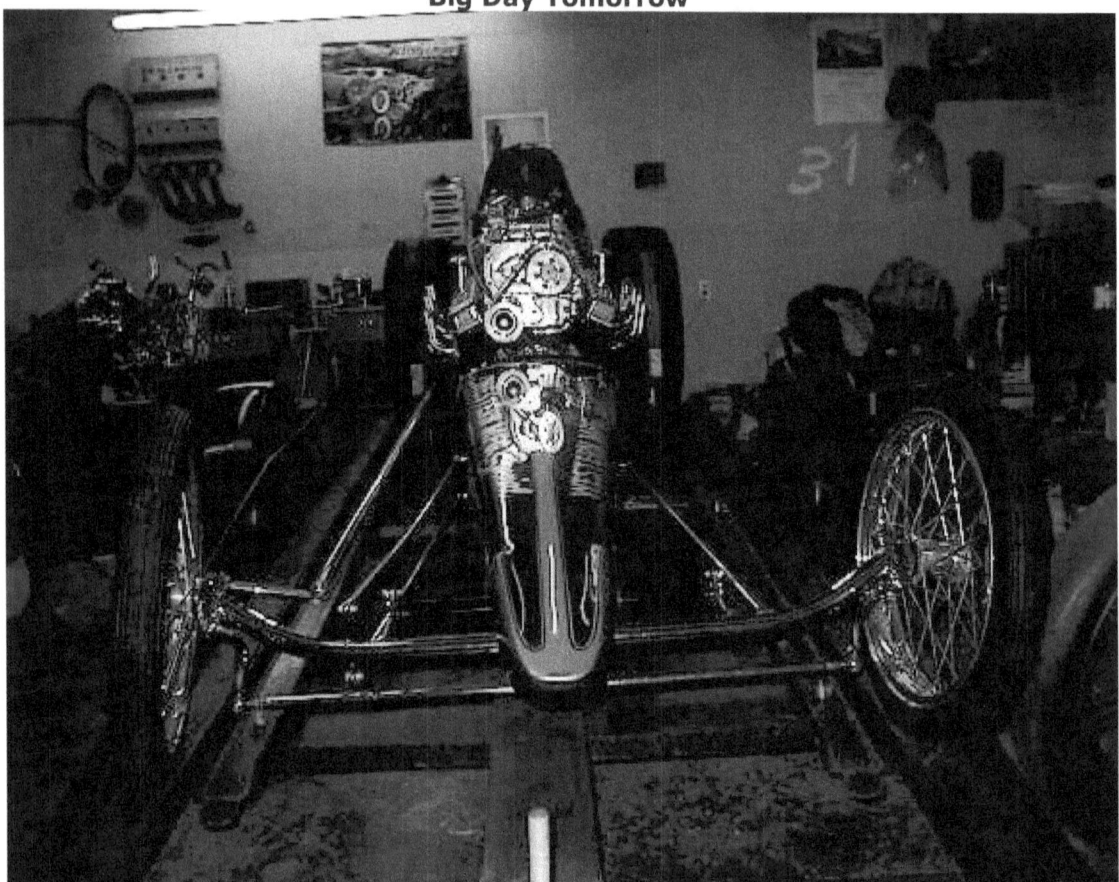

One quick 'Artsy' type shot ... "Ya know, I've dealt with just about every kinda car on this long strange, trip ... but there's still nothing that can hold a candle to one of these ... Ferrari's - Bugatti's - Delahaye's - Super Street Rods - messed with em' all ... still none of em' can compare with the cars that drew me into this whole deal in the first place ... DIGGERS!!! ... ... There should be at least one FULLER in every art gallery in the country... ... I spent a few days at the 'today' drags a few months ago ... and it was cool ... lotsa HP, and the cars go fast for sure ... But the cars are like bludgeons ... The delicateness and style are gone ... part of the past I guess.......... Fred

"Goodbye's"

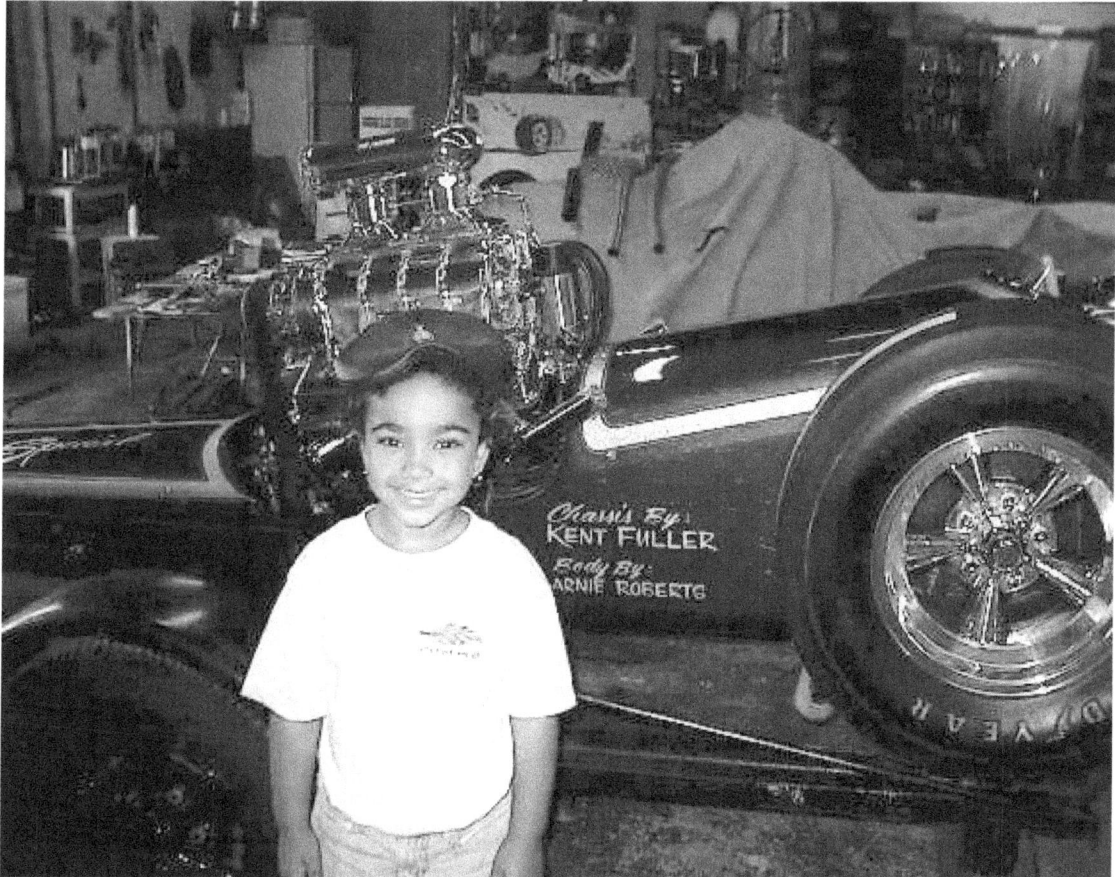

Arricka, (Eric's daughter), say's goodbye to her pal ... take note of the very stylish hat she's wearing - (The Fuller's 'Tony Nancy' injector cover)....

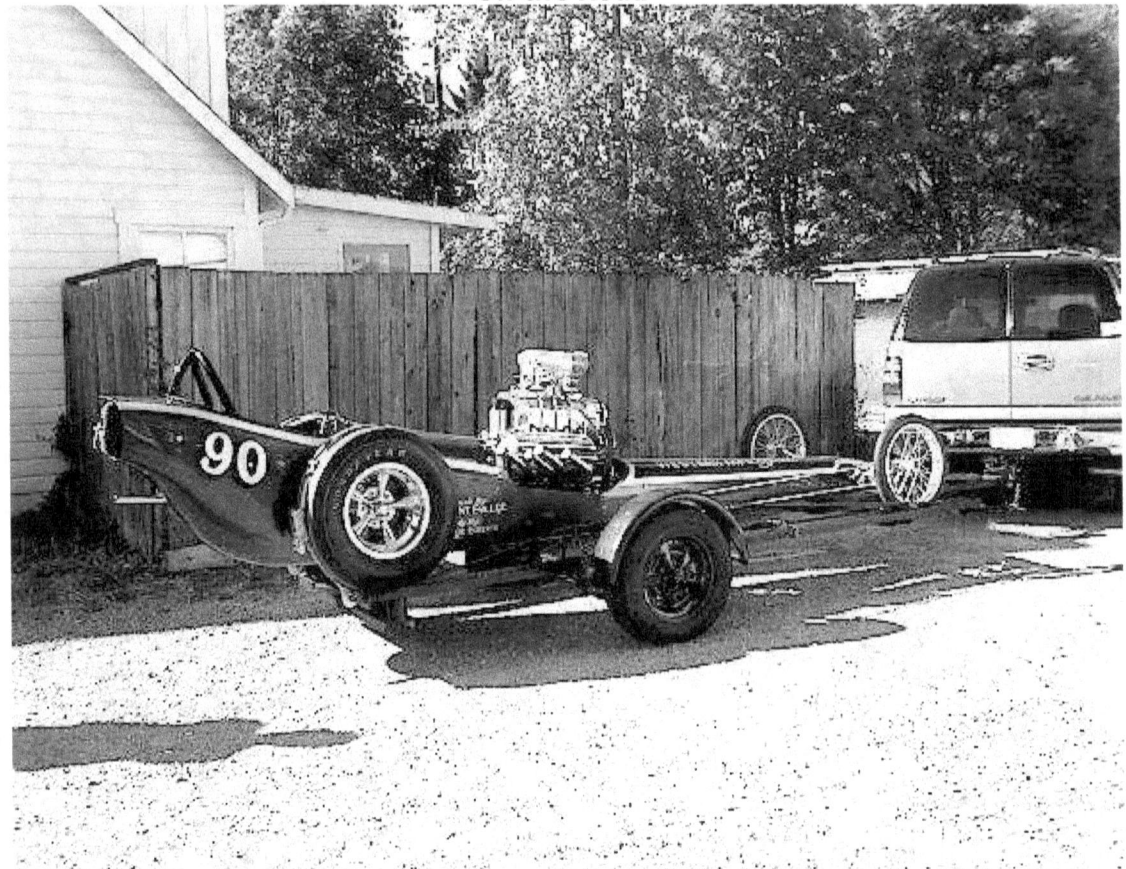

Is this traditional ... ... Or what!!! Well - - except for the new Tahoe tow car ... but you can pretend it's FULLER's 59 Rancharo.........

First Stop

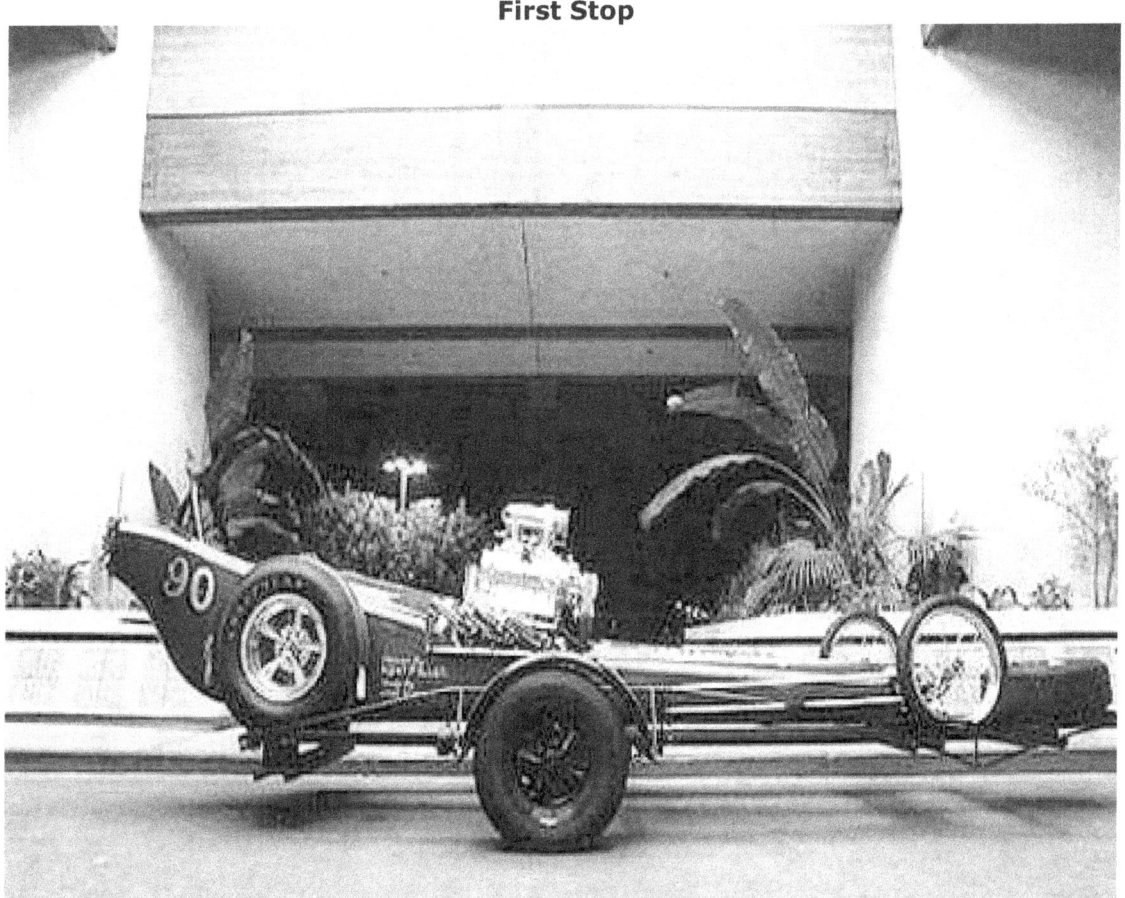

The first event to go to at the Reunion deal in Bakersfield is the big Standard 1320 gathering at The 'Double Tree Hotel' ... and guess who was parked out front - - The featured 'Guest of Honor'.............

"Fuller in the Shade"

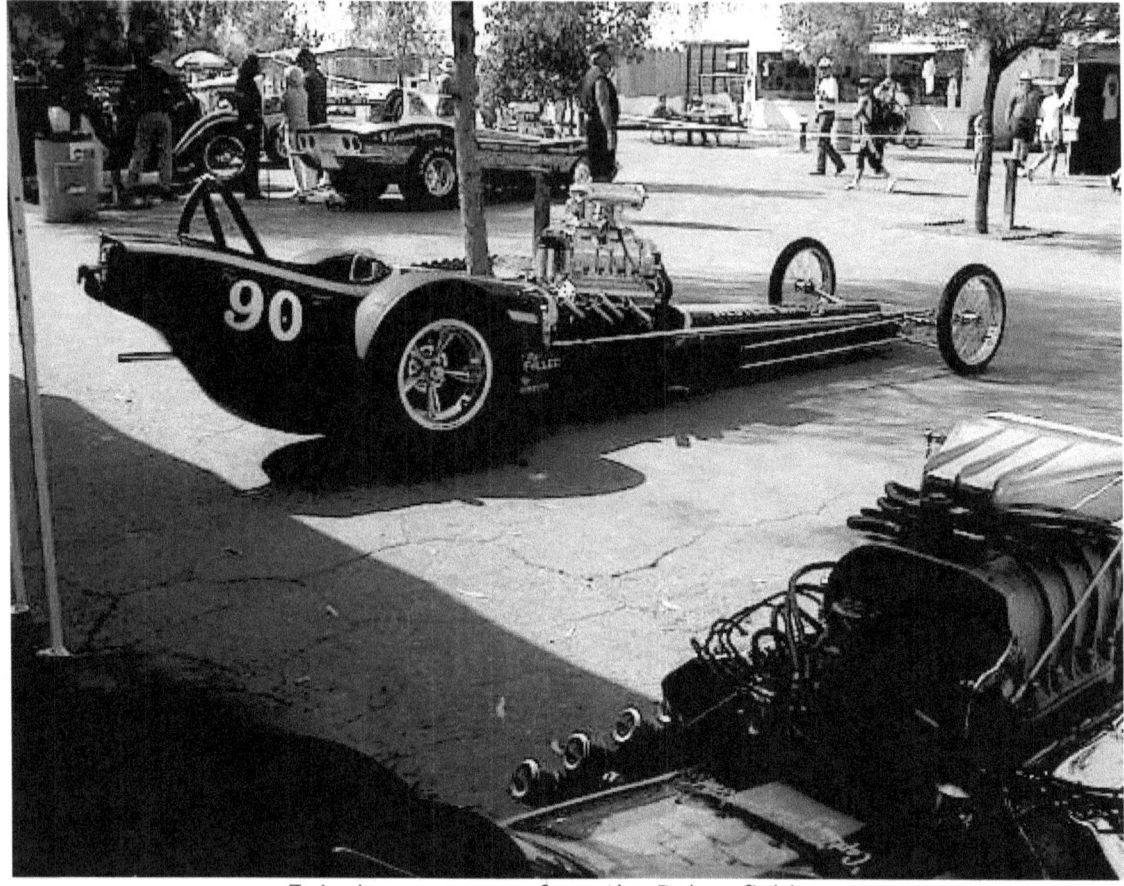

Enjoying an escape from the Bakersfield sun

Hi!!!!!!

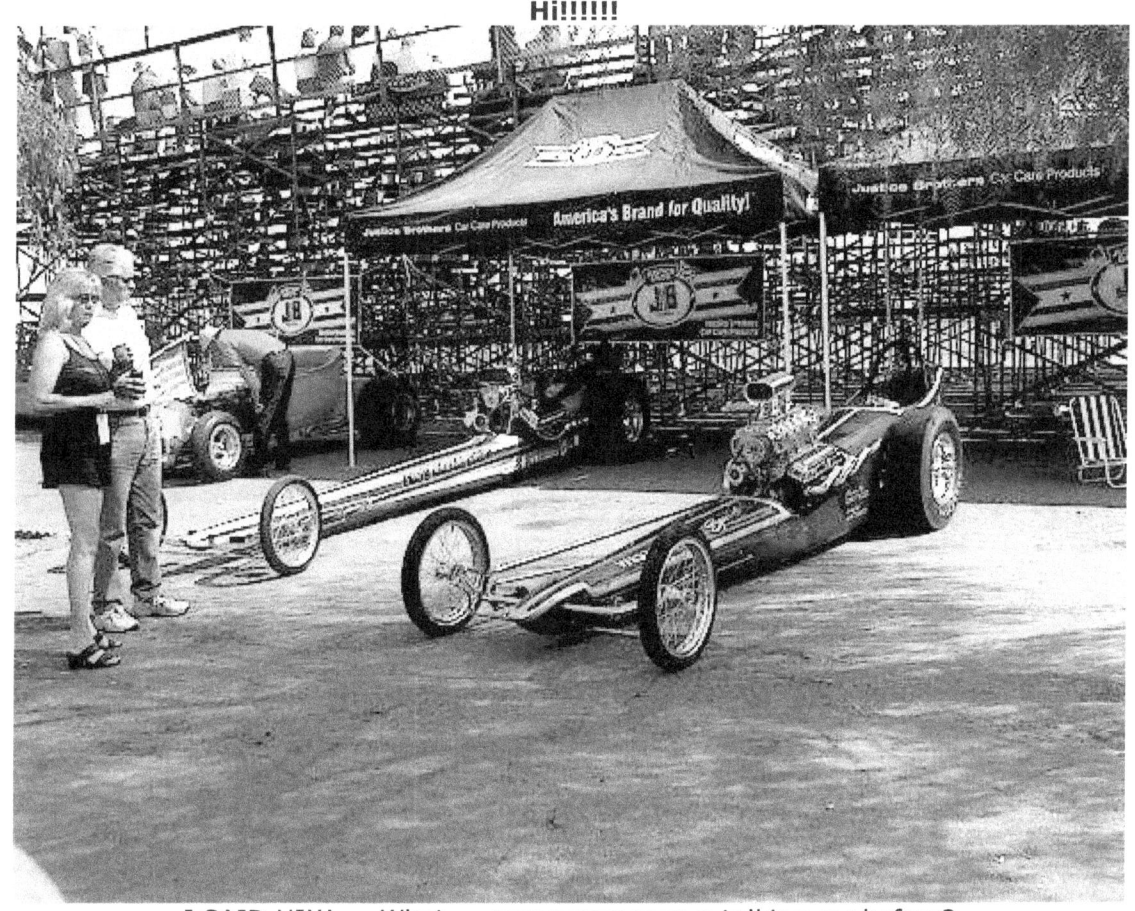

I SAID HI!!! ... What - - you never seen a talking car before?

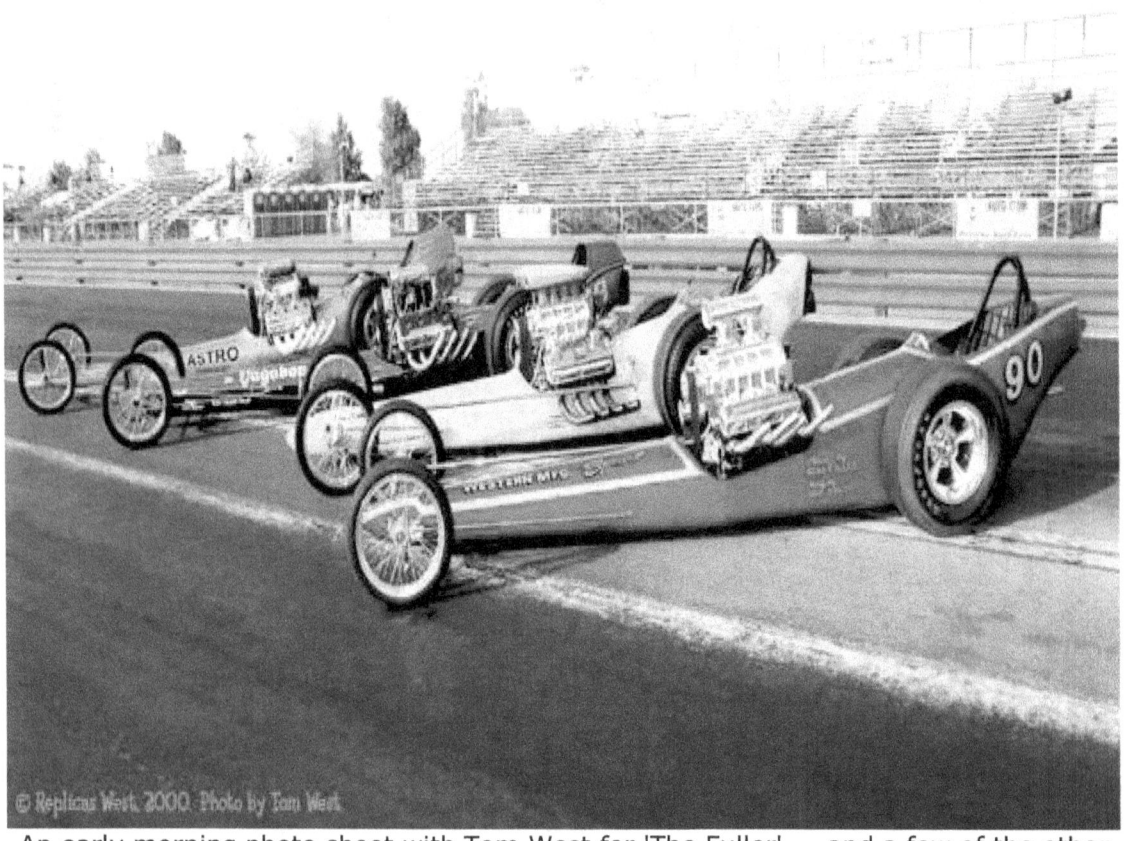

An early morning photo shoot with Tom West for 'The Fuller' ... and a few of the other FULLER creations in attendance...

"From Another Angle"

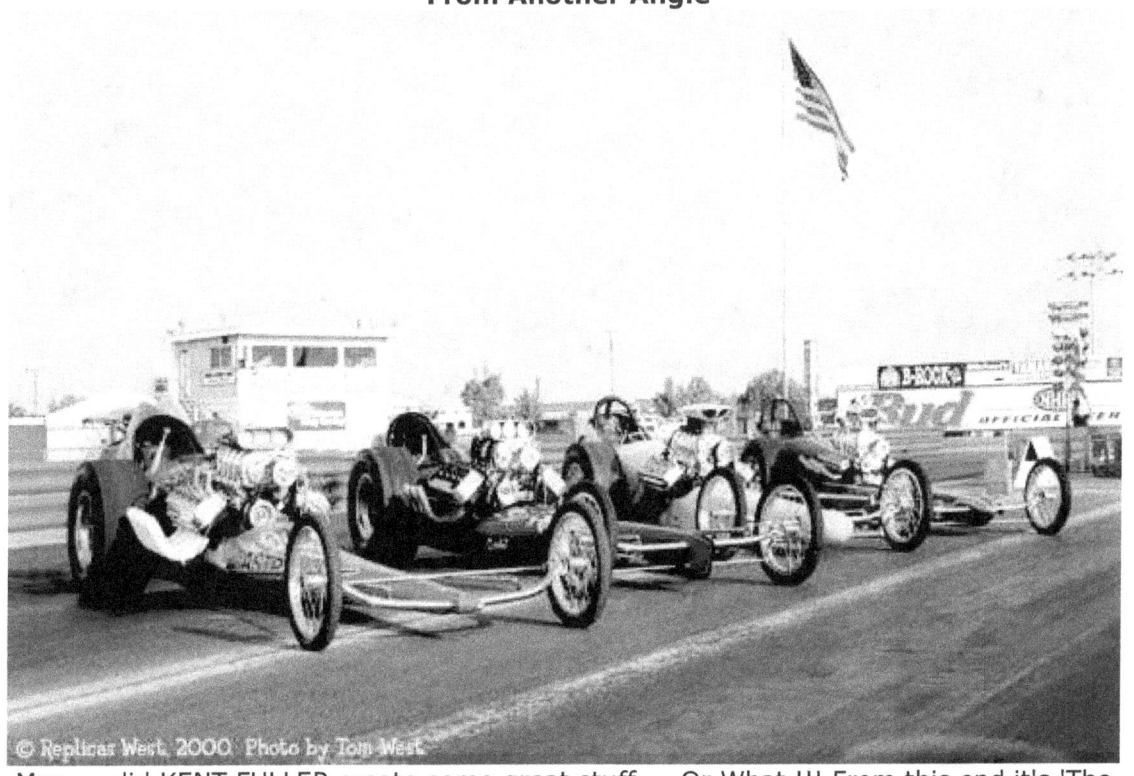

Man ... did KENT FULLER create some great stuff ... Or What !!! From this end it's 'The Magicar', 'Vagabond', 'Greer - Black & Prudhomme, and of course, 'The Fuller', (Western Manufacturing Special)

"What a Night"

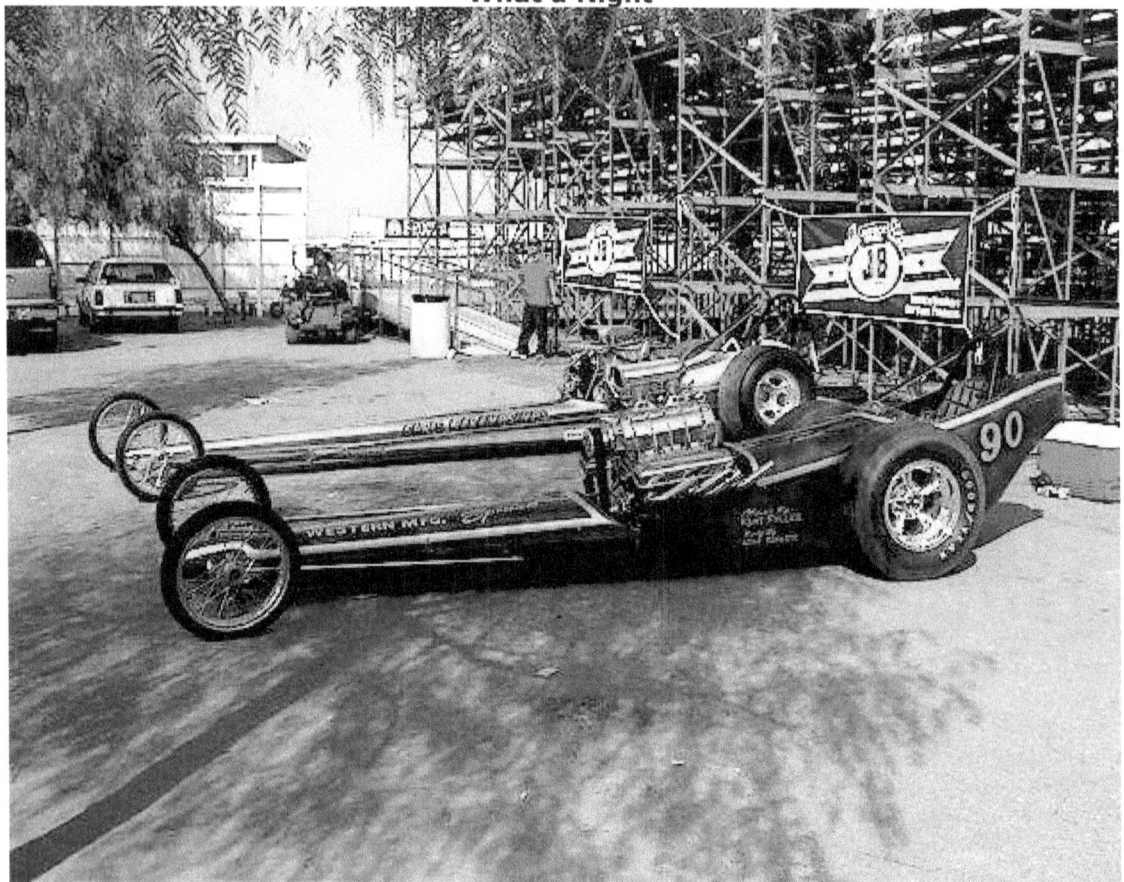

Man ... is this some kinda family reunion - - or what !!! Far beyond 'Most Cool' ... Here's The Fuller nursing a hangover on Sunday morning after partying the night before with a few of the other 'Fullers' at the reunion, including his 'kinda' crazy drinking buddy from Chicago ...... Geez - - hadn't seen him in years - - forgot what it was like to try and keep up with that guy... I mean he's gotta slow down - - He must be at least 100 years old........

"The Morning After"

The Fullers party pal shows off the Tattoo he got last night ... The Fuller thinks, "Uh-Oh, I think I got one too - - I'm afraid to look"......

"Roadster Nose"

The FULLER yells over at their bar hopping buddy from last night ... "You end up with any tattoos???" "Yeah man - I got a ton of em" ... comes the answer............

"Indoor Show"

'The Fullers' first big indoor show ... Seattle Roadster Show 2001 Here's our hero waiting for the crowd - with 'Supe' and 'The Rocket' in the background to give him moral support...

"The Fuller" & Friends

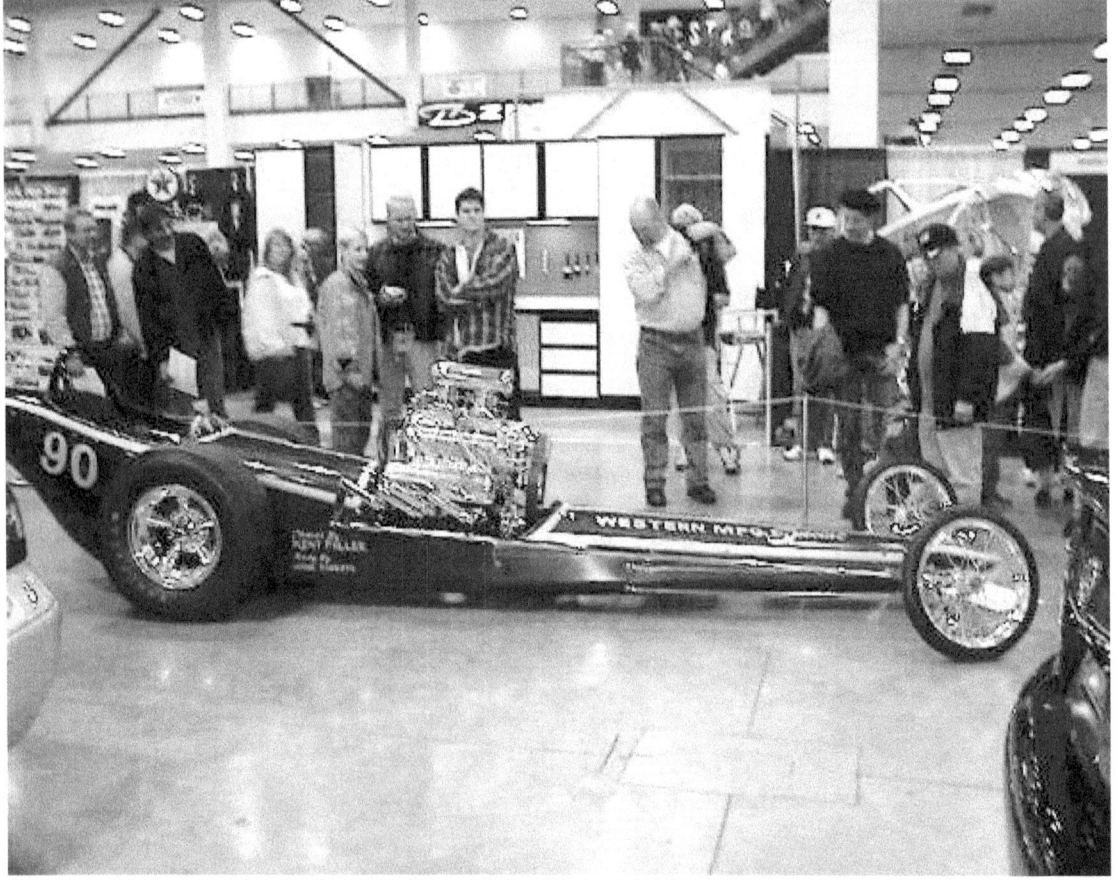

"Hmmmm"........ thinks 'The Fuller', "this deal of just parking someplace for a few days and being admired isn't bad at all"...........

HEY!!!! Burkey

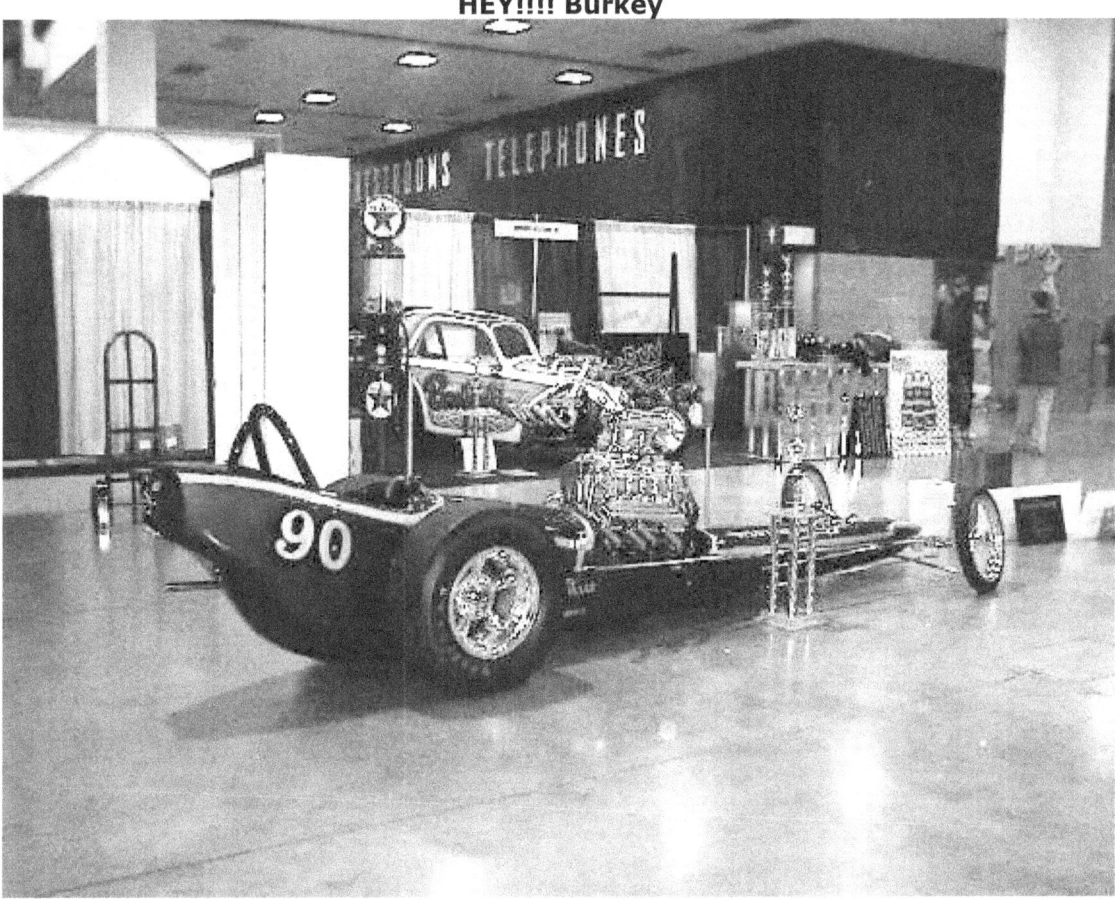

The Fuller compares trophy's with the Italian kid across the aisle after the show...

Campin Out

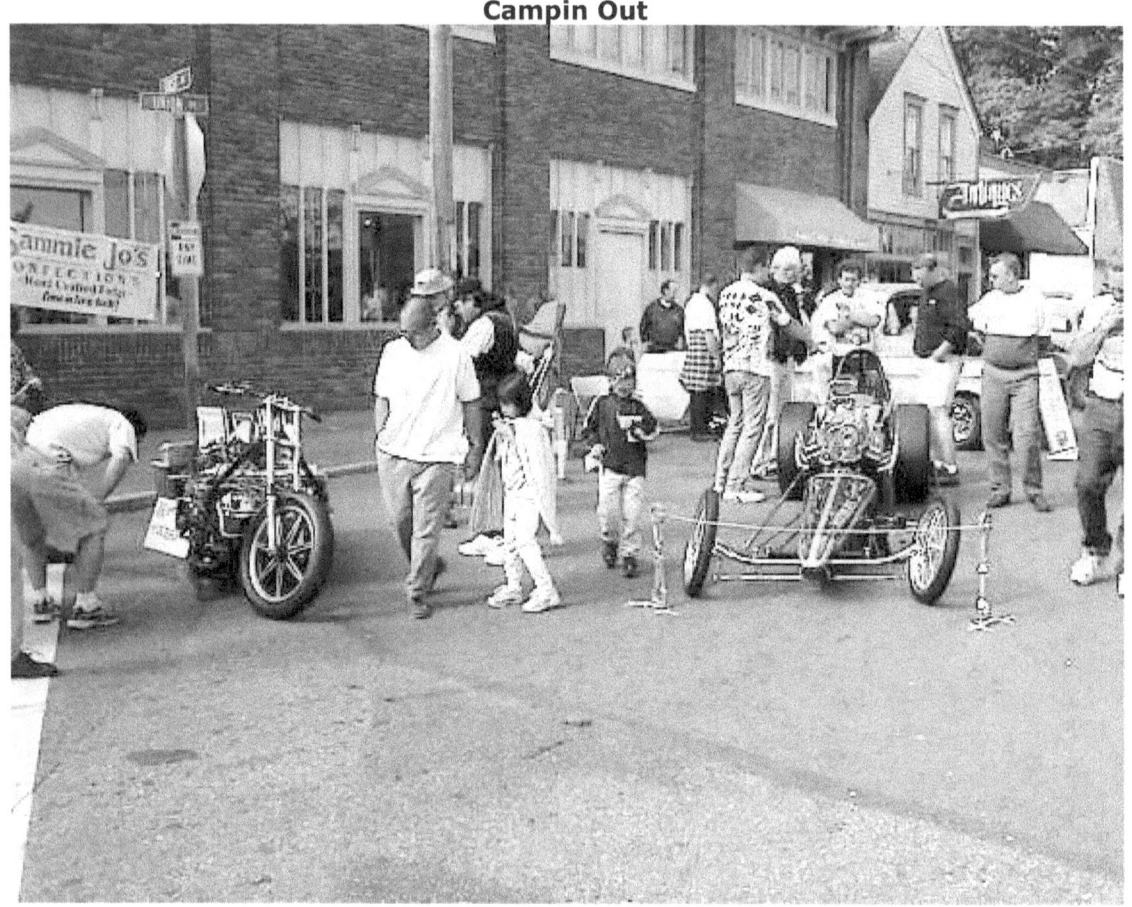

Here's 'Supe' and The Fuller workin' the crowd at the big hot rod show in Snohomish
Washington (Pit Crew's home town), The week before heading down to the next
Cailfornia Hot Rod Reunion (2001)

"Pit Crew" & Friends

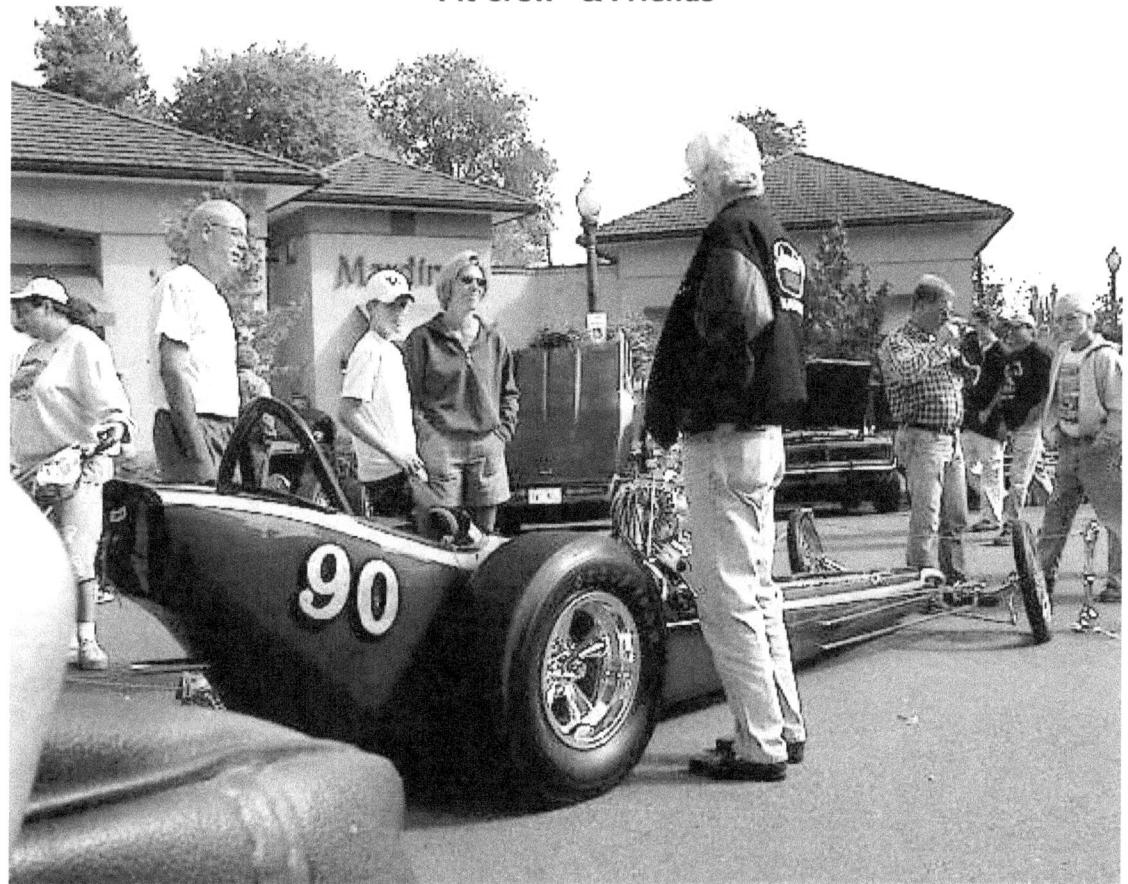

Here's Pete 'splaining the finer points of FULLER's art to a couple of fans.......

"IT Lives"!!!!!!!

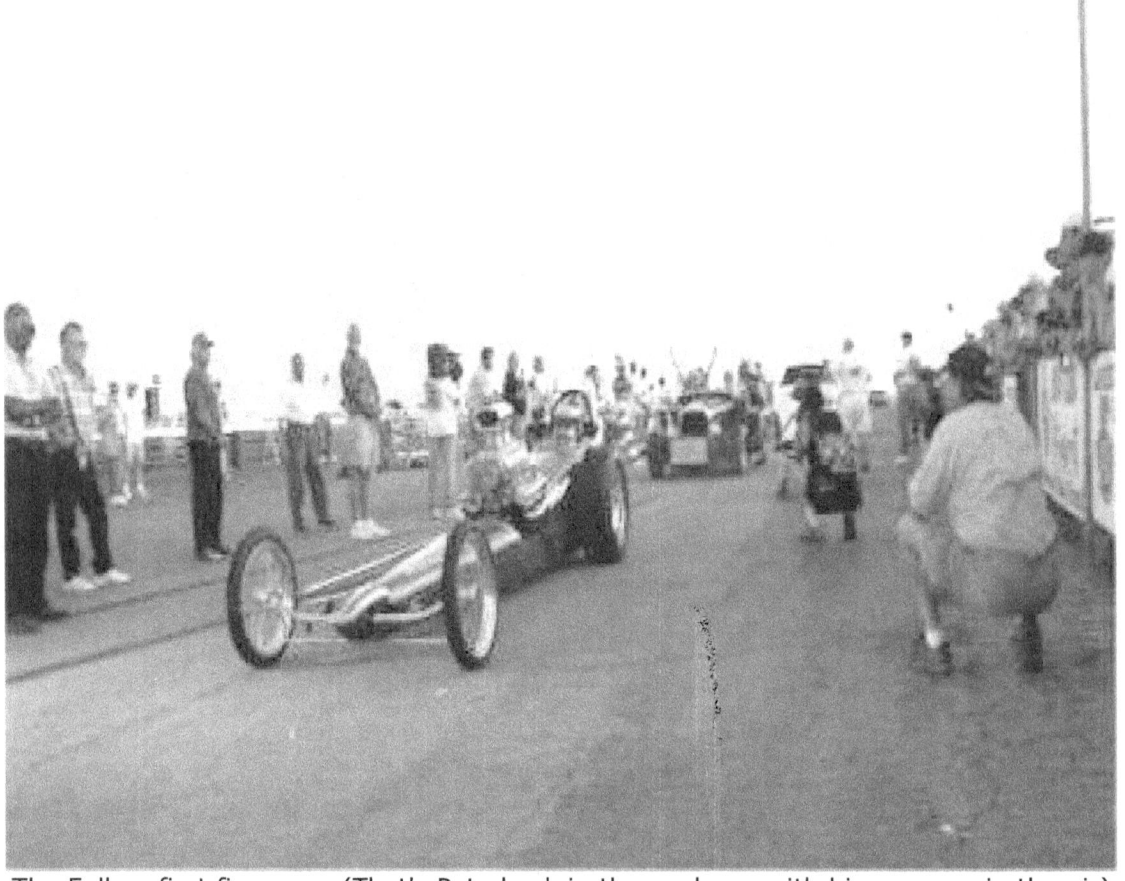

The Fullers first fire up ... (That's Pete back in the push car with his arms up in the air)

"Tech Talk"

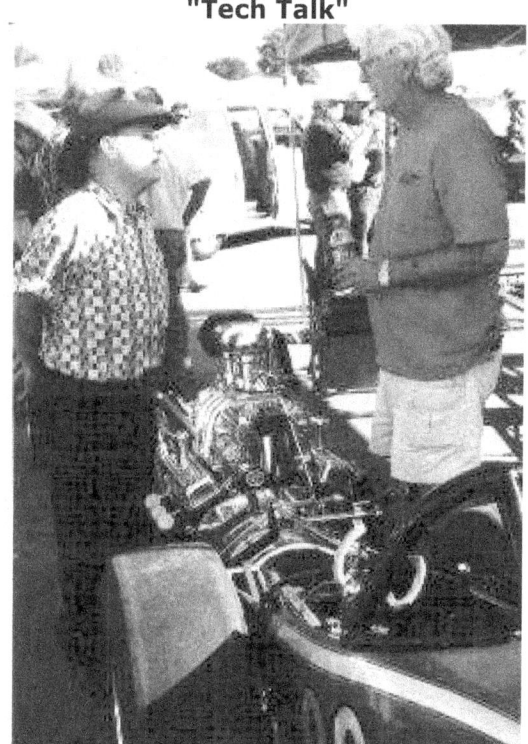

Pete talking engines with Texas racer Vance Hunt

"Museum Piece"

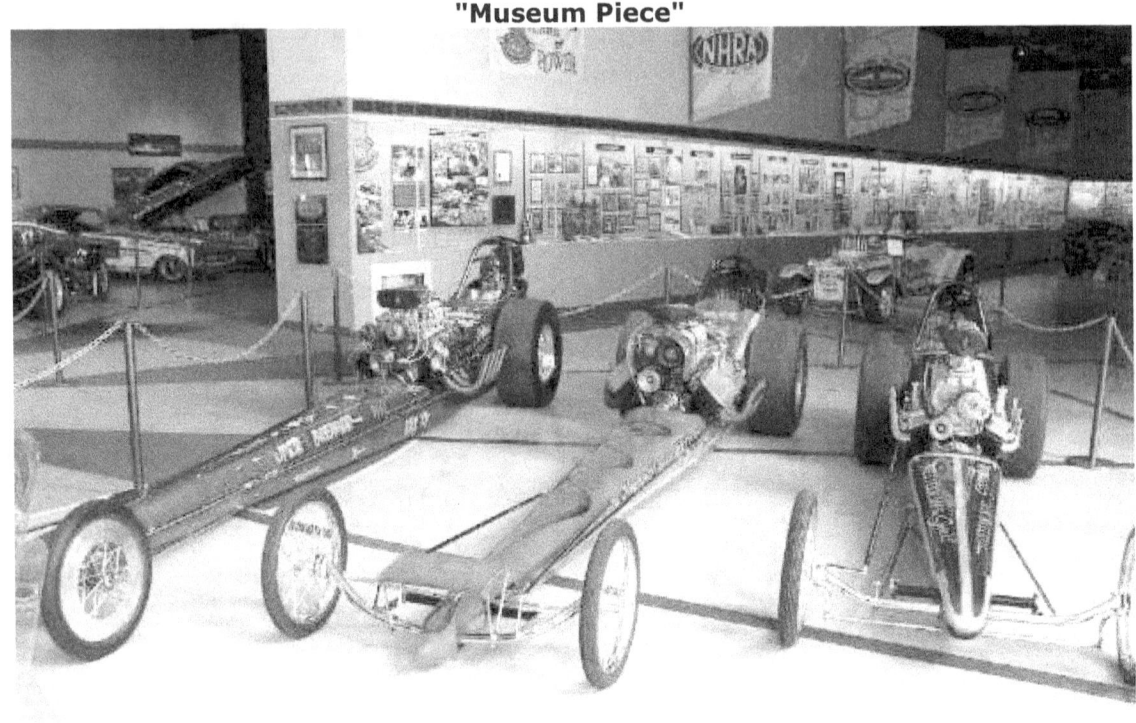

The Fuller moves into The NHRA Motorsport Museum in Pomona for the winter...

'The Jade Grenade', 'The Howard Cam Rattler', and 'The Fuller'... spend the winter at a pretty nice spa...

"The BIG SHOW"

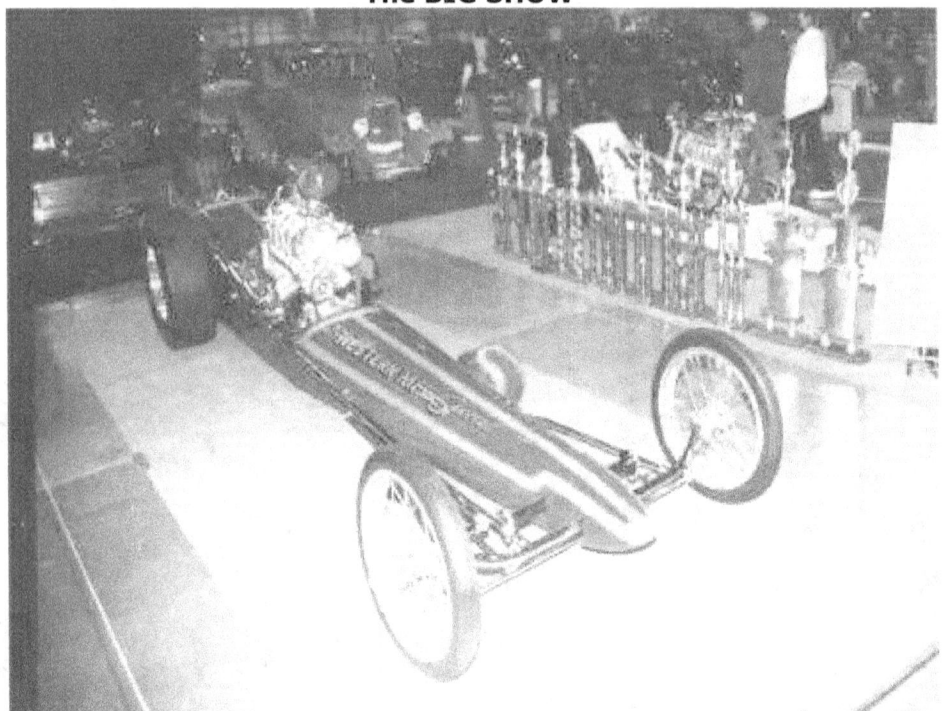

The Grand National Roadster Show, (2002) ... The Fuller knocks em' dead!!!

Red, White, and Blue

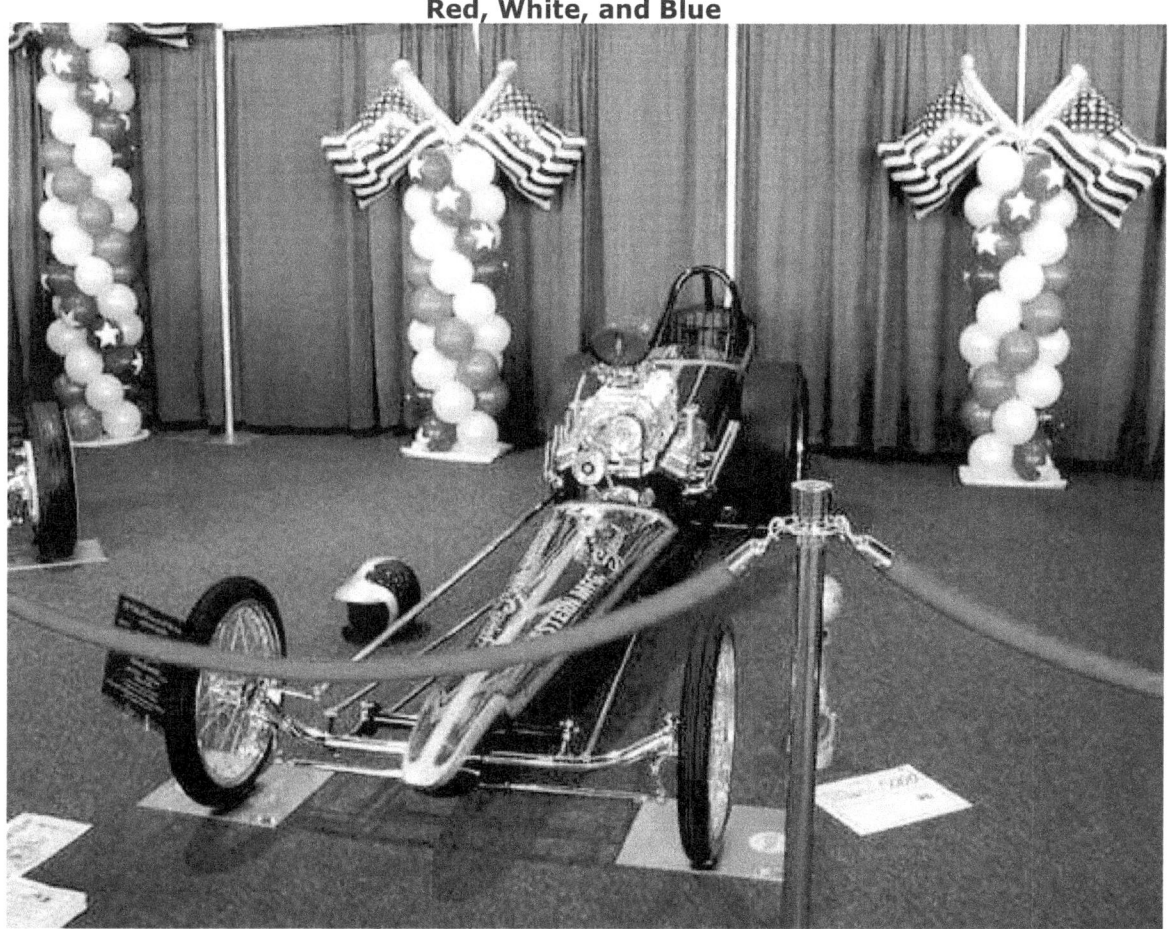

I thought the display was a little overdone ... but then hey - what do I know ... and besides - The Fuller was their feature car - and they did the display...

"Showing Off"

The Fuller doesn't like to boast ... and usually doesn't bring any of his hardware along to the shows - - but he is proud of the 'Best Paint' plaque's from 'The Grand National Roadster Show' ... and 'The Sacramento Autorama'...

Educator "Eric"

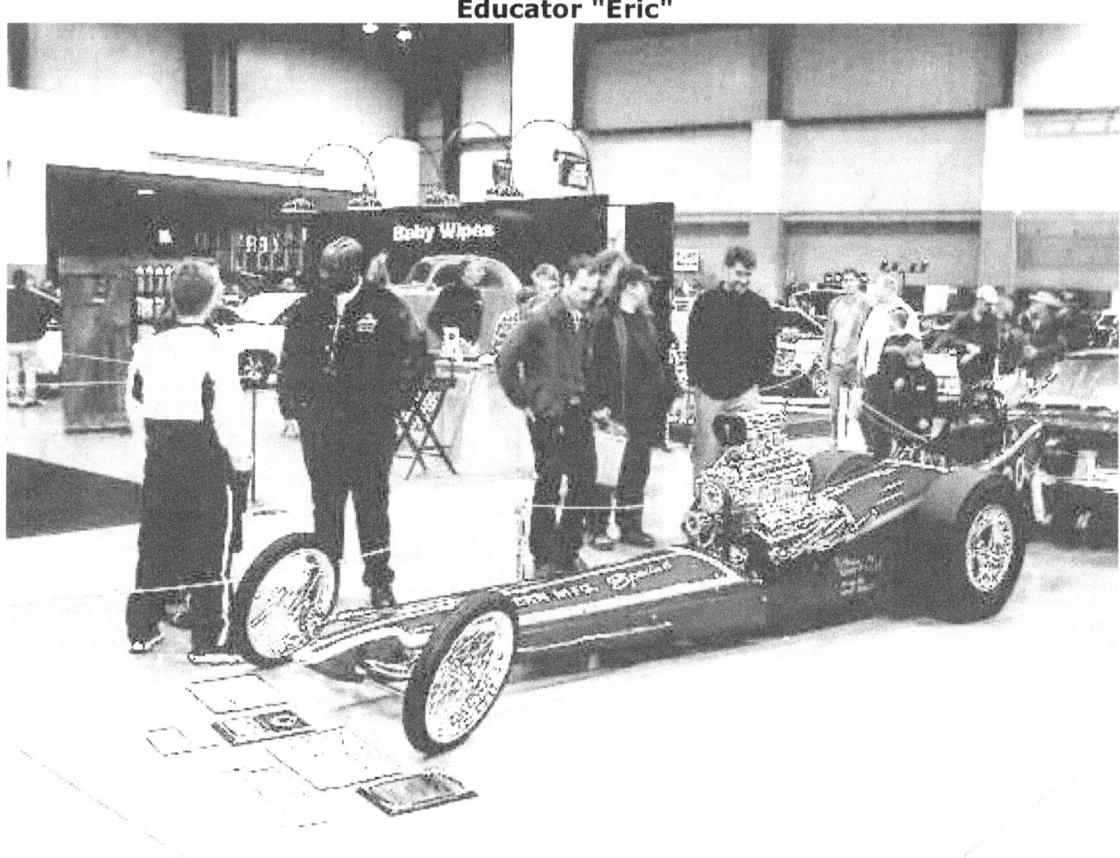

Here's a shot of Eric - (the guy in the black coat) - explaining the better points of 'The Fuller' to some young fans... The kids that come around at these deals are the most fun of all - - and they show a suprising amount of interest in the history of the sport...

"Tent Show"

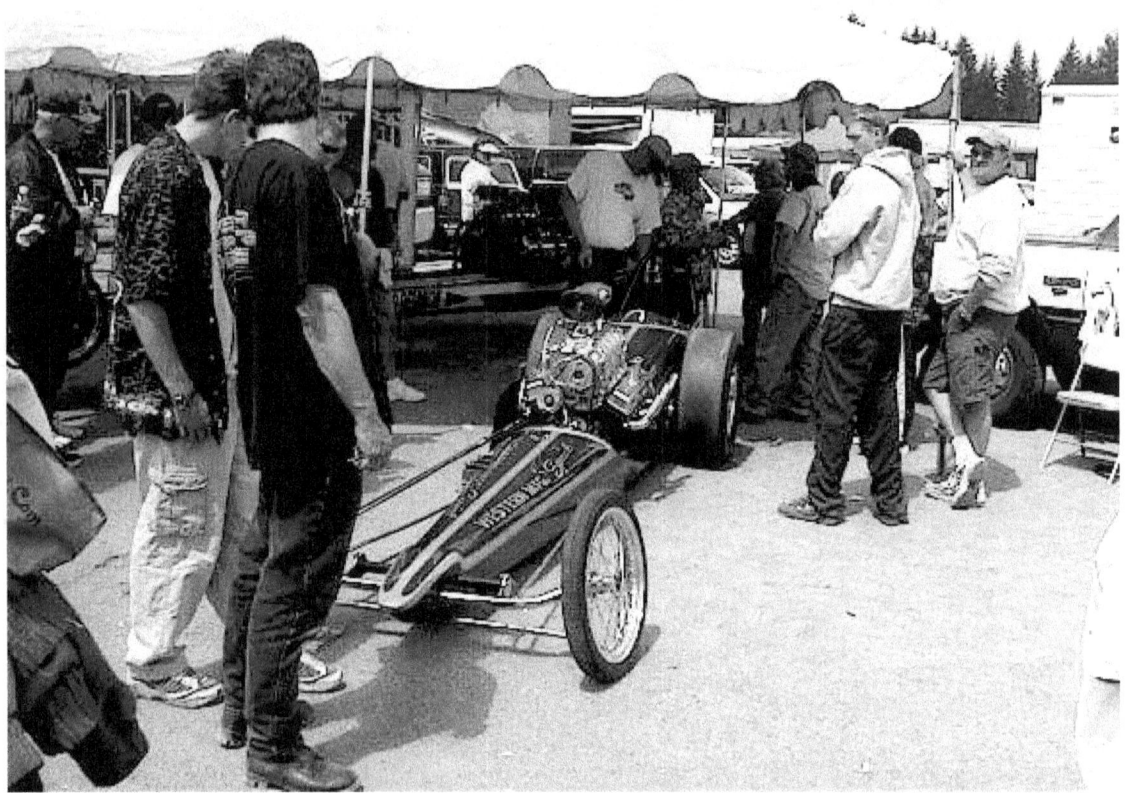

The Fuller takes time to do a display gig at the Seattle National Event for the CHRR and the Pomona Museum...

The "Grove"

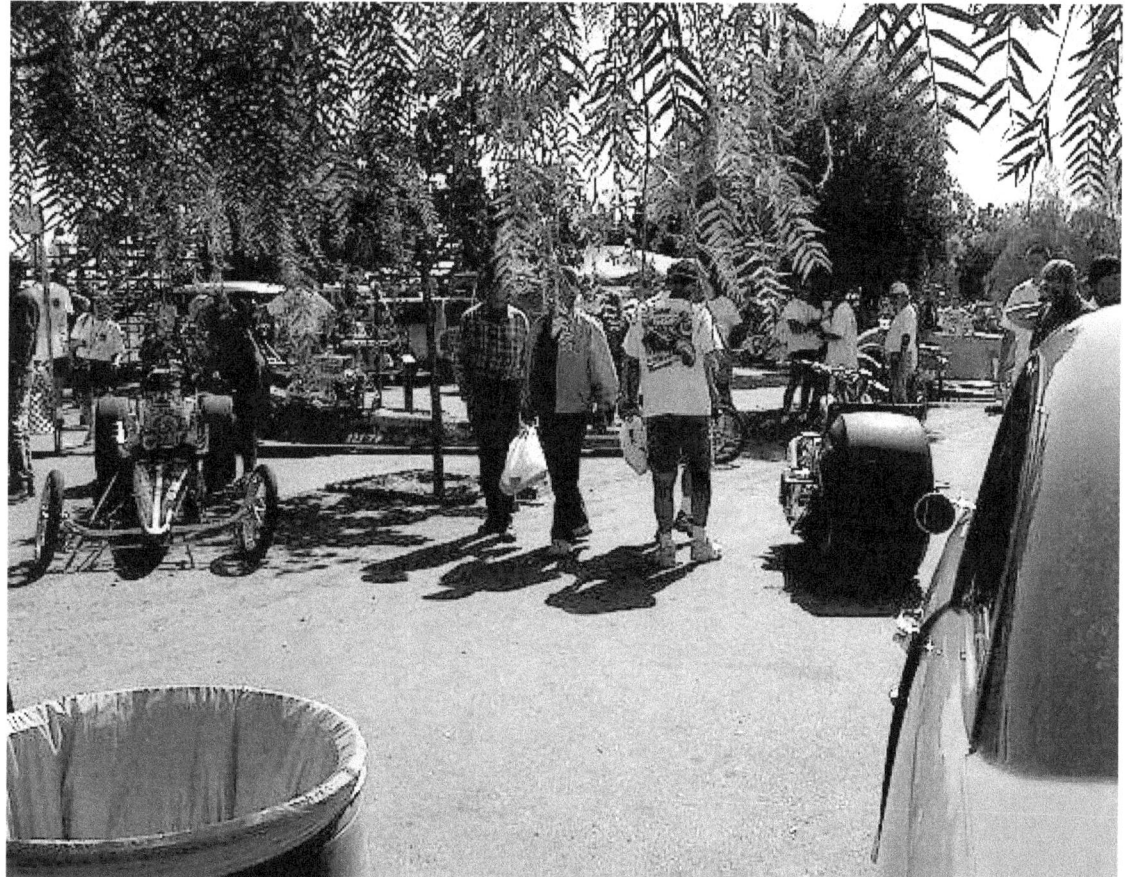

Man thinks 'The Fuller' is this a great place for a car show - or what! ... hard to believe it's in Bakersfield...

"Pit Crew" in the Sun

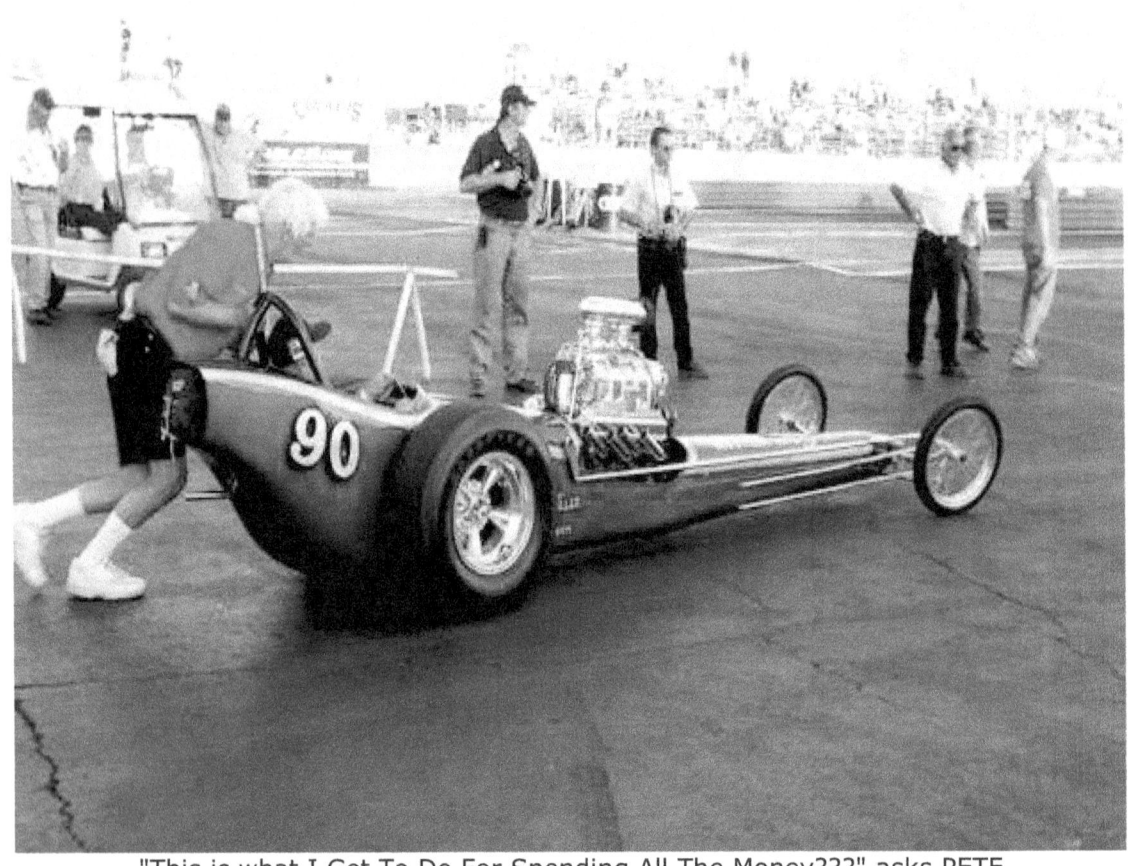

"This is what I Get To Do For Spending All The Money???" asks PETE

"Pete Holds Court"

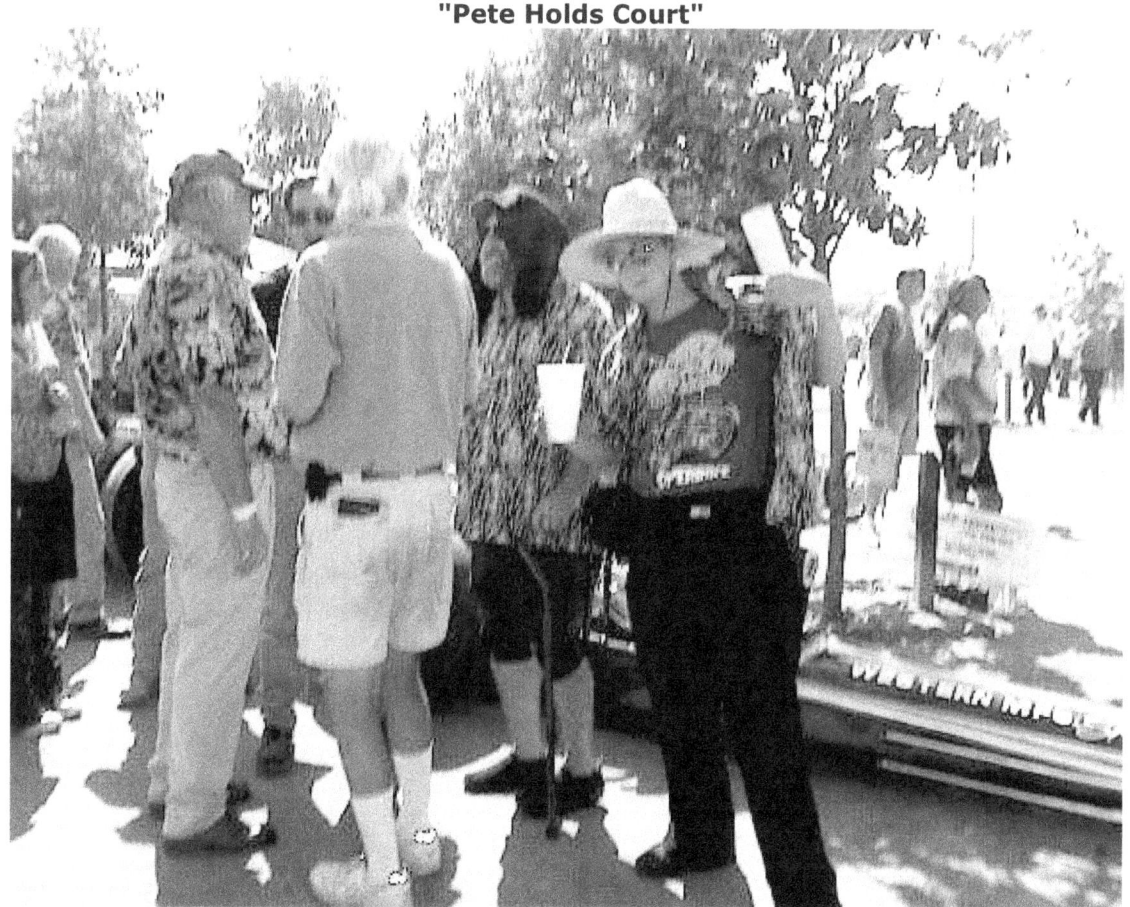

Pete visits with some of the guys...

"HEY Over Here!!!!"

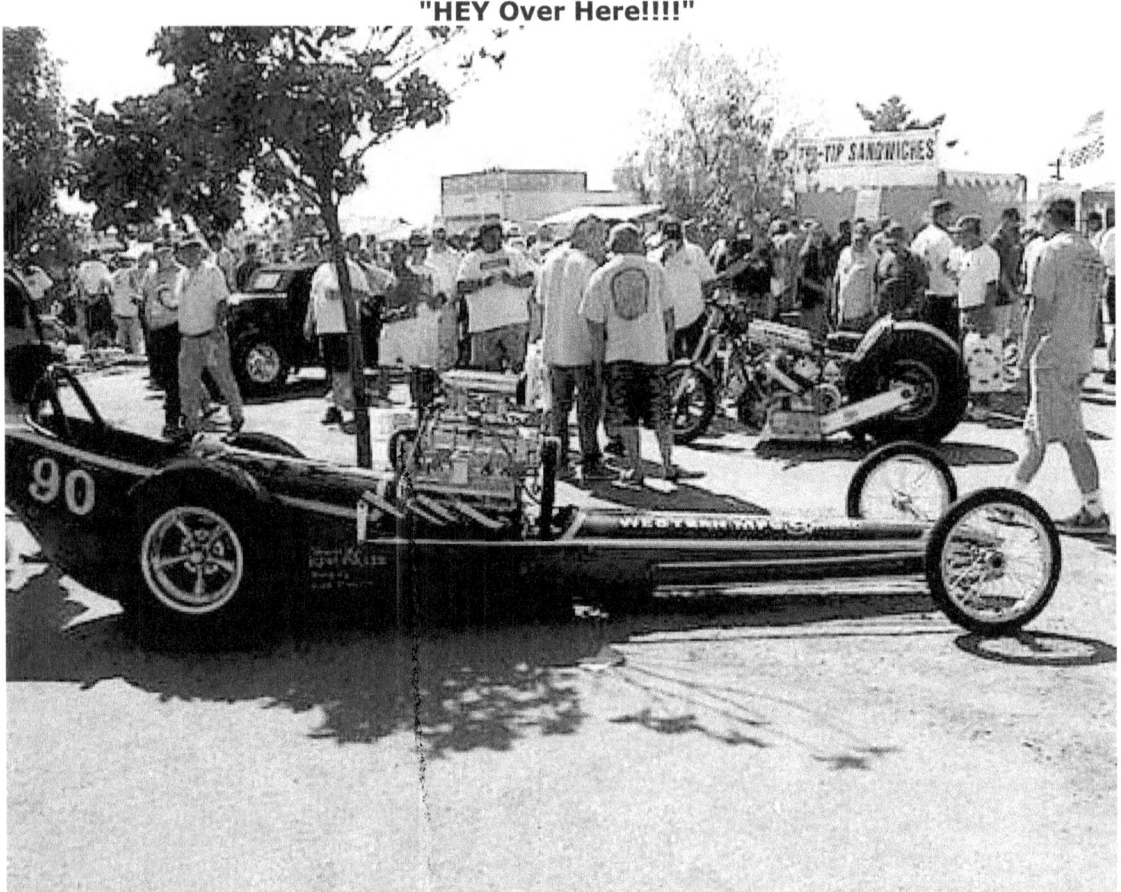

Whats the deal with this SuperBike guy anyway - - I mean I bring him along to the reunion this year - and the crowd just can't get enough of him...

He's Back

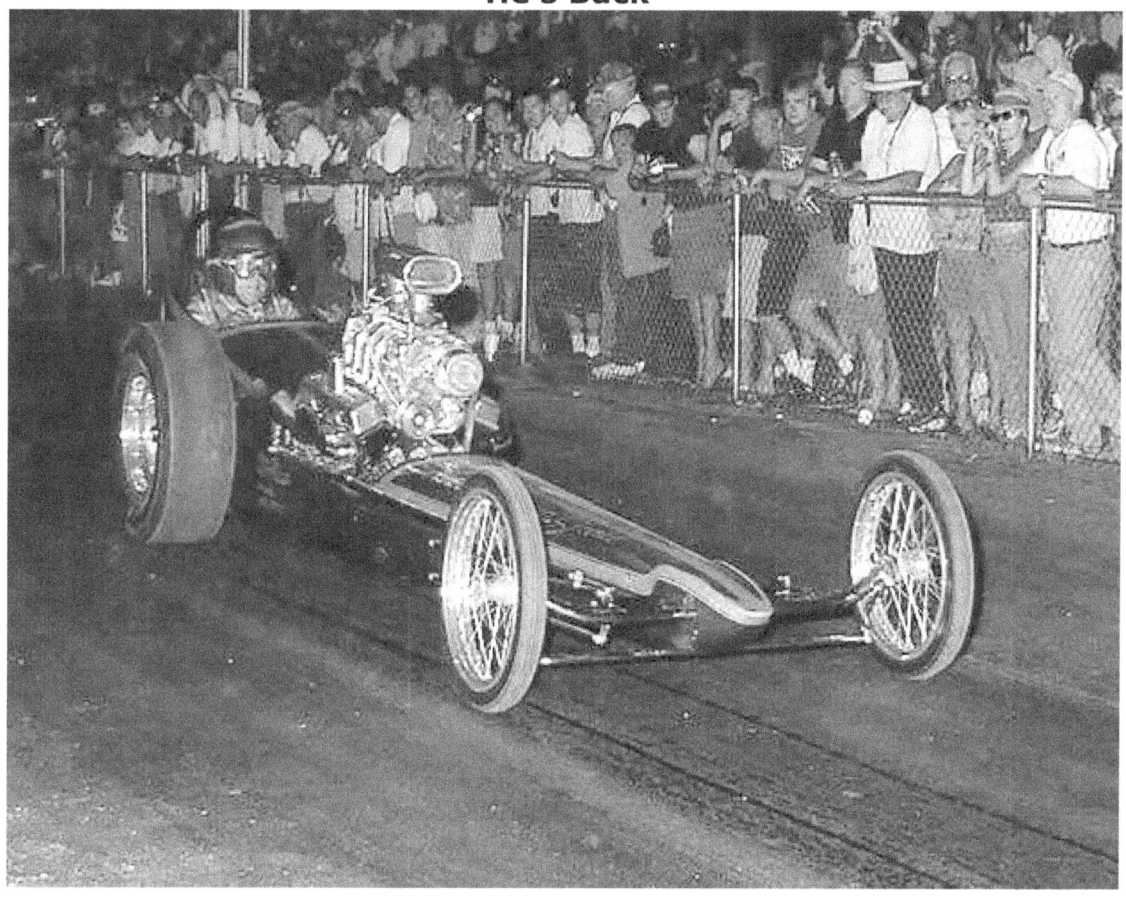

"Back being the darling of the crowd - - where I belong", thinks The Fuller ... "Life Is Good"...

"Ultimate Theatre"

ULTIMATE THEATER

Dragsters pushed down the track in front of the crowd

Lanes swapped as they turn around in front of the finish line ... crews out
for one last check

Then the sound of the cars being pushed back towards the starting line at
speed ... rattling tin ... cold clutch disks squeak and chatter ... the
chugging sound of compression

The suddeness of engines firing ... sometimes bursting to life at the very
last second

Next the turnaround behind the line ... both cars at a mean idle - swapping
lanes again

Drivers eyes meet as they cross ... sometimes a nod ... sometimes nothing

Then the starting line dance ... tuners tweek barrel valves ... glancing at
each other ... give the throttle a rap ... masters of the phyc-out

Crew wiping slicks ... drivers looking straight ahead

A pat on the hat ... a wave - and the cars pull forward

Bring the R's up - watch the flagman's eyes - - he makes the move ... And
all hell breaks loose!!!

Fred Vosk

http://bikesters.com

"Pit Crew" Pete Speaks:

What a long strange road we traveled to get to CHRR 2K. Normally I would have done my typical deal of showing up and hanging out for the weekend. Not this year!!! The March Meet changed all that. Jet Car Bob and I went to the March Meet (me for the first time in more years than I want to count) Bob and I had been trying to get our buddy, Jon Halstead to come to the reunion or The March Meet for a number of years without success. Things changed drastically this year, as Jon and his wonderful wife, Jeanne were in attendance and we had a wonderful time getting reacquainted again after so many years. Since I had committed to doing the restoration of Jon's first dragster, I was delighted to spend time with Jon and Jeanne getting a lot of research information for the project car. Jon also had a great time seeing lots of old friends. He called me a couple weeks later to tell me he was going Top Fuel racing and ask if I wanted to be part of the team. Wow, just like the old days. Hell Yes, I'll play!!

After the March Meet, I stopped at Fuller's place to pick up the car and started the long journey back to Snohomish, WA, with the car strapped to the roof of Pam's station wagon. Stopped off at Ewald's for a little rest, dinner and a tune up on his computer. The next day, stopped at Tom Wilford's place for coffee and a chat. Got home that afternoon late and unloaded some of the stuff I had gathered up for the project. You have to understand that I live in a very small neighborhood where I am probably the only motor-head around. No one around here ever seen a car like this and since it was still strapped to the roof rack, there was some amusing remarks about what it was. Best comment was from my Veterinarian friend's wife. She wanted to know if I was building a helicopter.

The next day, I set out for Hayes Classics in Kirkland to begin the process of restoring what is now commonly referred to as "THE FULLER", aptly named by Fred Vosk. At first it was a little intimidating to have the little car sitting among such classics as the Bugatti and the one off Ferrari as well as the rare Cadillac is being restored for the 100th anniversary Cadillac celebration (it will be a 100 point car). I won't bore you with all the details of the process of doing the car, since Fred has been chronicling the progress of it in his own inimitable and very humorous way. Yes we struggled with finding the right parts and I spent lots of long nights and early mornings searching the Internet.

The net result was what those of you that were at the reunion saw, either in front of The Doubletree on Thursday night or over the weekend, parked at the Fuller display. What did I get out of this, you might ask? First and foremost, I have been lucky enough to make a number of new friends, two of which, have put as much of their heart and soul into this project as I have. Fred Vosk and Eric Hayes, who are indeed artisans in their own right. The skills these guys process are unbelievable. You cannot appreciate Eric's polishing skills until you try to match it. Case in point is when Fred said to me, "Your not going to put that black anodized pump drive extension on this car, are you?" Well I decided to do the whole process of sanding it down to remove the anodizing and polish it up to match the rest of the car.. It took me about 5 hours to get it done, and when I was coming out of the polishing booth, Eric commented "Hey Pete, Now you look like one of the Bruthas'! I was covered with polishing stuff from head to toe. Eric can be my bro' any time he wants. He's so good at polishing, that when we needed to get some parts chromed, Eric did the polishing and and took the stuff to the chrome shop, and all they had to do was dip the pieces and get them back to us. It sure helped on turn-around time.

Fred's Rheumatoid Arthritis puts limits on what he can do physically, but it didn't stop him from doing the paint layout for the body and the polishing and assembly on some of the car. If you were to look closely at the paint scheme, you will see that there is no part strip between the silver strips and the silver coat and the line are immaculate. No bleed-over, anywhere. He also provided guidance to Eric in the painting process, since Eric had never done "metalflake" before. If you have seen the car, you can appreciate the quality of Eric and Fred's work.

If I sound like an Eric and Fred fan, it is only because, I am. Big Time!. If not for them, the car would still be way less complete than it is.

I want to personally thank everyone who stopped to admire the car and tell us how much they liked it. It was a work of art, that had come back to life. I'm not sure how to say this, since I don't want to offend anyone who took the time to comment about the car, however, from the time I rolled into the patch with it, I had high hopes we had accomplished all we set out to do. I guess my perfectionism sometimes gets in the way and I tend to reach beyond what is reasonable to accomplish in a given time. I wasn't happy with having to make the decision not to fire it up on Saturday, but I didn't want to make one of those last minute mistakes that would have spoiled it for us. Some of you may have known that Steve Gibbs, had ask Bob Smith and me to light it off for the Fuller presentation, out in front of the stands, and you will never know how much I wanted to do it. It wasn't possible to get done, so we pushed it out from the staging area.

I have been around the sport for a long time and seen some very nice cars built by some very talented people. I wanted to do this car with as much class as I have ever seen. I have told a few friends that I wanted it to surpass the GBP car for quality. I don't know if that got done or not, but when I got the kind of comments from my peers (That's the old guys from the 60's) whose workmanship I have always admired, I got chills up my spine.

The soft-spoken "metal master" from Wichita was the first to see it on Thursday, and although I can't remember his exact words, the impact on me was wonderful. Thanks for your opinion, Tom Steve Gibbs also say it on Thursday afternoon and was very impressed with the car. Enough so, that he told me to be sure and park it under the canopy at the entrance to the Doubletree. We told the clerk at the registration desk, when we were checking in that Mr. Gibbs had requested we do that and he said that would be just fine. Boy, does that Hook carry some weight around that place. Steve had also requested that the car make an appearance at his House of Hot Rods at the Fairplex at the earliest possible convenience. High praise, coming from the master of the Museum, also, Thursday afternoon, I needed to get some machine work done for one of the pieces of the blower drive (This was when I was still trying to get it ready to run). Well, after having been to the March Meet a number of times over the past forty years, I did what I would usually do when I needed help at Bakersfield. I went to see the Godfather of Bakersfield drag racing, Ernie Hashim. I ask if he could do a little machine work for me and with out a moments hesitation, he says, "what do you need?". I showed him the piece, he grabbed it, and told me, "I'll have it for you first thing in the morning". Now you have to understand, that first thing in the morning to Ernie is 7AM! He had it done exactly the way I needed it when I came to pick it up. He thought the car was beautiful and went on to tell his son (whose name escapes me at the moment) about the car that he had like this one. Ernie is 76 years old and was about to celebrate his 50th wedding anniversary that evening with upwards of 400 of his friends and family. I got a big hug and a pat on the back from Ernie. That made my day. I love Ernie Hashim.

Thursday evening at the Doubletree was a lot of fun and many folks stopped to look over the car. All that I talked with were very kind with their complements on the car. Dave McClelland stopped to chat about the car and ask some questions about it for reference material to use when he would interview Fuller later on Saturday. That worked out well, since Fuller is such a motor-mouth?

Dave Jeffers, who some of you may remember from his days at RCS, looked at the car and told me what a nice job we did restoring it. Last summer, I ran into Dave out at SIR at a match race. We hadn't seen each other in 30 years. His comments about the workmanship on the car were neat to hear, since I know what an excellent craftsman he is. Dave was also responsible for building the rear end that is in the car. He did it for a paperweight car he built while at the Ol' Man's place (RCS).

Most of you had an opportunity at some point, as I did, to spend some time looking over the Beebe & Mulligan recreation that Patty did for Dave West and can appreciate what an amazing craftsman that Foster really is. Patty's son, Cole has inherited these same talents and produced the super neat pick-up that was displayed next to the B&M car. I had the pleasure of getting a guided tour of the truck from Patty at the Doubletree. These guys are way above the standard for excellence when it comes to creating masterpieces. Both Patty and Cole were very complimentary to me about the car. It's hard to write what Patty said to me and convey the voice inflections of how he says it, however if you have ever talked to him, I think you know what I mean when he said to me in his deepest, most sincere voice "Thats an absolutely BITCHIN' car". Thank You Patty.

There's a guy who is a member of this group who has set the standard for excellence of dragsters both Gas and Fuel when he was racing, that has, in my estimation rarely been exceeded by anyone. For a guy who was a racer, week in and week out with solid results and always a class act, to hear him tell me "that's a really nice car". That's exciting for me and I want to thank you very much, Mr. C.

There are a few people who have gone through what I have just experienced and know exactly how much time and effort are need to reach the point that we are at currently. Bill Pitts and Tom Morris were very kind to make a point of telling me how nice the car turned out and how much they liked the work. Like Bill and Tom this was not a one man band kind of thing. I had super help from a lot of people to get it done. Eric and Fred are just as deserving as I am for any and all compliments regarding this effort. The Anderson's also know what it is like to go through this exercise and I appreciate their fine comments as well.

Some of the others involved in this project, that you may not know about, Randy Bradford who managed to get in a little machine work for me while thrashing on his own car to get ready for the reunion (not to mention letting me dig through his scrap barrel for material to make some of the components). Randy has a scrap barrel to die for. David Benjamin did a lot of machine work for us (lots of it was last minute bailout type work and if you saw some of Fred's postings about components that were made, Dave is our guy) Dave does fuel pumps and clutches for some of the hitters on the NHRA circuit. His ability as a machinist is super good.

Wayne King was very helpful in helping me find parts as well as Tom Wilford. Tom was a great resource for locating parts and is quite a historian on correct parts for a period correct restoration. Wayne also found a machine shop guy to do the blueprinting and balancing stuff on the motor (yes it is a sound motor and will run once I get some small details taken care of).

Bill Holland was also a great help in acquiring parts and getting work done. The heads are from World Products (one of Bill's clients) and were worked over by a friend of his by the name of Mike Slover. Bill's moral support and guidance were way more helpful than he may ever know.

Jim Hills participation as a genuine sponsor of this car is unquestionably one of the nicest things to happen to us. This car has never had anyone's decal on it and never will. Yet Jim made us a nice deal to put his product in the engine and went way beyond just being a supplier by giving us all the technical support to make sure we got it right the first time. Numerous phone calls and follow-ups to make sure everything worked for us. Well, if I haven't bored you all (is that Y'all?) yet and you got this far down the page, I would like to make sure that each and everyone of you understand that I am not minimizing anyone's kind and thoughtful comments about the results of this project. I truly appreciate them all, as do the other members of this team, Fred Vosk, Eric Hayes and Doug Pratt. I had a goal in mind and I think I met it.

Oh, yeah two more quick comments: Fred said to Fuller "Neat little car, huh Fuller" Fuller responded: "Yep, wish it was mine" Hopefully, I can fulfill your wish, my friend. Someone said to me on Saturday afternoon: "You have established a benchmark with this car" I don't remember who said it, but "Thank You"

"Pit Crew" Pete